Classroom Companion: Economics

The Classroom Companion series in Economics includes undergraduate and graduate textbooks alike. It welcomes fundamental textbooks aimed at introducing students to the core concepts, empirical methods, theories and tools of the field, as well as advanced textbooks written for students at the Master and PhD level seeking a deeper understanding of economic theory, mathematical tools and quantitative methods.

Leo Ferraris

Macroeconomic Theory

A Primer

Springer

Leo Ferraris
Department of Economics, Management
and Statistics
University of Milano-Bicocca
Milan, Italy

ISSN 2662-2882 ISSN 2662-2890 (electronic)
Classroom Companion: Economics
ISBN 978-3-031-88739-0 ISBN 978-3-031-88740-6 (eBook)
https://doi.org/10.1007/978-3-031-88740-6

This Springer imprint is published by the registered company Springer Nature Switzerland AG
The registered company address is: Gewerbestrasse 11, 6330 Cham, Switzerland

Preface

This is a textbook on macroeconomic theory for advanced undergraduate or introductory graduate courses. Its aim is to provide an introduction to modern macroeconomic theory, explaining its theoretical underpinnings and its conceptual evolution. The book guides the reader from the benchmark general equilibrium model with rational agents interacting in perfectly functioning competitive markets through scenarios with imperfect markets all the way to the polar opposite in which markets are absent and trade occurs over-the-counter in fully strategic situations.

The book is divided into four parts. In the first part, we present the standard macroeconomic model with a representative rational agent trading in competitive markets. We show that such a model can be used as a unified framework to address questions about the business cycle, economic growth, and asset pricing. In the second part, we introduce market imperfections to capture some phenomena that are beyond the purview of the standard model. We examine several economies in which there are market imperfections, including borrowing-constrained and incomplete-market economies. In the third part, we examine models in which private information and strategic effects are at work, hampering the smooth functioning of markets. In some cases, contractual arrangements between traders and financial intermediaries can help mitigate the effects of private information, offering the trading instruments that the market does not provide. In other cases, traders directly negotiate on the allocation of resources. We will use these non-market models to understand why the provision of liquidity by banks is useful but fragile, why money plays the role of means of payment, and why unemployment can emerge as an equilibrium phenomenon. In the fourth part, there is an introduction to the recursive methods that constitutes a bridge to more advanced material covered in graduate macroeconomic courses.

Leo Ferraris
Milan, Italy
January 2025

Competing Interests The author has no competing interests to declare that are relevant to the content of this manuscript.

Contents

Macroeconomic Theory and History

L. Ferraris, *Macroeconomic Theory*, Classroom Companion: Economics,
https://doi.org/10.1007/978-3-031-88740-6_1

1.1 Introduction

Macroeconomics is the discipline that studies the evolution of aggregate economic variables such as the Gross Domestic Product (GDP), namely, the amount of goods and services produced in a given country over a certain period of time. The evolution of GDP is of particular interest to the discipline as it corresponds to the income earned by the producers of goods and services over the same period. Thus, dividing GDP by the population of the country in the same period, one obtains income per person. Income per person represents a summary measure of the economic well-being of the country, reflecting the average availability of food and shelter, health care and education, access to water and electricity. Even a cursory look at the data on income per person of industrialized countries over the last hundred years reveals a profile of sustained growth with fluctuations around the trend and a few occasional recessions. The aim of macroeconomics is to come to grips with these phenomena, trying to understand the driving forces behind income growth, business fluctuations, and sudden recessions. Macroeconomic theory uses abstract mathematical models to help find qualitative and quantitative answers to these questions. Modern macroeconomic theory uses a specific type of mathematical model in which the aggregate economic variables are derived from the market interaction of a mass of dispersed individuals conceived as rational agents who act in their self-interest.

In this introductory chapter, we present modern macroeconomic theory, examining its conceptual foundations and its evolution in response to the historical events of the past century, starting from its inception with the Great Depression of the 1930s up to the Great Recession of 2008 and beyond.

1.2 Theory

Since macroeconomic theory studies the determination and evolution of aggregate economic variables arising from the interaction of many dispersed individuals making diverse economic decisions simultaneously in different markets, the underlying conceptual framework naturally involves a notion of *general economic equilibrium*, in which the relevant economic outcomes are all simultaneously determined (the general part) and are mutually compatible (the equilibrium part).

1.2.1 General Equilibrium

The search for a coherent mathematical representation of a competitive market economy started in the nineteenth century with the *Eléments d' économie politique pure* by French engineer turned economist Leon Walras. In his honor, perfectly competitive markets are still known as *Walrasian markets*. The notion of equilibrium adopted by Walras mimicked the physical notion of equilibrium of a system of interacting entities as a rest point of a dynamical process under the influence of market forces. Unfortunately, the mathematical difficulty of solving a dynamical system that is inherently non-linear due to the cross-market interactions left the problem unsolved except in special cases. The advances in mathematics in the first half of the twentieth century led to a complete change in perspective. The crucial new aspect of the theory was the different notion of *equilibrium*. Unlike physics, which studies the collision of particles under the influence of external forces, economics studies the behavior of free decision makers. The new notion of equilibrium, derived from the mathematical theory of games, conceives of the economic equilibrium as a situation in which decision makers have no incentive to unilaterally alter their behavior.

1.2.1.1 Foundations

The outcome of this change of perspective is the general equilibrium model, formulated by American economist Ken Arrow and French mathematician Gerard Debreu, hence known as the Arrow-Debreu model, which depicts a competitive market economy as a system in which rational consumers and producers with well-defined property rights over the available resources, exchange commodities and services through well-organized competitive markets for maximum personal benefit. In the Arrow-Debreu representation, there is a clear distinction between the exogenous economic characteristics of the traders, namely their preferences for consumption, their productive possibilities, and the property rights over initial resources, and the endogenous outcomes, namely allocations and prices, of the market system that is supposed to work competitively, that is, absent any market power by any trader.

1.2.1.2 Fundamentals vs Outcomes

The Arrow-Debreu model, by now the standard theory of the determination of economic value in general equilibrium, is the methodological foundation adopted by modern macroeconomic theory. The explanatory variables of the theory are the productive possibilities represented by the available technologies, the initial endowments of the commodities, and the preferences that people may have for their consumption. These are known as the *fundamentals*. The variables that need to be explained are the market *outcomes*, namely the allocation of commodities and services and their prices. The model determines the outcomes from the fundamentals.

1.2.1.3 Rationality

Market participants are assumed to be able to rationally plan their course of action for maximum personal benefit taking into account their endowment of commodities, private information over personal characteristics, their preferences over consumption and their production possibilities, and forming *rational expectations* over future economic outcomes, namely expectations that are not systematically wrong but correct at least on average. The adoption of the hypothesis that individual behavior is rational and coherent is closely connected to the purpose of the discipline. The aim of economics does not consist of changing personal goals to achieve some social objective. The aim of economics is to identify the best institutions that let people pursue their goals, affecting their behavior at most indirectly through the lever of economic incentives. According to this point of view, personal goals constitute a constraint on the identification of the best institutions. Hence, if the constraint is made more stringent, assuming that individuals pursue their goals in a coherent and rational manner rather than erratically and irrationally, the search for the best institution is perhaps more difficult, but once found, more robust to possible manipulations.

1.2.1.4 Equilibrium

The economic interaction of traders occurs through well-functioning markets. The relevant outcome of the economic interaction is the *equilibrium*, namely, a situation that occurs when the courses of action of all traders are mutually compatible and nobody has the incentive, individually, to change the planned course of action. Once equilibrium has been obtained, provided that it is uniquely determined, the model can be used to find out what would happen to the outcomes if the explanatory variables were to change, thus determining the endogenous response of the market outcomes to an exogenous change in the fundamentals. This conceptual exercise is known as comparative statics.

1.2.1.5 Efficiency

The famous Prisoners' Dilemma of game theory has shown that, surprisingly, individual rationality does not guarantee that the outcome of economic interaction is *socially* rational. Thus, modern macroeconomics is also interested in understanding whether market allocation can be improved socially by external intervention of public authorities. In order to answer this question, a criterion is needed to evaluate the potential improvements in market allocation obtained redistributing resources among the market participants. The accepted benchmark in economics is known as *Pareto efficiency*, a unanimity criterion that considers an alternative allocation an improvement over the current allocation only if the redistribution of resources benefits someone without hurting anyone. The welfare theorems guarantee that market outcomes cannot be improved according to the Pareto criterion by any type of external intervention if the market works smoothly under perfect competition. Perfect competition requires a full set of anonymous, well-functioning markets in which nobody has market power. In these circumstances, there is no scope for public intervention to improve market outcomes in terms of Pareto efficiency. The reason why market outcomes cannot be improved by external intervention is that the full set of available market instruments allows rational individuals to allocate their personal resources at the margin without distortions among all possible alternative economic uses.

1.2.2 Imperfections

In the second half of the twentieth century, a subsequent generation of general equilibrium theorists discovered that the appealing properties of the Arrow-Debreu model, in particular the welfare theorems, were heavily dependent on the assumptions that made the markets function perfectly. The first assumption that came under scrutiny was the presence of a full set of instruments to protect people against risk. The resulting model with partial insurance is known as the general equilibrium model with incomplete markets. The parallel discovery that the presence of private information about individual characteristics or behaviors could be used by traders to strategically manipulate economic outcomes, thus altering the allocation of resources, led to the incorporation of strategic considerations into the design of allocation mechanisms, including market ones. The literature that has dealt with the issue of optimally designing institutions that allow the smooth interaction of people with private information is known as mechanism design.

1.2.2.1 Externalities

The common element of models with market imperfections is the presence of *externalities*, either of the pecuniary type when markets are incomplete or of the strategic type when information is private, which distort the allocation of resources in the market relative to the efficient benchmark, generating market failures. With externalities, people do not fully capture the benefits or bear the costs of their choices, as a consequence, the welfare theorems do not hold, and efficiency is compromised. If the Arrow-Debreu model gives a picture of the market economy as a self-regulating mechanism that can only be disrupted by government intervention, the picture emerging from imperfect market models is more nuanced, allowing for several types of failure of the market mechanism that may invite government intervention to restore efficiency. Also, with market imperfections, fundamentals alone may not be enough to uniquely determine equilibrium allocations and prices, even if traders have rational expectations. In particular, when strategic elements matter, multiple Pareto-ordered equilibria may emerge, and the economy may be driven into a Pareto-dominated equilibrium akin to a crisis scenario by the private sector's self-fulfilling expectations that end up coordinating on pessimistic outcomes.

1.2.2.2 Policy

The point of view of modern macroeconomic theory is that the key role of the government consists in designing policy intervention that helps restore, or at least approximate, efficiency, correcting the externalities when markets are not functioning properly. This often requires designing institutions with comprehensive incentive schemes rather than adopting piecemeal interventions. As regards the way in which public policy should be designed, the theory provides two main ideas. First, when designing the policy, the authorities should take into account the possibility that the private sector may have relevant private information that may be used to gain an advantage by manipulating the intervention scheme. The lesson of mechanism design is that with private information, restoring full efficiency is too ambitious a goal for public intervention, as the information in most cases remains inscrutable also to the public authorities, and the intervention should be designed to try to elicit the information. Second, public intervention should take into account that the private sector has rational expectations of the possible effects of the intervention on its own behavior. The lesson of rational expectations is that discretionary intervention is a bad idea, since it ignores that the private sector tries to anticipate the moves of the public sector incorporating them in its decisions. In sum, policy intervention should be designed in a time-consistent, non-discretionary, and credible manner, taking into account that there may be attempts to manipulate the intervention scheme.

1.3 History

Macroeconomics, being less than hundred years old, is a relatively recent field within economics that is itself only two and a half centuries old, its birth being conventionally identified with the publication of Adam Smith's *Wealth of Nations* in 1776.

1.3.1 Humble Origins

The evolution of macroeconomics has been heavily influenced by the major events of the last hundred years, from the Great Depression to the Great Recession.

1.3.1.1 Great Depression

Macroeconomics was born in the 1930s, during the *Great Depression*, as a discipline whose aim was to try to make sense of the then dismal situation and to provide advice to policy makers to try to rescue it. Economic theory, at the time, had very little to say about recessions that were considered short-term phenomena of little practical importance. The decade that followed the financial crash of 1929 showed that recessions can be prolonged phenomena with widespread and persistent unemployment. A British economist, John Maynard Keynes, saw that the economic theory of his time could not reckon with a phenomenon of such scale and breadth and thought that a new approach was required to make sense of what was happening. His ambitious 1936 book entitled *The General Theory of Employment, Interest, and Money* contained, in narrative form, his views on what such an approach should be. According to Keynes, the new theory would have to rest on three pillars. First, aggregate demand and the price level would have to affect real output; second, unemployment should be seen as a persistent phenomenon that public intervention could help counteract; third, what Keynes called the animal spirits of the speculators should be factored in to explain market instability. These views, which were incompatible with the economic orthodoxy of the time, initially met with resistance from the profession. The Great Depression lasted until World War II, followed by a prolonged period of economic expansion known as the *Golden Age of Capitalism*, during which many countries recovered from the effects of the war and began to grow at fast rates for the best part of two decades. During this period, Keynes' views were accepted and became the new orthodoxy. After Keynes' premature death, his narrative was turned, by a new generation of then young, mostly American macroeconomists, into a quantitative econometric model based on a large system of statistical relations that were meant to describe the workings of the economy as a whole and were used to guide public policy intervention. By the 1960s, Keynesian macroeconomists had identified what seemed, at the time, a robust, but later turned out to be spurious, trade-off between inflation and unemployment known as the Phillips curve, whereby sustained inflation would keep unemployment at bay.

1.3.1.2 Great Inflation

The attempt to exploit the Phillips curve led to a cavalier use of expansionary monetary policy by monetary authorities around the world for quite some time, until, in the 1970s, most developed economies experienced a prolonged period of low growth, rising unemployment, and high inflation, a phenomenon now known as the *stagflation*, that is, stagnation with inflation. This unexpected phenomenon that lasted for more than a decade, a period now known as the *Great Inflation*, stunned the profession and eventually led to a change in theoretical perspective. The turning point came with the work of American economist Robert Lucas, who pointed out that the restrictions imposed by the Keynesians on their econometric model were implying an unreasonable shortsightedness of the economic agents, who were assumed to form their expectations about future economic variables in a myopic way. Even more dangerous for the purpose of designing public policy interventions, it was assumed that the private sector was blind to the effects of changes in policy on its own behavior. The implication was that the unwarranted Keynesian assumptions on the passive expectations of the private sector were responsible for the abuse of monetary policy that had caused the then rampant stagflation. This was the beginning of the rational expectations revolution. To incorporate rational expectations, that is, expectations that are not systematically wrong, into macroeconomics the Keynesian approach had to be abandoned to break new theoretical ground.

1.3.2 Great Expectations

After the failure of Keynesian macroeconomics to predict stagflation, a new paradigm inspired by the Arrow-Debreu general equilibrium model has emerged. Over time, the paradigm has incorporated several advances from the game-theoretic literature.

1.3.2.1 Great Moderation

The Arrow-Debreu representation of a market economy as a coherent mathematical model of general economic equilibrium whose outcomes turn out to be unimprovable by external intervention, scaled down to a more manageable aggregate version with a rational representative consumer and just a few key commodities, became the foundation of the new approach to macroeconomics, developed by the mostly Chicago-based *New Classical* economists. The New Classical model replaced the Keynesian model as a laboratory to study both long-term economic growth and short-term business cycles. The golden age of the New Classical Paradigm, between the mid-1980s and mid-2000s, was the period known as the *Great Moderation*, during which the American economy experienced minimal fluctuations of economic activity around a stable trend of income growth. During the Great Moderation bonanza, even a new generation of Keynesian macroeconomists, known as the New Keynesians, came to accept the new paradigm, with the only proviso that wages may not be free to adjust in the short run to clear the labor market, thus generating, temporarily, some unemployment. Coupled with a reason for money to have a role in the allocation of resources, wage rigidity opens up the possibility that monetary policy may help correct the ensuing distortions in the short run, thus, putting Keynesian icing on the New Classical cake. The party came to an abrupt end in 2008 when the Great Recession broke out.

1.3.2.2 Great Recession

The *Great Recession* originated from a liquidity crisis that began in mid-September 2008 when the investment bank Lehman Brothers went bust. During the summer of 2008, investors lost confidence in the ability of investment banks to redeem their short-term loans. As many financial institutions were simultaneously looking for liquidity to be able to meet the demand of their customers who were asking to liquidate their positions, liquidity began to dry up. Investment banks started liquidating their assets at fire sale prices, whose collapse tightened borrowing constraints, generating a credit crunch that led to a major contraction of GDP. As in the Great Depression of the 1930s, the Great Recession has changed the theoretical landscape, reviving interest in situations in which traders' expectations are not uniquely pinned down by the equilibrium, giving rise to recessions driven by self-fulfilling pessimistic beliefs. Government intervention may be able to play a helpful role when the economy is entrapped in a situation of self-confirming negative expectations. The unconventional intervention of the Federal Reserve Bank and the European Central Bank through the so-called quantitative easing has helped the recovery from the Great Recession that, however, has dragged on into the following decade with relatively high unemployment rates and meager income growth for the best part of the 2010s. The Covid-19 and the somewhat unexpected comeback of inflation in the early 2020s are recent history.

1.4 Conclusion

Macroeconomic theory has evolved from its narrative inception in the 1930s into its current applied general equilibrium form in response to the stagflation of the 1970s. During the last fifty years it has incorporated theoretical advances from game theory and mechanism design, especially in response to the events that have surrounded the Great Recession of the end of the 2000s. The rest of the book provides the details of the evolution of the discipline.

1.5 Literature

An excellent introduction to the general equilibrium Arrow-Debreu model is contained in Gerard Debreu's *Theory of Value*. An enjoyable read on the evolution of macroeconomic theory is Roger Farmer's *How the Economy Works: Confidence Crashes and Self-Fulfilling Prophecies*. The turning point of the rational expectations revolution in macroeconomics is the paper by Robert Lucas entitled *Econometric Policy Evaluation: A Critique*.

References

Debreu G (1959), Theory of Value. An Axiomatic Approach, Yale University Press

Farmer R (2010), How the Economy Works: Confidence Crashes and Self-Fulfilling Prophecies, Oxford University Press

Keynes J M (1936), The General Theory of Employment, Interest and Money, Palgrave Macmillan

Lucas R Jr (1976), Econometric Policy Evaluation: A Critique, Carnegie-Rochester Conference Series on Public Policy, 1: 19–46

Smith A (2008), An Inquiry into the Nature and Causes of the Wealth of Nations, Oxford University Press

Walras L (2003), Elements of Pure Economics, Routledge

A Perfect World

The first part of the book introduces the reader to the workhorse macroeconomic model with rational economic decision makers interacting through competitive markets. We will show the analytical properties that characterize such a model, in particular, the strong link between the allocations delivered by market trade and the efficient allocations. We will also show how the same unified model can be used to address questions about short-run fluctuations of employment and income, the relationship between inflation and monetary policy, the long-run evolution of income, and the pricing of financial assets. Ultimately, the aim of macroeconomics is to try to understand the determinants of the evolution of income per person, the unemployment rate, and the inflation rate over time. Questions about the short-run, considering changes in economic variables relative to the previous year or quarter, are studied by the theory of business cycles, while questions about the long-run, considering averages of the economic variables over long stretches of time, are studied by the theory of economic growth. The study of business cycles and economic growth that have long been considered separate fields using different methodologies are now fully integrated areas of macroeconomic research, using essentially the same analytical tools, namely the macroeconomic model with rational traders operating in competitive markets, which we will describe in this first part.

In the first chapter, we present the two basic models to be used in the rest of this part. The first model examines the intratemporal trade-off between labor supply and consumption used to study short-run economic fluctuations. The second model examines the intertemporal trade-off between current and future consumption through the saving decision that is the basis for the study of long-run economic growth.

In the second chapter, we discuss the business cycle. The main business cycle facts for many developed economies are the following: employment and income fluctuate substantially in the short-run, moving together; changes in the labor input and productivity are the major drivers of economic fluctuations in the short-run, while changes in the capital input play a negligible role as determinants of short-run fluctuations in employment and income.

In the third chapter, we discuss long-run economic growth. The main growth facts about developed economies are the following: income per person has been growing steadily at positive rates for over a century; income, productivity, and capital all grow at about the same long-run rate; the growth in the capital input and productivity are the major drivers of economic growth in the long run, while the labor input does not play any substantial role as determinant of long-run income growth.

In terms of asset pricing, which we discuss in the fourth chapter, the benchmark model gives rise to two anomalies when used to match the available evidence. First, the long-run equity premium, namely the spread between the average returns of stocks and the risk-free rate of short term government bonds over long stretches of time, has been large in many countries for a long time. The model can make sense of a large equity premium only conceiving the private sector as extremely, some would say unreasonably, risk averse. This is known as the equity premium puzzle. Second, the standard model can reconcile the long run risk-free rate and consumption growth rate in several countries with the risk aversion needed to match the long run equity premium, only by conceiving the private sector as extremely, some would say unreasonably, patient. This is known as the risk-free rate puzzle. These anomalies point toward a model with market imperfections that we will examines in the rest of the book.

Concerning inflation, the evidence shows that changes in the price level are driven almost entirely by monetary factors with virtually no effect on real variables in the long run, while in the short run there is a significant non-neutrality of money. The business cycle and growth facts can be explained and reproduced surprisingly well using the standard model. The observed short-run non-neutrality of money can be incorporated into the model adding nominal rigidities.

Basic Macroeconomic Model

L. Ferraris, *Macroeconomic Theory*, Classroom Companion: Economics,
https://doi.org/10.1007/978-3-031-88740-6_2

2.1 Introduction

There are two key trade-offs in macroeconomics: the intratemporal decision of how much to work to earn a wage that serves to finance current consumption; and the intertemporal decision of how much current income to save to finance future consumption. In this chapter, we present the two benchmark macroeconomic models that address these two basic decisions. The first static model introduces the topic of the determination of employment and income by companies and workers in a market setting that will serve as the foundation for the discussion of short-run fluctuations, namely the business cycle. We compare the market outcomes obtained with unfettered competition and with various distortions, including market power by companies, price rigidity, and taxation. With unfettered markets, the allocation of resources turns out to be efficient according to the Pareto criterion, public intervention is at best irrelevant, often distortionary. With distortions, the allocation of resources is no longer efficient and public intervention may help correct the inefficiency. We use this model to discuss the effect of an unexpected change in productivity on the wage, employment and income. In the monetary version of the model, the stock of money determines the price level but is neutral with respect to real allocations, unless there is nominal rigidity. We also use the model to discuss the disincentive effect that income taxation has on labor supply, leading to the non-monotonicity of the tax revenue known as the *Laffer curve*; and to introduce the discussion of time inconsistency of public policy that we will pursue further in the rest of the book. The second two-period model introduces the topic of the determination of savings through capital accumulation in a market setting that will serve as the foundation for the discussion of long-term income growth. We show that the effect of changes in productivity extend to capital accumulation. We use this model to address the issue of the neutrality of the public debt, also known as the *Ricardian equivalence*. We show that productive externalities open the door to endogenous income growth and endogenous income fluctuations.

2.2 Employment

We begin our exposition with a simple static macroeconomic model that determines employment, income, consumption, and the market wage. First, we consider a model without distortions of any type; then, we introduce market power and income taxation.

2.2.1 Unfettered Market

There is one company that is endowed with a technology to produce one type of commodity using labor and one worker who offers labor to earn income to be spent on consumption of the commodity produced by the company. The company and the worker are representative of a large number of identical companies and workers and operate to maximize their private benefits, namely, the profits that the company earns selling its product and the preferences of the worker for consumption and labor. Trade occurs through competitive markets, in which no one has market power. The worker is the owner of the company and hence receives any profits that its activity may generate. We begin by describing the behavior of the agents that populate the economy, namely, the company and the worker. Then, we define and derive the competitive equilibrium.

2.2.1.1 Company

The company has a technology that serves to produce the final output of a single commodity using labor hired from the labor market. The purpose of the company is to maximize the profits obtained from selling the commodity on the market. Since the labor and production markets are competitive, the company takes the wage and price of the commodity as given. The company has a technology that uses labor, ℓ, to produce final output of the commodity, y, represented by the production function

$$y = zf(\ell), \tag{2.1}$$

where z is a parameter that measures the company's productivity. The function $f(\ell)$ is differentiable and satisfies the following requirements.

Assumption 1

i. $f'(\ell) > 0 > f''(\ell)$ for $\ell \geq 0$; ii. $f(0) = 0$, $f'(0) = \infty$ and $f'(\infty) = 0$.

Thus, production increases at decreasing rates in the labor input; moreover, nothing can be produced without any labor input, and a marginal increase in the labor input from zero is extremely productive but almost useless starting from large amounts. The two last requirements are known as *Inada conditions*. Define the elasticity of the production function as $\epsilon_f(\ell) \equiv f'(\ell)\ell/f(\ell)$ and the elasticity of the marginal product of labor as $\epsilon_{f'}(\ell) \equiv -f''(\ell)\ell/f'(\ell)$.

Let p be the market price of the final product, and ω be the wage, denominated in abstract units of account. The purpose of the company is to maximize profits, defined as the difference between revenue py and cost $\omega\ell$, by choosing the input of labor ℓ and the output y, that is, $\Pi(y, \ell) = py - \omega\ell$. Inserting the production function (2.1) into the profit, we obtain the profit as a function of labor demand alone

$$\Pi(\ell) = pzf(\ell) - \omega\ell.$$

Defining the real wage as $w \equiv \omega/p$, the first-order condition for the optimal labor demand $\Pi'(\ell) = 0$ gives the necessary condition for the optimum

$$zf'(\ell) = w, \tag{2.2}$$

which equates the marginal product of labor with the real wage. The condition is also sufficient for the optimum since the production function is strictly concave. Since the marginal product of labor is monotonically decreasing by Assumption 1.i and, hence, invertible, the necessary and sufficient condition for the optimal choice of the company (2.2) can be solved for the labor demand

$$\ell(w) = f'^{-1}(w/z), \tag{2.3}$$

which is differentiable and strictly decreasing in the real wage, with $\ell'(w) = -\epsilon_{f'}(\ell)^{-1}\ell(w)/w < 0$. A higher salary reduces the company's labor demand.

2

Example 2.1

A production function that meets all the conditions of Assumption 1 is $f(\ell) = \ell^{1-\alpha}$ with $\alpha \in (0, 1)$. The elasticity of production is $\epsilon_f(\ell) = 1 - \alpha$ and that of marginal productivity is $\epsilon_{f'}(\ell) = \alpha$. The optimality condition (2.2) becomes $z(1-\alpha)\ell^{-\alpha} = w$ and the labor demand is $l(w) = [(1-\alpha)z/w]^{1/\alpha}$.

2.2.1.2 Worker

The worker has some time that can be used to work in order to earn income to be spent on consumption. The aim of the worker is to satisfy the preferences for consumption and labor. The worker has preferences over consumption, c, and labor supply, l, represented by the differentiable utility function

$$U(c, l) = u(c) - v(l), \tag{2.4}$$

that assigns utility to consumption $u(c)$ and disutility to labor $v(l)$. The utility function satisfies the following assumptions.

Assumption 2

i. $u'(c) > 0 > u''(c)$ for any $c \geq 0$; ii. $v'(l) > 0, v''(l) \geq 0$ for any $l \geq 0$; iii. $u'(0) = \infty$ and $u'(\infty) = 0$.

Thus, increasing consumption is beneficial but at decreasing rates and working is costly at non-decreasing rates. We also assume the marginal utility of consumption to be, respectively, infinite for zero consumption and zero for infinite consumption. In analogy to the previous assumption, these are also known as *Inada conditions*. Define the elasticity of the marginal utility of consumption as $\epsilon_{u'}(c) \equiv -u''(c)c/u'(c)$, and the elasticity of the marginal disutility of labor as $\epsilon_{v'}(l) \equiv v''(l)l/v'(l)$.

Through the choice of consumption and labor supply, the worker aims at maximizing the utility subject to the budget constraint, which represents the limit imposed on the expenditures for consumption by the income, given by the labor income and the profit received from the company, that is, $pc \leq \omega l + \Pi$. The worker spends entirely the income on consumption, since the utility is strictly increasing in consumption and there is no alternative use of resources. Hence, using the real wage $w \equiv \omega/p$ and the real profit $P \equiv \Pi/p$, the budget constraint can be written in real terms as $c = wl + P$. Substituting for consumption from the budget constraint into the utility function (2.4), we obtain utility as a function of labor supply alone

$$U(l) = u(wl + P) - v(l).$$

Computing the first-order condition for the optimal labor supply $U'(l) = 0$, we obtain the necessary condition for the optimum

$$\frac{v'(l)}{u'(c)} = w, \tag{2.5}$$

that equates the marginal rate of substitution between labor and consumption with the real wage, where $c = wl + P$. Work generates disutility, but allows the worker to earn labor income that can be spent on consumption. Hence, there is a trade-off for the worker between reducing the disutility of work and increasing consumption. The opportunity cost of such a decision is represented by the wage. The condition (2.5) is also sufficient for the optimum, due to the strict concavity of the utility of consumption and the convexity of the disutility of labor in Assumption 2.i & ii. The necessary and sufficient condition for the optimum (2.5) implicitly defines the worker's labor supply as a function of the real wage, $l(w)$. By implicit differentiation of (2.5), we obtain

$$l'(w) = \frac{l(w)}{w} \frac{1 - \epsilon_{u'}(c)wl/c}{\epsilon_{v'}(l) + \epsilon_{u'}(c)wl/c}.$$

Whether the labor supply increases or decreases in the wage depends on the strength of the substitution relative to the income effect. On the one hand, a higher wage makes labor more attractive, but, on the other hand, at a higher wage, the income of the worker will be higher, making labor less necessary to finance additional consumption. The former is the substitution effect, and the latter is the income effect of a change in the wage. Since $wl \leq c = wl + P$, if the marginal utility elasticity $\epsilon_{u'}(c) < 1$, the substitution effect certainly prevails and the labor supply of the worker increases with the real wage.

Example 2.2

A utility function that meets all the conditions of Assumption 2 is $U(c,l) = (1-\epsilon)^{-1}c^{1-\epsilon} - l$ with $\epsilon \geq 0$. The elasticity of marginal utility is constant equal to ϵ, and the elasticity of marginal disutility is nil. The optimality condition (2.5) becomes $c^{\epsilon} = w$ which gives consumption $c(w) = w^{1/\epsilon}$ and labor supply $l(w) = w^{(1-\epsilon)/\epsilon} - P/w$.

2.2.1.3 Competitive Equilibrium

At a competitive equilibrium, neither the company nor the worker should be willing to change their decisions, and the markets should clear. Market clearing in the commodity market requires consumption to equate production, that is, $c = y$, and in the labor market, demand and supply of labor must be equated, that is, $\ell = l$. Notice that substituting the profit of the company $P = y - w\ell$ into the budget constraint of the worker $c = wl + P$, we obtain $c = w(l - \ell) + y$. Assuming that the labor market clears with $l = \ell$, the commodity market also clears $c = y$. In other words, provided the company maximizes its profit and the worker fulfills the budget constraint, if one market, for instance, the labor market, clears, the other market, in this case the commodity market, automatically clears. This is known as *Walras law*. As a consequence, there is actually only one independent equation between $\ell = l$ and $c = y$. We focus on the labor market.

2

Definition 2.1

A *competitive equilibrium* is an allocation of labor between the company and the worker and a real wage such that: *i.* the labor demand of the company and the labor supply of the worker are optimally determined given the wage; *ii.* the wage clears the labor market.

The optimal demand and supply for labor have been determined as functions of the real wage. Let us now determine the real wage that equates labor demand and supply. Using the optimal labor demand of the company $\ell(w)$ given by (2.3), the optimal labor supply of the worker $l(w)$ implicitly determined by (2.5) with $c = wl + P$, the company's profit $P = y - w\ell$, the production function (2.1), and market clearing in the labor market $l = \ell$, we obtain the equilibrium condition

$$\Phi(w, z) \equiv v'\left(f'^{-1}(w/z)\right) - wu'\left(zf(f'^{-1}(w/z))\right) = 0, \tag{2.6}$$

that determines the competitive equilibrium wage. The following proposition proves that there is a unique equilibrium wage that satisfies equation (2.6) for any productivity level.

Proposition 2.1

There exists a unique competitive equilibrium wage for every positive productivity level.

Proof The function $\Phi(w, z)$ is continuous in w. By Assumptions 1.ii and 2.iii, we have $\Phi(0, z) = \infty$ and $\Phi(\infty, z) = -\infty$. Hence, by the intermediate value theorem, a $\tilde{w} \in (0, \infty)$ that satisfies $\Phi(w, z) = 0$ exists for any $z > 0$. Also, by Assumptions 1.i and 2.i & ii, the partial derivative $\Phi_w(w, z) = v''(l)/[zf''(l)] - u'(c) - wu''(c)f'(l)/f''(l) < 0$ for any $z > 0$, hence $\tilde{w}$ is unique for any $z > 0$. □

Thus, we have obtained the equilibrium wage function $w(z)$. Using the equilibrium wage function $w(z)$ in the labor demand (2.3), we obtain the equilibrium employment as a function of productivity, $l(z)$. Substituting employment into the production function (2.1), we obtain equilibrium income and consumption $c(z) = y(z) = zf(l(z))$.

Example 2.3

Continuing with the production function $y = zf(\ell) = \ell^{1-\alpha}$ and the utility function $U(c, l) = (1-\epsilon)^{-1}c^{1-\epsilon} - l$, the equilibrium condition (2.6) becomes $[z^{1/\alpha}(1-\alpha)^{(1-\alpha)/\alpha}/w^{(1-\alpha)/\alpha}]^{\epsilon} = w$, which we can solve for w, obtaining the equilibrium wage $w(z) = z^{\epsilon/[\alpha+(1-\alpha)\epsilon]}(1-\alpha)^{(1-\alpha)\epsilon/[\alpha+(1-\alpha)\epsilon]}$. Plugging the equilibrium wage into the labor demand, we obtain the equilibrium employment $l(z) = z^{(1-\epsilon)/[\alpha+(1-\alpha)\epsilon]}(1-\alpha)^{1/[\alpha+(1-\alpha)\epsilon]}$, which we can insert into the production function, obtaining the equilibrium income $y(z) = z^{(1+\alpha)/[\alpha+(1-\alpha)\epsilon]}(1-\alpha)^{(1-\alpha)/[\alpha+(1-\alpha)\epsilon]}$, which coincides with consumption.

2.2.1.4 Comparative Statics

We can use the model to determine the effect of a change in productivity on the wage, employment, and income in the competitive equilibrium. By implicit differentiation of the equilibrium condition (2.6), we obtain

$$w'(z) = \frac{w(z)}{z} \frac{\epsilon_{v'}(l(z)) + [\epsilon_{f'}(l(z)) + \epsilon_f(l(z))]\epsilon_{u'}(c(z))}{\epsilon_{v'}(l(z)) + \epsilon_{f'}(l(z)) + \epsilon_f(l(z))\epsilon_{u'}(c(z))},$$

that is strictly positive. The change in employment as a consequence of the change in productivity can be determined from the optimality condition of the company (2.3) with $w(z)$ as

$$l'(z) = \frac{l(z)}{z} \frac{1 - \epsilon_{u'}(c(z))}{\epsilon_{v'}(l(z)) + \epsilon_{f'}(l(z)) + \epsilon_f(l(z))\epsilon_{u'}(c(z))},$$

whose sign depends on $\epsilon_{u'}(c(z))$. If $\epsilon_{u'}(c(z)) < 1$, the marginal utility of consumption is relatively inelastic, making employment respond directly to changes in productivity. On the other hand, if $\epsilon_{u'}(c(z)) > 1$, the marginal utility of consumption is relatively elastic, causing employment to respond inversely to changes in productivity. In the knife-edge case $\epsilon_{u'}(c(z)) = 1$, productivity does not have any effect on employment. With regard to income $y(z) = zf(l(z))$, differentiating it with respect to productivity with the derivative of the labor supply $l'(z)$, we obtain

$$y'(z) = \frac{y(z)}{z} \frac{\epsilon_{v'}(l(z)) + \epsilon_{f'}(l(z)) + \epsilon_f(l(z))}{\epsilon_{v'}(l(z)) + \epsilon_{f'}(l(z)) + \epsilon_f(l(z))\epsilon_{u'}(c(z))},$$

which is strictly positive. When $\epsilon_{u'}(c(z)) < 1$, a drop in the productivity parameter z can be interpreted as a recession with a corresponding drop in wages, income, and employment. A drop in productivity lowers the real wage, which, provided the substitution effect dominates the income effect, induces a contraction in the labor supply, which, in turn, depresses employment, income, and consumption.

Example 2.4

Continuing with the previous example, we obtain the wage elasticity $w'(z)z/w(z) = \epsilon/[\alpha + (1-\alpha)\epsilon]$, which is strictly positive; the employment elasticity $l'(z)z/l(z) = (1-\epsilon)/[\alpha + (1-\alpha)\epsilon]$, which is positive if and only if $\epsilon < 1$; and the income elasticity $y'(z)z/y(z) = 1/[\alpha + (1-\alpha)\epsilon]$ which is strictly positive.

2.2.1.5 Efficiency

The notion of efficiency that we adopt is *Pareto efficiency*. In our context, Pareto efficiency requires the allocation of existing resources without wasting any of them to maximize the benefit to the worker. In other words, the objective is to

2

select consumption and employment to maximize utility (2.4) subject to the resource constraint $c = y = zf(\ell)$. Inserting the resource constraint into the utility function, we obtain $U(\ell) = u(zf(\ell)) - v(\ell)$. Computing the first-order condition for the optimal choice of employment ℓ, $U'(\ell) = 0$, we obtain

$$\frac{v'(\ell)}{u'(zf(\ell))} = zf'(\ell). \tag{2.7}$$

Condition (2.7) equates the marginal rate of substitution between labor and consumption to the marginal product of labor. Employment is the same as in competitive equilibrium, since the latter is determined implicitly by equating the marginal rate of substitution between labor and consumption to the wage, equation (2.5) with $c = y = zf(\ell)$, and the wage to the marginal product of labor, equation (2.2). Using the resource constraint with the solution for employment, we get the efficient level of output and consumption.

The market allocates the resources efficiently, in the sense that no external agency can improve upon the market allocation. This occurs because the market allows us to equate separately the marginal product of labor to the real wage on the side of the company and the marginal rate of substitution between labor and consumption to the real wage on the side of the worker, thus equating them indirectly to each other. This holds even when productivity drops unexpectedly. Employment and income will drop as a consequence, but will remain efficient for the new productivity level. Thus, the model gives rise to recessions that are efficient responses to exogenous disturbances in productivity.

The one-to-one correspondence between efficient and competitive equilibrium allocations suggests an alternative, often simpler, strategy to derive the equilibrium. First, derive efficient employment using equation (2.7). Then, claim that this must also be the competitive equilibrium employment and use it in the optimality condition of the company, equation (2.2), to obtain the equilibrium wage.

2.2.1.6 Linear Production Function

We will often consider a technology with constant returns to scale, represented by a linear production function, that is, with $f(\ell) = \ell$ in (2.1). The optimal labor demand by the company is decided as follows. If the real wage is higher than the productivity $w > z$, the profit is negative unless the company closes, therefore the optimal choice of the company's labor demand is nil $\ell = 0$. If the real wage is smaller than the productivity $w < z$, the company's profit is greater the larger its size, hence, its optimal labor demand is infinite $\ell = \infty$. If the real wage equals the productivity, $w = z$, the profit is nil for any size, therefore the optimal labor demand of the company is perfectly elastic, $\ell \in [0, \infty]$. This argument determines the company's labor demand as a weakly decreasing function of the real wage $\ell(w)$. Both infinite and zero labor demand are incompatible with a competitive equilibrium; hence, the only relevant case is the perfectly elastic labor demand that arises when $w = z$. The equilibrium condition reflects the labor supply decision of the worker with the wage $w = z$. Therefore, we have $v'(l) = zu'(zl)$, which uniquely determines equilibrium employment as a function of productivity. The comparative statics with respect to productivity is qualitatively the same as before, and the allocation is efficient.

Example 2.5

Suppose that the production function (2.1) is linear. As a consequence, the optimal labor demand is perfectly elastic for $w = z$ and the company's profit is nil. The utility of the worker is $U(c, l) = (1 - \epsilon)^{-1}c^{1-\epsilon} - l$. The worker anticipates that the company's profit is nil and, therefore, the budget constraint is $c = wl$. The optimality condition (2.5) reduces to $(wl)^{\epsilon} = w$, which gives the labor supply as a function of the wage $l(w) = w^{\frac{1-\epsilon}{\epsilon}}$, whose derivative is $l'(w) = (\epsilon^{-1} - 1)l(w)/w$, which is positive if and only if $\epsilon < 1$. This is the case in which the substitution effect prevails over the income effect. Consumption is $c(w) = wl(w) = w^{\frac{1}{\epsilon}}$, with derivative $c'(w) = \epsilon^{-1}c(w)/w$. Thus, ϵ^{-1} is the elasticity of changes in consumption with changes in wages, also known as the *elasticity of substitution* between labor and consumption. Using $w = z$ in the labor supply, obtain equilibrium employment $l(z) = z^{\frac{1-\epsilon}{\epsilon}}$, which increases with productivity if and only if $\epsilon < 1$. Consumption and income are $c(z) = y(z) = z^{\frac{1}{\epsilon}}$, which increase in z for any ϵ.

2.2.1.7 Representative Consumer

The assumption that there is a single representative consumer seems restrictive. It turns out that this is not the case in economies in which markets work perfectly. To see the point, suppose, for simplicity, that the production function is linear in labor and that there are a number of consumers indexed by i with preferences represented by the utility function $U^i(c^i, l^i) = u^i(c^i) - v^i(l^i)$. It is well known that, with perfectly functioning markets, competitive equilibrium achieves an allocation that maximizes $\sum_i \vartheta^i U^i(c^i, l^i)$ using a positive weight ϑ^i for each i such that $\sum_i \vartheta^i = 1$, subject to the resource constraint $\sum_i c^i = z \sum_i l^i$. Now, define the utility of consumption of the representative consumer as $u(c) \equiv \max \sum_i \vartheta^i u^i(c^i)$ with $\sum_i c^i = c$ and the disutility of labor as $v(l) \equiv \min \sum_i \vartheta^i v^i(l^i)$ with $\sum_i l^i = l$. Since efficient allocation, which coincides with competitive equilibrium allocation, is a pair (c, l) that maximizes $U(c, l) = u(c) - v(l)$ subject to resource constraint $c = zl$, the two problems coincide. Therefore, in an economy in which the welfare theorems hold, the representative consumer is just a convenient simplifying assumption made without loss of generality to focus on the aggregate outcomes. Similar logic applies to the representative company.

2.2.1.8 Public Expenditures

Let us now introduce a public sector that needs to finance public expenditures, G, through a lump-sum tax from the worker, T, balancing the budget, $G = T$. The budget constraint of the worker now becomes $c = wl - T$, since the taxation reduces the income available to be used for private expenditures. Lump-sum taxation does not distort the worker's optimal choice since it does not affect the margins. For simplicity, we assume that the production function is linear in labor. Using the public budget condition $G = T$, maximization of the utility of the worker

2

leads to the optimality condition for the labor supply $wu'(wl - G) = v'(l)$, which gives the supply of labor by the worker as a function of the wage and public expenditures $l(w, G)$. Since the company is not taxed, the condition $w = z$ still holds. Therefore, the competitive equilibrium satisfies equation $zu'(zl - G) = v'(l)$, leading to equilibrium employment $l(G)$, income $y(G) = zl(G)$, and consumption $c(G) = zl(G) - G$ as functions of public expenditures. We can now determine the impact of public spending on the equilibrium allocation and the worker's well-being. Define the function $h(G) \equiv y(G)/c(G)$. The derivative of equilibrium employment with respect to public spending is

$$l'(G) = \frac{1}{z}\frac{h(G)\epsilon_u(c(G))}{h(G)\epsilon_u(c(G)) + \epsilon_v(l(G))},$$

which is positive. Hence, public spending increases employment and also income, since $y'(G) = zl'(G)$, but crowds out consumption, since the derivative

$$c'(G) = zl'(G) - 1 = -\frac{\epsilon_v(l(G))}{h(G)\epsilon_u(c(G)) + \epsilon_v(l(G))},$$

is non-positive. In competitive equilibrium, the well-being of the worker as a function of public expenditures is $U(G) = u(c(G)) - v(l(G))$, whose derivative with respect to G, using the derivatives above and the optimality condition $zu'(c(G)) = v'(l(G))$, is $U'(G) = -u'(c(G))$, which is strictly negative. Since the economy with $U(0)$ corresponds to the case without public spending considered above, public intervention is detrimental to society's welfare.

It may be conjectured that the negative impact on welfare is due to the fact that public spending has been assumed to have no direct utility benefit for the worker. To see that this conjecture is incorrect, consider the case in which public services give a direct benefit to the worker, and, hence, the utility of the worker is $U(c, G, l) = u(c) + u(G) - v(l)$. In this case, public spending is optimally determined by the optimality condition $u'(c) = u'(G)$, which gives $c = G$. The marginal effects of G on the equilibrium allocation remain the same, but the marginal effect on welfare is nil, $U'(G) = -u'(c(G)) + u'(G) = 0$, by the optimal choice of G. Hence, even in this more favorable case, public spending has no strict beneficial effect on the worker's welfare.

2.2.1.9 Price Level

The model examined so far does not determine the absolute price level p, which can, however, be pinned down adding money to it. Suppose that there is a nominal stock M of fiat money, namely unbacked currency. The real balances m give the worker utility $u(m)$, representing the benefit that money generates for its transaction services. The worker's preferences are represented by the utility function $U(c, m, l) = u(c) + u(m) - v(l)$. The worker holds the entire initial stock of money; therefore, the budget constraint is $c + m = wl + M/p + P$, where the company's profit is $P = y - w\ell$. The first-order condition for the optimal choice of real balances is $u'(c) = u'(m)$, which implies $c = m$. The equilibrium wage and the allocation are the same as before. From the optimality condition for real balances and the budget constraint with the company's profit, using market clearing in the labor market $\ell = l$ and in the money market $m = M/p$, we obtain the equation that gives the price level $p = M/y$, with income that has been determined before in equilibrium. Money is neutral as regards real variables, and its nominal stock determines the price level. An increase in the nominal money stock increases the price level without real effects.

2.2.2 Distortions

Next, we examine some features that distort market allocations relative to the efficient benchmark. We consider market power and distortionary taxation. The effect is similar, since both market power and distortionary taxation act as wage cuts, reducing labor supply, which, in turn, decreases employment and income relative to efficiency.

2.2.2.1 Market Power

Let us modify the model to discuss the effect of market power. Suppose that a representative company produces the final product using $J \geq 1$ intermediate inputs, whose vector is denoted by $\mathbf{x}$ with the j-th component denoted by x_j. The technology of the company is represented by the production function $y = zf(x)$ with the usual assumptions, where $x = g(\mathbf{x})$ is an aggregator of intermediate inputs to be specified below, whose first and second partial derivatives with respect to the j-th input are $g_j(\mathbf{x}) > 0$ and $g_{jj}(\mathbf{x}) < 0$ respectively. The final output market is competitive, while there is market power in the input market. Each input x_j is produced by a company that uses a technology represented by a linear production function that uses labor as input $x_j = \ell_j$. Each company is a monopolist of its own input and, therefore, sets its price p_j expressed in units of the final output. There is monopolistic competition in the market for inputs, since each input is produced by a monopolist, but the inputs are substitutes in the final production. The labor market, in contrast, is perfectly competitive with the wage w. There is a representative worker who is the owner of all companies with preferences for consumption c, real balances m, and labor l represented by the utility function $U(c, m, l) = u(c) + u(m) - v(l)$, which is differentiable, strictly increasing, and strictly concave with respect to each item.

The demand for the input j by the company that produces final output satisfies the optimality condition $p_j(x_j) = zf'(x)g_j(\mathbf{x})$, which equates the price of the input to its marginal productivity. The profit function of the intermediate input producer j is $p_jx_j - w\ell_j$, where the wage is competitively determined on the labor market and is uniform between companies, so that workers are indifferent among jobs, ensuring that all intermediate input producers can hire workers. Inserting the price of the input from the optimality condition of the final good producer and the production function $x_j = \ell_j$, we obtain the profit as a function of the supply of the input, $p_j(x_j)x_j - wx_j$. The supply of the input by the intermediate producer j satisfies the optimality condition $p_j(x_j) + p_j'(x_j)x_j = w$, which equates the marginal revenue of the company with its marginal cost represented by the wage. Inserting the derivative of the price with respect to the input, we obtain the optimality condition

$$zf'(x)g_j(\mathbf{x})\left[1 - \epsilon_{f'}(x)\epsilon_g(x_j) - \epsilon_{g'}(x_j)\right] = w, \tag{2.8}$$

where $\epsilon_g(x_j) \equiv g_j(\mathbf{x})x_j/g(\mathbf{x})$ is the elasticity of the aggregator function and $\epsilon_{g'}(x_j) \equiv -g_{jj}(\mathbf{x})x_j/g_j(\mathbf{x})$ the elasticity of its derivative. Notice that, by the properties of the aggregator function which is increasing and strictly concave in each input, the term in brackets is lower than 1, therefore, the input price is above the marginal cost represented by the real wage. In other words, there is a *mark-up* of input prices over marginal cost. With competition over perfectly substitutable inputs, the mark-up would disappear since the market price cannot be directly altered by the actions of any single market participant, which implies that the wage reflects the marginal productivity of the input, which, in turn, is equal to its market price. Instead, with monopolistic competition, the price can be manipulated by the input producer, exploiting the demand elasticity of the final good producer to charge a price above marginal cost, obtaining a positive mark-up and profit. The mark-up depends on the elasticity of the aggregator function with respect to changes in the input and the curvature of the aggregator. Together with the distortion induced by market power, there is a strategic externality at work, due to monopolistic competition among the input producers, as can be seen from (2.8), where the optimal choice of each input producer depends on the other inputs, through the aggregate $x = g(\mathbf{x})$. By comparison, a monopolist that sells the entire input to the producer of the final output would not suffer this externality while still enjoying a positive mark-up.

The worker chooses consumption, real balances, and labor supply to maximize utility subject to the budget constraint $c + m = wl + M/p + P$, where p is the price level calculated from the prices of the inputs using the same aggregator and P represents the profits generated by all companies and returned to the owner. Denoting by $\ell = \sum_j l_j$ the aggregate labor demand of the input production sector, the profits are $P = y - w\ell$, since the revenues of the input producers correspond to the cost of the final good producer. The optimality condition for the labor supply is

$$\frac{v'(l)}{u'(c)} = w, \tag{2.9}$$

that equates the marginal rate of substitution between labor and consumption to the wage; the optimality for the real balances is $u'(c) = u'(m)$, that is, $c = m$, together with the budget constraint that, using the profits, is given by $c + m = w(l - \ell) + M/p + y$.

At a monopolistic competitive equilibrium, all agents determine optimally their choices and all markets clear. Market clearing requires $c = y$ for the final commodity, $m = M/p$ for real balances, and $l = \ell$ for the labor market. We consider symmetric equilibria in which identical agents behave the same, with $x_j = \hat{x}$, $\ell_j = \hat{\ell}$ and $p_j = \hat{p} = p$ for all input producers.

Using the optimality condition (2.9) of the worker with $c = y = zf(x) = zf(l)$ and the optimality condition (2.8) of the companies in symmetric equilibrium with $\hat{\ell} = \ell/J = l/J$, dropping the wage we obtain

$$\frac{v'(l)}{u'(zf(l))} = zf'(l)\xi(l/J), \tag{2.10}$$

where $\xi(l/J) \equiv g'(l/J)\left[1 - \epsilon_{f'}(l)\epsilon_g(l/J) - \epsilon_{g'}(l/J)\right]$. The condition (2.10) determines equilibrium employment, equating the marginal rate of substitution between labor and consumption for the worker with the marginal product of labor altered by the term that reflects the market power of intermediate input producers.

Efficiency requires the equality of the marginal rate of substitution between labor and consumption with the marginal productivity of labor, as in equation (2.7). With perfect competition in all markets, both the marginal rate of substitution between labor and consumption and the marginal productivity of labor would be equated to the wage, achieving efficiency. The presence of market power distorts the allocation, reducing the wage that creates a disincentive to supply labor, in turn reducing employment and income relative to perfect competition.

▪▪ Example 2.6

Suppose that the production function is $f(x) = x^{1-\alpha}$ and the input aggregator has the following constant substitution elasticity of form

$$g(\mathbf{x}) = J^{\frac{\epsilon-1}{\epsilon}} \left(\sum_{j=1}^{J} x_j^{\varepsilon} \right)^{\frac{1}{\varepsilon}},$$

where $\varepsilon \in (0, 1)$ represents the degree of substitution of the inputs, which we assume is sufficiently substitutable, with $\varepsilon > 1 - \alpha$. The function contains a scaling factor that is included to limit the effect of the number of inputs J on equilibrium. In symmetric equilibrium, the derivative is $g'(l/J) = 1$, and the elasticities are $\epsilon_{f'}(l/J) = \alpha$, $\epsilon_g(l/J) = 1/J$ and $\epsilon_{g'}(l/J) = (1-\varepsilon)(J-1)/J$. Inserting these conditions into the equilibrium condition (2.10), we find that the marginal product of labor is reduced by the factor $\xi(J) \equiv [1 - \alpha + \varepsilon(J-1)]/J \leq 1$. The distortion with respect to efficiency is maximal with a monopolist, in which case $\xi(1) = 1 - \alpha$, and decreasing in the number of competitors, since $\xi'(J) > 0$, with $\varepsilon > 1 - \alpha$. When the number of competitors is large, we have $\xi(\infty) = \varepsilon$. Perfect competition corresponds to the benchmark case in which the number of competitors is large and the inputs are perfect substitutes $\varepsilon = 1$, in which case the distortion is nil, leading to $\xi(\infty) = 1$.

2.2.2.2 Price Rigidity

In the model with market power, by the optimality condition for real balances and the budget constraint of the worker with market clearing in the labor market

2

$l = \ell$, and in the money market $m = M/p$, we obtain the equation $p = M/y$ which determines the price level for a given money stock once income has been determined in equilibrium. Notice that the money supply only determines the price level without any real effect. The price level is proportional to the money stock as in the competitive version of the model.

Suppose now that the monetary authority changes marginally the stock of money M after the companies have set their price optimally. Companies can modify their price, but face a small cost of adjusting the price. These are the so-called small *menu costs*. Since companies have optimized with respect to their price, by the envelope theorem the effect of a change in M through the price is nil to first order. Therefore, a small cost is enough to offset the incentive to change prices following a marginal change in the money stock. With unchanged prices, the price level p remains the same, and therefore an increase in the money supply leads to higher income and employment through the equation $y = M/p$. With price rigidity, monetary policy is no longer neutral, giving rise to real effects.

2.2.2.3 Taxation

We can use the model to think about the effects of distortionary taxation on the private sector. Consider the model with perfect competition without money and assume, for simplicity, that the production function is linear and the profit is nil. Suppose that there is a public sector that needs to finance public expenditures G, defined in real terms, through taxation. The public sector maintains the balance of the budget throughout the period. Since lump-sum taxation has no effect on the optimal choice of the company and worker, as it does not affect their income at the margin, we consider taxation as a function of personal income that is distortionary. Consider a taxation scheme, $\tau(wl)$, whose marginal tax rate increases with labor income, that is, $\tau'(wl) > 0$. There are three possibilities for marginal tax rates. Taxation may be regressive, with decreasing marginal tax rates as income increases, $\tau''(wl) < 0$, flat, with constant marginal tax rates at all income levels, $\tau''(wl) = 0$, or progressive, with increasing marginal tax rates in the income profile, $\tau''(wl) > 0$. Real-world taxation is typically progressive for extra-economic reasons. For simplicity, from now on we will limit our attention to the flat tax case, with a flat and time-invariant marginal tax rate, $\tau \in [0, 1]$. The worker's budget constraint in real terms becomes $c = (1 - \tau)wl$, as the income available after tax payment is only a fraction $1 - \tau$ of the labor income. The optimality condition of the worker is

$$\frac{v'(l)}{u'((1-\tau)wl)} = (1-\tau)w,$$

which equates the marginal rate of substitution of labor and consumption to the after-tax wage. Therefore, the tax acts as a wage cut. Everything else remains the same. The allocation is distorted with respect to efficiency, since the wage is reduced by the taxation of labor income. The company is not affected by taxation; therefore, before tax, the wage will reflect productivity $w = z$. Substituting $w = z$ into the previous condition, we obtain equilibrium employment as a function of the flat tax rate, $l(\tau)$, as well as income, $y(\tau) = zl(\tau)$ and consumption, $c(\tau) = (1-\tau)zl(\tau)$. The derivative of the equilibrium employment with respect to the tax rate is

$$l'(\tau) = -\frac{l(\tau)}{1-\tau}\frac{1-\epsilon_u(c(\tau))}{\epsilon_u(c(\tau)) + \epsilon_v(l(\tau))}, \tag{2.11}$$

that is negative if and only if $\epsilon_u(c(\tau)) < 1$. Taxation reduces the wage, and hence the labor income available for consumption expenditures. This, in turn, discourages the labor supply of the worker, when the substitution effect dominates the income effect, thus reducing employment and income.

▪▪ Example 2.7

Consider the example with linear disutility of labor and constant elasticity of substitution of consumption $\epsilon = 1/2$. The equilibrium employment is $l(\tau) = (1-\tau)z$ and the derivative with respect to the marginal tax rate is $l'(\tau) = -z$.

2.2.2.4 Laffer Curve

The tax revenue of the public sector serves to finance entirely public expenditure $G(\tau) = \tau zl(\tau)$, whose derivative with respect to the tax rate is

$$G'(\tau) = z[l(\tau) + \tau l'(\tau)],$$

where equilibrium employment is positive but its derivative (2.11), may be negative depending on the value of the substitution elasticity. Hence, the revenue of the public sector may be non-monotonic in the tax rate because of the disincentive of taxation on the labor supply. Hence, the same tax revenue may be collected with a low and a high tax rate. This is known as the *Laffer curve*.

▪▪ Example 2.8

Continuing with the previous example, the tax revenue of the public sector is $G(\tau) = \tau(1-\tau)z^2$, whose derivative with respect to the tax rate is $G'(\tau) = (1-2\tau)z^2$. Hence, tax revenue increases when the rate is smaller than 50%, reaches a maximum at 50%, then decreases for higher rates.

2.2.2.5 Time Consistency

Suppose the public expenditures affect positively the well-being of people, perhaps through the financing of a public health care system, so that utility is given by

$$U(c, G, l) = u(c) + u(G) - v(l).$$

A benevolent public authority will try to maximize the utility of the worker by choosing the marginal tax rate, knowing that the private sector determines the optimal use of consumption and labor supply operating in a market system. Us-

2

ing the equilibrium employment $l(\tau)$ derived above, the equilibrium consumption $c(\tau) = (1-\tau)zl(\tau)$ and the public expenditures $G(\tau) = \tau y(\tau) = \tau zl(\tau)$ into the utility function of the worker, we obtain

$$U(\tau) = u((1-\tau)zl(\tau)) + u(\tau zl(\tau)) - v(l(\tau)).$$

Thus, the public authority selects the marginal tax rate τ to maximize $U(\tau)$. Taking into account that the consumer will choose optimally consumption and labor supply, hence, the first-order condition $(1-\tau)zu'((1-\tau)zl(\tau)) = v'(l(\tau))$ holds, the optimality condition for the choice of the tax rate by the public authority reduces to

$$u'((1-\tau)zl(\tau))zl(\tau) = u'(\tau zl(\tau))[zl(\tau) + \tau zl'(\tau)],$$

that equates the marginal benefit of private consumption and public expenditures that are substitute from the point of view of the consumer, taking into account the distortion on labor supply induced by the taxation needed to finance the public expenditures, as reflected in the derivative of the employment with respect to the tax rate. The optimality condition gives a tax rate lower than 50% when the substitution effect prevails over the income effect, since in this case the derivative of employment with respect to the tax rate is negative.

Suppose now that the public authority ignores the indirect effect of taxation on the labor supply, considering only the direct effect of the tax rate on the income and the tax revenue. Considering l independent of τ, the optimality condition for the tax rate to maximize the private sector utility is

$$u'((1-\tau)zl)zl = u'(\tau zl)zl,$$

that is, $1-\tau = \tau$, with the optimal marginal tax rate at 50%.

The first scenario, in which the public sector takes into account that the worker's labor supply decision will be affected by the tax rate, corresponds to the policy that would be chosen by picking the tax rate beforehand and committing to stick to the choice. This policy decision is governed by a rule of intervention that is adopted initially and maintained throughout. The second scenario, in which the public sector ignores the effect of taxation on the worker's labor supply, corresponds to the policy that would be chosen changing the tax rate in a discretionary manner after the private sector has already determined its labor supply. This would be a scenario in which the public authority cannot commit to sticking to the long-term optimal taxation plan. Under discretionary policy, the tax rate ends up being higher since the discouraging effect of taxation on the labor supply is ignored. If the private sector anticipates that the public authority will intervene in a discretionary manner, it will respond by reducing its labor supply in the first place, thus depressing economic activity. This is the problem of *time inconsistency* of the public sector that imposes a burden on the private sector arising from the temptation to intervene in a discretionary manner, which may come, for instance, from electoral considerations, rather than following time-consistent rules.

Example 2.9
Continuing with the previous example with $\epsilon = 1/2$, the optimality condition for the tax rate factoring in the distortion on labor supply can be written as $\sqrt{\tau(1-\tau)} = 1 - 2\tau$, whose solution gives an optimal tax rate $\tau^* < 1/2$. Ignoring the effect on labor supply, the optimal tax rate is $\hat{\tau} = 1/2$.

2.3 Saving

The previous static model concerned the intratemporal trade-off between consumption and labor supply, that is, how much leisure to give up to earn wage income to be spent on current consumption. The other key economic decision concerns the intertemporal trade-off between current and future consumption, that is, how much of current income to save for the future. We present a simple two-period model with a single durable commodity that can be accumulated for the future in the form of capital to capture this intertemporal trade-off.

2.3.1 Capital

We describe the technology available to produce output and the preferences for consumption of the saver in the two periods. Then, we determine the efficient allocation of resources and use it to derive the competitive equilibrium appealing to the welfare theorems. There are two time periods indexed by $t = 1, 2$.

2.3.1.1 Technology

In the second of the two periods, a technology is available that uses capital K, and labor L, to produce the output Y, represented by the differentiable production function $Y = zF(K, L)$ that satisfies the following requirements.

Assumption 3
i. $F_K(K,L) > 0 > F_{KK}(K,L)$; ii. $F_L(K,L) > 0 > F_{LL}(K,L)$; iii. $F_K(0,L) = F_L(K,0) = \infty$;
iv. $F(xK, xL) = xY$ for any $x > 0$.

Thus, each input has a positive and decreasing marginal productivity and the production function exhibits constant returns to scale, in the sense that, say, by doubling both inputs, the output also doubles. Due to constant scale returns, expressing production and capital per capita as $y \equiv Y/L$ and $k \equiv K/L$, we can write the production function in intensive form

$$y = zf(k),$$

where $f(k) \equiv F(K/L, 1)$, $f'(k) > 0 > f''(k)$, with $f(0) = 0$ and the boundary condition $f'(0) = \infty$, by Assumption 3. Capital depreciates completely in production. The model encompasses partial depreciation by interpreting $f(k)$ as gross production with the surviving capital stock.

Example 2.10

The Cobb-Douglas production function $Y = zF(K,L) = zK^{\alpha}L^{1-\alpha}$ with $\alpha \in (0,1)$ meets all the requirements of Assumption 3. Due to constant scale returns, we can rewrite the production function in intensive form as $y = f(k) = zk^{\alpha}$.

2.3.1.2 Preferences

There is a representative saver with a positive initial endowment e of resources, a unit time endowment in the second period entirely devoted to work and consumption preferences in the first period, denoted by c_1, and the second period, denoted by c_2, represented by the utility function

$$U(c_1, c_2) = u(c_1) + \beta u(c_2),$$

with time discount $\beta < 1$, where the utility function is differentiable and satisfies the following requirements. Time separable utility with discounting encapsulates the notion that the saver is relatively impatient, favoring current relative to future consumption.

Assumption 4

i. $u'(c_t) > 0 > u''(c_t)$ for $c_t \geq 0$ at $t = 1, 2$; ii. $u'(0) = \infty$.

Thus, utility is strictly increasing, and strictly concave and satisfies the boundary condition at zero consumption.

Example 2.11

The utility function $u(c_t) = (1-\epsilon)^{-1}c_t^{1-\epsilon}$ with $\epsilon \geq 0$ for $t = 1, 2$ meets the requirements of Assumption 4. When $\epsilon = 1$, one obtains the logarithm.

2.3.1.3 Efficiency

Since the economy has no imperfections, the welfare theorems apply. Therefore, the efficient allocation can be decentralized by market trade. We use a short-cut to derive the competitive equilibrium, computing first the efficient allocation and then using it to derive the rental rate of capital and the wage. The efficient allocation maximizes the saver's life-time utility subject to the resource constraint in the first period, $c_1 + k = e$, and in the second period, $c_2 = y = zf(k)$. Substituting these constraints into the utility function, we obtain $U(k) = u(e-k) + \beta u(zf(k))$. Calculating the first-order necessary condition for the optimal choice of capital k, $U'(k) = 0$, we obtain

$$u'(e-k) = \beta z f'(k) u'(zf(k)), \tag{2.12}$$

which gives the efficient stock of capital. The investment in capital reduces current consumption but increases future consumption boosting productivity. The condition is also sufficient by the strict concavity of the production and utility functions. This condition can be written as

$$\frac{1}{\beta}\frac{u'(c_1)}{u'(c_2)} = f'(k),$$

which equates the intertemporal marginal rate of substitution between consumption in the two periods with the marginal productivity of capital. The efficient allocation optimally trades off the consumption substitution between the two periods with the marginal productivity gain of additional savings. The next proposition proves the existence of a unique efficient capital stock that solves equation (2.12).

Proposition 2.2
There is a unique efficient capital stock for any productivity level.

Proof According to Assumptions 3.iii and 4.ii, the RHS of (2.12) is infinite and the LHS finite when $k = 0$; when $k = e$, the LHS of (2.12) is infinite and the RHS finite. Therefore, by continuity, there is a $k^* \in (0, e)$ that satisfies (2.12) for any z. Due to the strict concavity of the utility and production functions in Assumptions 3.i and 2.i, k^* is unique for any z. □

We denote by $k(z)$ the efficient capital stock as a function of productivity. The efficient consumption for the first period is given by $c_1(z) = e - k(z) > 0$ and the efficient consumption for the second period by $c_2(z) = zf(k(z))$.

2.3.1.4 Competitive Equilibrium

Suppose that the technology is owned by a company that rents capital at a competitive real rental rate r and pays a competitive real wage w in the second period. Maximization of profits $y - rk - w$ with technology $y = zf(k)$ leads to the optimality condition that equates the marginal product of capital with its rental rate $zf'(k) = r$. Competition with constant return-to-scale implies zero profits; therefore, the wage is $w = z[f(k) - f'(k)k]$. The competitive equilibrium allocation coincides with the efficient one by the welfare theorems. Thus, the competitive rental rate is $r = zf'(k(z))$, and the competitive wage is $w = z[f(k(z)) - f'(k(z))k(z)]$.

Example 2.12
Consider the production function $y = k^\alpha$ with $\alpha \in (0, 1)$, $z = 1$, and the utility function $u(c_t) = \ln c_t$ for $t = 1, 2$. The efficient allocation has the capital stock $k^* = \alpha\beta e/(1 + \alpha\beta)$, consumption in the first period is $c_1^* = e/(1 + \alpha\beta)$ and in the second period $c_2^* = [\alpha\beta e/(1 + \alpha\beta)]^\alpha$. The competitive rental rate is $r = \alpha[\alpha\beta e/(1 + \alpha\beta)]^{\alpha-1}$ and the wage is $w = (1 - \alpha)[\alpha\beta e/(1 + \alpha\beta)]^\alpha$.

2.3.1.5 Ricardian Equivalence

Suppose that the public sector needs to finance public expenditure G in the first period. The options available are immediate lump-sum taxation T_1 or the issuance of public debt in the form of government bonds of a period, whose stock is D, reimbursed in the second period with gross real interest R financed by lump-sum taxation T_2. The government budget for the first period is $G = T_1 + D$ and in the second period $RD = T_2$. Substituting for the public debt from the latter constraint into the first, we obtain the intertemporal budget constraint of the government

$G = T_1 + T_2R^{-1}$, where public expenditure appears to be financed through discounted and future taxation.

The demand for bonds by the saver in each period for the next is denoted by d. The budget constraint of the saver in the first period is $c_1 + k + d = e - T_1$ and in the second period $c_2 = rk + Rd - T_2$, since the debt is paid with interest R and there is a lump-sum tax in each period. For the saver to be willing to save using both capital and public debt, it must be $r = R$. Solving the second budget constraint for the demand for debt by the saver and inserting it into the first budget constraint, we obtain the intertemporal budget constraint of the saver $c_1 + c_2 = e - (T_1 + T_2R^{-1})$. Using the government budget into this constraint, we obtain

$$c_1 + c_2 + G = e.$$

In other words, the choice of the saver as far as consumption is concerned depends on the amount of public expenditure G of the government, but not on the way the government decides to finance them, whether through immediate taxation or public debt issuance financed by postponed taxation. The saver anticipates that any government debt issuance while reducing current taxation will have to be financed with extra taxation in the future that is equivalent in discounted terms. In sum, public debt is neutral as regards the equilibrium determination of the real allocations.

2.3.1.6 Employment

We now consider the simultaneous determination of savings and labor supply within the two-period market model. Suppose that the representative saver can decide the supply of labor in the second period l. The utility function of the saver is

$$U(c_1, c_2, l) = u(c_1) + \beta[u(c_2) - v(l)],$$

where the disutility of labor satisfies $v'(l) > 0, v''(l) \geq 0$ for all $l \geq 0$. The budget constraint of the saver in the second period is $c_2 = wl + rk$. The optimality condition for labor supply is $wu'(wl + rk) = v'(l)$. Labor supply is optimally adjusted to the point where it equates the marginal rate of intratemporal substitution between labor and consumption to the real wage. The zero-profit condition of the company is $wl + rk = zf(k)$ and the rental rate is $r = zf'(k)$. The optimality condition becomes

$$z[f(k) - f'(k)k]u'(zf(k)) = v'(l)l,$$

which determines the equilibrium employment once the capital stock is obtained from equation (2.12). Since the derivative of the function $h(l) \equiv v'(l)l$ is increasing monotonically, it is invertible. Therefore, the equilibrium employment is $l(z) = h^{-1}(z[f(k(z)) - f'(k(z))k(z)]u'(zf(k(z))))$

2.3.1.7 Productivity

The effect of a change in productivity on capital accumulation is given by

$$k'(z) = \frac{k(z)}{z} \frac{1 - \epsilon_u(c_2(z))}{\epsilon_u(c_1(z))k(z)/c_1(z) + \epsilon_{f'}(k(z)) + \epsilon_f(k(z))\epsilon_u(c_2(z))},$$

which is positive if and only if $\epsilon_u(c_2(z)) < 1$. The same applies to $l'(z)$. Thus, when the substitution effect prevails on the income effect, a drop in productivity has an adverse effect on capital accumulation and employment.

2.3.2 Externality

Suppose now that the productivity z depends on the average capital stock in the economy, denoted by $\mathcal{K}$, through the differentiable function $z(\mathcal{K})$, which is non-negative and strictly increasing in $\mathcal{K}$. There is a unit continuum of identical companies and savers who make exactly the same decisions as before, without internalizing the effect of their decisions on the average capital stock. The optimization of the companies gives the rental rate $r = z(\mathcal{K})f'(k)$ and the wage $w = z(\mathcal{K})[f(k) - f'(k)k]$. The optimization of the saver, ignoring the labor decision, gives $u'(e-k) = \beta z(\mathcal{K})f'(k)u'(z(\mathcal{K})f(k))$. In symmetric equilibrium, since all identical traders are treated equally and there is a unit continuum of traders, the individual and average capital stock are equal $k = \mathcal{K}$. Therefore, the equilibrium condition that determines the capital stock is

$$u'(e-k) = \beta z(k)f'(k)u'(z(k)f(k)). \tag{2.13}$$

Next, we consider two scenarios that contain in a nutshell the theories of endogenous long-term growth and endogenous business fluctuations to be addressed later in the book.

2.3.2.1 AK Model

Suppose that the productivity is such that, when combined with the production function, it comes out linear with a constant productivity factor $z(k)f(k) = Ak$. The equilibrium condition (2.13) becomes

$$u'(e-k) = \beta A u'(Ak).$$

Under the maintained assumptions, an equilibrium capital stock that satisfies this equation exists and is unique. Since marginal utility decreases in consumption, people consume more later than earlier in time if and only if $A > \beta^{-1}$. The extension of the model to the long term with an infinitely lived dynasty of savers, known as the AK model, generates an indefinite growth of consumption, income, and capital accumulation at a positive net rate $g = \beta A - 1$. The productive externality at the aggregate level compensates for the decreasing returns to scale of capital at the individual level, leading to long-term growth.

2

2.3.2.2 Multiple Equilibria

Consider now the equilibrium condition (2.13). An equilibrium capital stock that satisfies this equation exists, by the boundary conditions on the production and utility functions. However, the equilibrium is not necessarily unique. Taking the derivative with respect to the capital stock and evaluating it at an equilibrium capital stock $\tilde{k}$, we find that its sign is negative if

$$\frac{\epsilon_{u'}(e-\tilde{k})\tilde{k} + [\epsilon_{f'}(\tilde{k}) + \epsilon_f(\tilde{k})\epsilon_{u'}(z(\tilde{k})f(\tilde{k}))](e-\tilde{k})}{(e-\tilde{k})[1-\epsilon_{u'}(z(\tilde{k})f(\tilde{k}))]} < \epsilon_z(\tilde{k}),$$

where $\epsilon_z(k) \equiv z'(k)k/z(k)$ is the elasticity of productivity with respect to capital. If such a condition is satisfied at some equilibrium, there are multiple capital stocks that are compatible with the competitive equilibrium. In this case, the productive externality results in an equilibrium multiplicity that can give rise to situations in which the traders coordinate their expectations on different scenarios, with different levels of capital accumulation and income. This phenomenon forms the basis for the endogenous business cycle literature.

2.4 Conclusion

The standard market model even in its simple static or short-run form already contains the main features that will emerge from its infinite-horizon version. The allocation is efficient; a drop in productivity leads to a drop in equilibrium wage, employment, income, and capital when the substitution effect dominates the income effect. Money determines the price level but is neutral as regards real allocations, unless there are nominal rigidities. Public debt is also neutral with respect to real allocations. Market power and income taxation distort the allocations away from efficiency. Public policy may suffer from time inconsistency. Capital is accumulated efficiently to save resources for the future to compensate lower current consumption with higher future consumption financed by higher productivity. Externalities in production can give rise to permanent economic growth or endogenous economic fluctuations.

2.5 Literature

The possibility of time inconsistency of public policy was first pointed out by Finn Kydland and Ed Prescott in their celebrated paper *Rules rather than Discretion: the Inconsistency of Optimal Plans*. The model with monopolistic competition is a simplified version of the model contained in the paper *Monopolistic Competition and the Effects of Aggregate Demand* by Olivier Blanchard and Nobuhiro Kiyotaki. The Ricardian equivalence, which takes its name from the nineteenth-century British economist David Ricardo, who first formulated it, has been shown to hold in a general equilibrium intertemporal model by Robert Barro in the paper entitled *Are Government Bonds Net Wealth?* The version of the model with the productive externality is inspired by the paper *Increasing Returns and Animal Spirits* by Philippe Weil.

Exercises

1. Let the company production function be $y = f(\ell) = \sqrt{\ell}$.
   a. Calculate the marginal product of labor.
   b. Calculate the optimal labor demand as a function of the wage w.
   c. Calculate the effect of a change in the wage on labor demand.
2. Let the utility function of the worker be $U(c, l) = \log c - l$.
   a. Calculate the marginal utility of consumption and the disutility of labor.
   b. Calculate the optimal labor supply as a function of the real wage w.
   c. Calculate the effect of a change in the wage on labor supply.
3. Let the utility function of the worker be $U(c, l) = 2\sqrt{c} - l$.
   a. Calculate the marginal utility of consumption and the disutility of labor.
   b. Calculate the optimal labor supply as a function of the real wage w.
   c. Calculate the effect of a change in the wage on labor supply.
4. Let the utility function of the worker be $U(c, l) = \log c - l$ and the production function of the company $y = f(\ell) = z\sqrt{\ell}$.
   a. Calculate the competitive equilibrium.
   b. Calculate the efficient allocation.
   c. Calculate the effect of a change in z on employment and income.
5. Let the utility function of the worker be $U(c, l) = 2\sqrt{c} - l$ and the production function of the company $y = f(\ell) = z\ell$.
   a. Calculate the competitive equilibrium.
   b. Calculate the efficient allocation.
   c. Calculate the effect of a change in z on employment and income.
6. Let the company production function be $Y = f(K, L) = \sqrt{KL}$.
   a. Calculate the marginal product of capital and labor.
   b. Calculate the optimal demand for capital and labor.
   c. Calculate the effect of a change in the rental rate on the demand for capital per capita.
7. Let the utility function of the worker be $U(c_1, c_2) = \log c_1 + \beta \log c_2$.
   a. Calculate the marginal utility of consumption for the two periods.
   b. Calculate the optimal savings decision.
8. Let the utility function of the worker be $U(c_1, c_2) = \log c_1 + \beta \log c_2$, $e = 1$, and the production function of the company $Y = f(K, L) = \sqrt{KL}$.
   a. Calculate the competitive equilibrium.
   b. Calculate the efficient allocation.

2

References

Barro R (1974), Are Government Bonds Net Wealth? Journal of Political Economy, 82: 1095–1117

Blanchard O, Kiyotaki N (1987), Monopolistic Competition and the Effects of Aggregate Demand, American Economic Review, 77: 647–666

Kydland F, Prescott E (1977), Rules Rather than Discretion: The Inconsistency of Optimal Plans, Journal of Political Economy, 85: 473–492

Weil P (1989), Increasing Returns and Animal Spirits, American Economic Review, 79: 889–894

Exogenous and Endogenous Cycles

L. Ferraris, *Macroeconomic Theory*, Classroom Companion: Economics,
https://doi.org/10.1007/978-3-031-88740-6_3

3.1 Introduction

Employment and income fluctuate together over time. This short-run phenomenon is known as the *business cycle*. In this chapter, we will identify the main driving forces of business cycles. We will discuss three different points of view on this issue.

First, we will present the view that business cycles originate from the aggregation of random events that affect productivity. This is the view associated with the so-called *Real Business Cycle* theory. According to this view, business cycles are the efficient response of a well-functioning market economy to supply-side disturbances.

Second, we will discuss the view that business cycles originate from aggregate demand shocks driven by monetary policy contractions, in economies with price rigidities. This view, sometimes referred to as the *Monetary Business Cycle* theory, considers the business cycle as an inefficient response of an economy with nominal rigidities in the short run destined to be corrected in the long run. Both of these views consider business cycles as driven by forces that are external or exogenous with respect to the private sector and presume that the expectations of the private sector are firmly pinned down by the equilibrium. For this reason, these are known as *Exogenous Business Cycle* theories.

Finally, we will examine the alternative view that business cycles arise from within the private sector as a consequence of the problematic coordination of its expectations that may become unhinged. This is the view that is associated with the so-called *Endogenous Business Cycle* theory. According to this view, business cycles are driven by the potentially erratic market beliefs of people who coordinate their expectations using extrinsic events known as *sunspots*, turning their fears that the economy may end up in recession into self-fulfilling prophecies. The exogenous theory of the business cycle requires the substitution effect to prevail over the income effect, while the endogenous theory requires the income effect to prevail over the substitution effect.

3.2 Exogenous Business Cycle

The model we have discussed in the previous chapter can be immediately extended to an infinite time horizon with an infinitely lived dynasty of workers. For this reason, the model is called dynastic. The dynastic model leads to the same behavior as the static model repeated over time when there are no imperfections. The model can be used to study the effect of changes in productivity on employment, income, and consumption, as in the *Real Business Cycle* theory, which attributes recessions to negative productivity shocks. With money and nominal rigidities, recessions can be attributed to monetary policy contractions, as in the *Monetary Business Cycle* theory.

3.2.1 Real Business Cycle

The time is indexed by the variable $t = 1, 2, ...$ that runs over the integers. A representative company and a representative dynasty trade labor in a competitive labor market every period without distortions.

3.2.1.1 Competitive Equilibrium

The company operates every period a technology represented by the linear production function

$$y_t = f(\ell_t) = z_t \ell_t.$$

By maximization of the company, the optimal labor demand will be perfectly elastic when the wage equalizes the productivity, $w_t = z_t$ at all times, resulting in zero profit for the company.

The dynasty of workers maximizes its life-time utility, representing its preferences for sequences of consumption $\mathbf{c}$ and labor $\mathbf{l}$, given by

$$U(\mathbf{c}, \mathbf{l}) = \sum_{t=1}^{\infty} \beta^{t-1} [u(c_t) - v(l_t)], \tag{3.1}$$

where $\beta < 1$ is the time discount factor, that represents the preference of the dynasty for current relative to future consumption. The utility function satisfies Assumption 2. Since the profit is null, the budget constraint at each point in time will be $c_t = w_t l_t$, which can be inserted into (3.1), to calculate the condition that determines the optimal choice of labor supply at any time $w_t u'(w_t l_t) = v'(l_t)$, which equates the marginal rate of substitution between labor and consumption with the real wage at each point in time.

Competitive equilibrium requires the company and the dynasty to make optimal choices every period with perfect foresight of future wages, and the labor market to clear every period. Using the optimality condition of the dynasty with $w_t = z_t$, we obtain the same equilibrium condition that we had in the static model holding at all times, $v'(l_t) = z_t u'(z_t l_t)$. Therefore, the model has exactly the same properties as the static model, including efficiency. When productivity is time-invariant, so is the allocation and the wage.

3.2.1.2 Productivity Shocks

The model can be extended to include uncertainty, adding shocks to productivity, for example $z_t = Z z_{t-1} + \varepsilon_t$, with $Z < 1$ and ε normally distributed with zero mean and finite variance. In this case, the life-time utility (3.1) becomes an expected life-time utility. The requirement that the dynasty has perfect foresight of future wages becomes a requirement that the expectations of the future wages of the dynasty are rational, that is, correct on average. The model can generate fluctuations in employment and income over time. In particular, a negative shock to productivity would lower the real wage, which in turn would negatively affect the supply of labor, when the substitution elasticity is lower than 1. This would de-

3

press employment and income. The full model has capital as additional productive input which can be accumulated over time by the dynasty that gives up current consumption to invest for the future. Capital accumulation introduces in the model an intertemporal transmission mechanism that operates through the investment decision of the dynasty that propagates the shocks to the future, with a mild degree of persistency. Once the productivity shock is passed on to current income, investment will adjust affecting future production. The change in investment turns out to be relatively larger than consumption, which therefore turns out to be smoother than income. The complete model is then calibrated; that is, the preference and technology parameters are set to be consistent with the long-term behavior of the economy and used to generate a profile of consumption, investment, employment, and income to be compared with actual data.

3.2.1.3 Euler Equation

Suppose that a one-period bond is available that is reimbursed with a net real interest payment r_t for every period. The budget constraint of the dynasty becomes $c_t + b_{t+1} = w_t l_t + (1 + r_t) b_t$, where b_{t+1} is the demand for the bond. The choice of the bond adds another optimality condition that governs the portfolio decision of the dynasty, equating the gross interest payment to the marginal rate of substitution of consumption over time

$$1 + r_{t+1} = \frac{u'(c_t)}{\beta u'(c_{t+1})}. \tag{3.2}$$

Current consumption is forfeited at the margin to increase future consumption, factoring in the interest payment. This intertemporal condition that governs the saving decision through the bond is known as the *Euler equation*. In a stationary equilibrium with time-invariant productivity, employment, income, and consumption remain constant over time. By equation (3.2), this requires the interest rate $r = \beta^{-1} - 1$. Employment is determined by $zu'(zl) = v'(l)$. Consumption and income are given by $c = y = zl$.

3.2.2 Monetary Business Cycle

Now, we introduce money into the dynastic model using the money-in-the-utility short-cut. With nominal rigidities, the model can give rise to monetary non-neutrality.

3.2.2.1 Utility of Money

Money can be added to the model to generate a quantity theory equation that determines the price level and inflation, assuming that real cash balances give a utility benefit to the dynasty that is symmetric with respect to consumption as seen before. This is the model with *money in the utility function*, which implicitly captures its transaction services. Suppose that the nominal money stock is constant over time $M_t = M$ at all times and that the productivity is also constant over time $z_t = z$ at all times. The life-time utility of the dynasty, representing its preferences for sequences of consumption $\mathbf{c}$, real money balances $\mathbf{m}$ and labor supply $\mathbf{l}$, is given by

$$U(\mathbf{c}, \mathbf{m}, \mathbf{l}) = \sum_{t=1}^{\infty} \beta^{t-1}[u(c_t) + u((1+\rho_{t+1})m_{t+1}) - v(l_t)],$$

where $1 + \rho_t \equiv p_t/p_{t-1}$ is the gross inflation rate. The real balances accumulated for the end of the period m_{t+1}, need to be adjusted using the inflation rate to make them comparable to the real balances at the beginning of the period. The budget constraint of the dynasty in real terms is given by

$$c_t + (1 + \rho_{t+1})m_{t+1} = w_t l_t + m_t,$$

in every period, since the labor income and the real balances accumulated from the past can be spent on consumption and new real balances. The optimality condition for the choice of real balances, m_{t+1}, is

$$[u'(c_t) - u'(m_{t+1})](1 + \rho_{t+1}) = \beta u'(c_{t+1}),$$

and the optimality condition for labor supply is $w_t u'(c_t) = v'(l_t)$ as before. The wage is still determined as before by the optimization of the company as $w_t = z$. The equilibrium in the money market requires $m_t = M/p_t$ in every period.

Consider a stationary equilibrium with time-invariant real variables. With a constant stock of money, the price level remains constant over time and, therefore, the inflation rate is nil $\rho_t = 0$ in every period. Thus, the optimality condition for the real balances above becomes $u'(m) = (1 - \beta)u'(c)$ and the budget constraint becomes $c = wl$. Hence, the equilibrium condition for employment is $zu'(zl_t) = v'(l_t)$. The price level is pinned down by the condition $p = M/u'^{-1}((1 - \beta)u'(y))$, which is a version of the quantity theory of money, since the price level is proportional to the nominal money stock.

3.2.2.2 Inflation

Suppose now that there is a monetary authority that has the control of the money stock. Define the gross growth rate of the money stock as the current stock relative to the previous period stock, namely $1 + \gamma_t \equiv M_t/M_{t-1}$, which we assume to be constant over time, with $\gamma_t = \gamma$ at all times. The money stock is altered by the monetary authority through lump-sum taxes and transfers. In a stationary equilibrium, the inflation rate is now given by $\rho_t = \gamma$ at all times. In other words, inflation is governed by the growth rate of the money stock.

Notice that the money stock and its growth rate, while determining the price level and the inflation rate, are neutral with respect to the real variables, in the sense that changes in its stock do not alter the equilibrium allocations, and also superneutral, in the sense that changes in the growth rate of its stock do not alter the equilibrium allocations.

Example 3.1

In the example with constant substitution elasticity and linear disutility of labor, assuming for simplicity $\epsilon = 1/2$, the quantity theory holds and the price level is $p = (1 - \beta)^2 M/z^2$.

3.2.2.3 Fisher Equation

3 In addition to the real bond, there is also a nominal bond available refunded in the following period in cash with net nominal interest payment $i_t \geq 0$. For the dynasty to hold both instruments, it should be impossible to make profits arbitraging between them. This is guaranteed by the condition known as the *Fisher equation* that equates the real rate to the nominal rate discounting the effect of inflation

$$1 + r_t = \frac{1 + i_t}{1 + \rho_t}. \tag{3.3}$$

If the stock of money remains constant, the inflation is bound to be zero and, therefore, the nominal and the real rates are the same and equal to $i = r = \beta^{-1} - 1$. With a stock of currency that changes at a constant rate γ over time, the nominal interest rate is given by $i = (1 + \gamma)\beta^{-1} - 1$.

3.2.2.4 Nominal Rigidity

Real-world monetary authorities use the nominal interest rate rather than the stock of liquidity as a policy instrument. Consider a version of the model in which the companies have market power. Suppose that the price is rigid in the short run, that is, in the first period, but not in the long run, from the second period onward. The optimality condition for the labor supply of the worker equates the marginal rate of substitution of labor and consumption with the real wage, which is lower than the marginal productivity of labor due to the market power of the companies. There is a nominal bond whose Euler condition equates the interest rate with the marginal rate of substitution between current and future consumption. Suppose that the monetary authority uses the monetary instrument to maintain price stability with zero inflation and controls the nominal interest rate of the bond. By the Fisher equation (3.3), the nominal and real interest rates are the same when inflation is nil. The Euler condition in the first period is

$$u'(y_1) = \beta u'(\tilde{y})(1 + i_2),$$

where $y_2 = \tilde{y}$, since from the next period onward the economy will operate without price rigidity, with long-term output level $\tilde{y}$. Suppose that $i_2 > \beta^{-1} - 1$, so that the short-run employment is lower than its long-run value. From the next period on, $i_t = \beta^{-1} - 1$ for $t \geq 3$. Since the utility function is strictly concave, lowering the nominal interest rate increases short-run income. On the other hand, since the companies cannot adjust the prices in the short run, the profit margin has to decrease to maintain equilibrium. Thus, a lower interest rate has real effects in the short run, increasing income and eroding the market power of companies. In contrast, a monetary contraction with an increase in the nominal interest rate induces a recession. In the long run, without price rigidity, monetary policy determines the price level and is neutral as regards allocations.

3.2.2.5 Interest Rate Rule

Let us now see how a monetary authority that controls the nominal interest rate of the bond instead of the money stock can pin down the inflation rate. Assume also that the price and wage are flexible at all times and that all the markets are perfectly competitive.

In equilibrium, the Euler condition (3.2) with $c_t = y_t$ expresses the growth of income as a function of discounting and the real interest rate. Income is time-invariant; hence, the real interest rate is also time-invariant and is pinned down by the equation $\beta(1+r) = 1$. Applying a logarithmic transformation to both sides of this equation, we obtain

$$r = -\ln\beta, \tag{3.4}$$

since $\ln(1+r) \approx r$ for small r. The nominal and the real interest rate are related through the inflation rate by the Fisher equation (3.3). The only variable that may not be time-invariant is inflation, whose expectations may alter the nominal rate. Applying the same logarithmic transformation with the approximation $\ln(1+x) \approx x$ valid for small x, we obtain the nominal rate as the sum of the real rate and expected inflation $i = r + \mathbb{E}\rho$. Plugging into the Fisher equation the real interest rate from the Euler condition, (3.4), we obtain

$$i = \mathbb{E}\rho - \ln\beta. \tag{3.5}$$

Suppose that the monetary authority follows the so-called *Taylor rule*, whereby the nominal interest rate is increased if current inflation is above its target, which for simplicity, we set to zero. Thus, the nominal rate is given by

$$i = \upsilon\rho - \ln\beta, \tag{3.6}$$

with a reaction parameter $\upsilon > 0$ and a constant term that reflects time discounting. Equating the nominal rate from the Taylor rule, (3.6), and the Fisher equation (3.5), we obtain the equilibrium condition

$$\mathbb{E}\rho = \upsilon\rho,$$

in which the expected future inflation is a linear function of current inflation. Clearly, the only stationary solution has zero inflation. If $\upsilon < 1$ the stationary solution is globally stable, hence indeterminate with a continuum of trajectories converging to it, if $\upsilon > 1$ the stationary solution is globally unstable, hence determinate, while case $\upsilon = 1$ is knife edge. Hence, the dynamic path of inflation is determinate if and only if $\upsilon > 1$.

Therefore, to pin down the inflation path and maintain price stability, the monetary authority should adopt a policy rule that responds aggressively to any inflation episode, increasing the nominal rate more than one-for-one with current inflation. Essentially, the monetary authority maintains price stability, threatening to let the inflation rate explode if inflation diverges from its target.

Notice that should the monetary authority fix the nominal interest rate at a constant value independent of inflation, setting $i = \iota - \ln \beta$, the dynamic equation that governs the evolution of inflation would become $\mathbb{E}\rho = \iota$, which does not pin down the inflation path for any value of ι as a continuum of inflation rates are compatible with a constant expected inflation. This is the well-known proposition that states that the inflation path is indeterminate if monetary policy pegs the nominal interest rate.

3.3 Endogenous Business Cycle

The static model can be embedded into a dynamic framework in a model in which the time horizon is infinite, but people live finite lives, known as the life-cycle or *overlapping generations* model.

3.3.1 Life-cycle Model

There is a company with a technology represented by the production function $y_t = \ell_t$, where for simplicity it is assumed that productivity is unitary. The optimization of the company leads to $w_t = 1$.

Every period, starting from the first date, a new consumer is born who will live for two periods. On the first date, there is a consumer who is already alive and lives only in that period. The model has overlapping generations in the sense that in every period there are two consumers who are alive and belong to two consecutive generations. Each generation has preferences represented by the utility function

$$U(c_{t+1}, l_t) = \beta u(c_{t+1}) - v(l_t),$$

in other words, people can work when young, experiencing disutility of labor, but enjoy consumption when old. The utility function satisfies Assumption 2. Suppose that there is an asset, in fixed supply, that allows traders to transfer income over time. The young agent born at time t works for a wage that is invested in the asset. In real terms, the worker gets $w_t l_t = m_t$, where m_t is the demand for the asset. When old, the agent can spend his or her savings on consumption, $(1 + r_{t+1})m_t = c_{t+1}$, where $r_{t+1} \geq 0$ is the interest rate. Substituting consumption and labor for the demand of the asset and computing the first-order condition for the optimal choice of the savings, obtain

$$v'(m_t w_t^{-1}) w_t^{-1} = \beta(1 + r_{t+1}) u'((1 + r_{t+1}) m_t), \tag{3.7}$$

where, as usual, the current marginal disutility of labor per unit of the wage is equated to the future marginal benefit of consumption factoring in the interest payment of the asset.

3.3.1.1 Competitive Equilibrium

The equilibrium requires clearing the market for the commodity and the asset, in particular $c_t = y_t$. The optimality of the company implies $w_t = 1$, with the production function y_t in every period. Together with the equilibrium conditions, the budget constraints of the agent give $c_t = y_t = l_t = m_t$ and $(1 + r_{t+1})m_t = c_{t+1} = y_{t+1} = l_{t+1} = m_{t+1}$. Substituting these equations in the optimality condition (3.7), we obtain

$$m_t v'(m_t) = \beta m_{t+1} u'(m_{t+1}). \tag{3.8}$$

An equilibrium is a sequence of real asset balances m_t that satisfies equation (3.8). A stationary equilibrium is invariant in time, with $m_t = m$ at all times. The existence of a unique $m > 0$ that satisfies $v'(m) = \beta u'(m)$ is established by continuity under Assumption 2. This equilibrium value of real balances determines consumption, income, and employment, since $m = c = y = l$. There is also a stationary equilibrium in which $m = 0$. In stationary equilibrium, the interest rate is nil, since $(1 + r)m = m$. Therefore, we can interpret the asset as a fiat object similar to money, used as a *store of value* or saving instrument to transfer income over time.

Example 3.2

Consider the utility of consumption with constant elasticity, ϵ, and the linear disutility of labor. The dynamic equation (3.8) becomes $m_{t+1} = (m_t/\beta)^{\frac{1}{1-\epsilon}}$. The stationary equilibrium with trade has $m = \beta^{\frac{1}{\epsilon}}$. Employment, consumption, and income are $l = y = c = \beta^{\frac{1}{\epsilon}}$.

3.3.1.2 Efficiency

The stationary equilibrium with trade that satisfies the equilibrium condition $v'(m) = \beta u'(m)$ is efficient, as can be seen by computing the stationary efficient allocation that is obtained maximizing the utility function subject to the feasibility constraint. There is still, however, a stationary equilibrium without trade that is inefficient, as well as all the non-stationary equilibria that are also inefficient. The reason for the inefficiency of some of the equilibria of the life-cycle model is that there is an overall infinite amount of resources available for redistribution, due to the presence of an infinite number of generations overlapping over time.

Example 3.3

Continuing with the previous example, the efficient allocation is $l^* = y^* = c^* = \beta^{\frac{1}{\epsilon}}$.

3.3.2 Self-Fulfilling Prophecy

There are also non-stationary, time-changing, equilibria in this model, some of which are cyclical. When the map describing the equilibrium dynamics, (3.8), linearized around the stationary equilibrium has a slope equal to -1, its solutions alternate deterministically around the steady state.

3.3.2.1 Cycles

From the equilibrium condition (3.8), by implicit differentiation, we obtain the derivative evaluated at the steady state

3

$$\left.\frac{dm_t}{dm_{t+1}}\right|_m = \frac{1-\epsilon_{u'}(m)}{1+\epsilon_{v'}(m)}, \tag{3.9}$$

where we consider the inverse dynamics, since the map $mu'(m)$ may be non-monotonic and, hence, not invertible. For the dynamical system to generate endogenous cyclical behavior, the derivative (3.9) should be sufficiently negative, so that the equilibrium variables oscillate deterministically above and below their stationary equilibrium value. In particular, to have a cycle of period two near the stationary state, namely an equilibrium in which the real balances alternate deterministically around their stationary equilibrium value, it has to be that the derivative (3.9) equals -1, that is, $\epsilon_{u'}(m) = 2 + \epsilon_{v'}(m)$. Therefore, the endogenous business cycle theory requires the income effect to dominate the substitution effect.

Example 3.4

Consider the following specification of the fundamentals, with $v(l_t) = l_t$ and $u(c_t) = -e^{-ac_t}$ with $a > \beta^{-1}$. This is a case with non-constant substitution elasticity that is linear in consumption, since $\epsilon_u(c) = ac_t$. The equilibrium condition (3.8) is $m_t = \beta a m_{t+1} e^{-am_{t+1}}$. There are two stationary equilibria, one without trade and one with $m = \ln a\beta / a$. Approximating linearly the previous dynamic equation around m, the derivative (3.9) is $1 - \ln a\beta$, which is equal to -1 for $\ln a\beta = 2 \Leftrightarrow a = \beta^{-1}e^2$. When the parameter a crosses this value, an endogenous cycle of period two arises. Notice that $\epsilon_{u'}(m) = am = \ln a\beta = 2$.

3.3.2.2 Sunspots

Since there are no changes in the fundamentals, in particular, the productivity is fixed at unity, these cycles are entirely driven by expectations and can be interpreted in terms of *sunspot equilibria*, as follows. Suppose that, in every period, a public event may occur. There are two possible states for each period, with or without the event, indexed by $s = 1, 2$ with a constant transition probability between the states s and s' given by $\pi_{ss'}$. The uncertainty is extrinsic, in the sense that it does not affect the fundamentals, but its realization is public. Therefore, sunspot events have no direct effect on the preferences or production possibilities but their realization can be ascertained by anyone. The workers have rational expectations over future interest rates and believe that the interest rate is perfectly correlated with the occurrence of the sunspot event. A sunspot equilibrium is a rational expectations equilibrium in which this belief is self-fulfilling and the allocation oscillates between two different values. The conditions for a stationary sunspot equilibrium are

$$m_s v'(m_s) = \beta \sum_{s'=1,2} \pi_{ss'} m_{s'} u'(m_{s'}),$$

for every current state $s = 1, 2$, with $m_1 \neq m_2$. A deterministic cycle of period two satisfies these equations when the switching probability between different states is equal to 1. By continuity argument, a sunspot equilibrium with switching probability close to but strictly smaller than 1 exists whenever the deterministic cycle exists.

Notice that neither preferences nor endowments or technologies are hit by shocks, yet the equilibrium allocations fluctuate over time. The fluctuations are driven by the belief that becomes self-fulfilling that the occurrence of random exogenous events will affect economic outcomes.

Example 3.5

Let us continue with the previous example. The conditions for a stationary sunspot equilibrium are $m_s = \beta a \sum_{s'} \pi_{ss'} m_{s'} e^{-am_{s'}}$ for every current state $s = 1, 2$, with $m_1 \neq m_2$. Consider the case $\pi_{ss} = 0$ for each s. Solving the two equilibrium conditions, we obtain $m_s(1 + a\beta e^{-am_s}) = 2m$ and $m_{s'} = 2m - m_s$ for $s' \neq s$, where $m = \ln a\beta / a$ is the stationary equilibrium value that satisfies these conditions. Evaluating in the stationary state the derivative $\frac{dm_s(1+a\beta e^{-am_s})}{dm_s}|_m = 2 - \ln a\beta$, which is zero precisely when $a = \beta^{-1}e^2$, namely the condition for the existence of a deterministic cycle. For slightly larger and slightly smaller values of a, $m_1 \neq m_2$. By continuity, a sunspot equilibrium exists for $\pi_{ss} \neq 0$.

3.4 Great Moderation

The *Great Moderation* is the prolonged period of stable income growth with little volatility and stable low inflation that has interested the United States and other developed economies between 1985 and 2005.

3.4.1 Calm After the Storm

The period between 1965 and 1985 is known as the Great Inflation, during which income was very volatile and inflation rose to double-digit figures. This period of high volatility culminated with the so-called stagflation, a combination of high inflation and rising unemployment. The end of stagflation in the 1980s, brought about by a tightening of monetary policy, was followed by a long period of stable income growth with moderate fluctuations and very low and steady inflation that lasted until the mid-2000s. By the end of the period, the variability of growth in real income had declined by half since the mid-1980s, while the variability of inflation had declined by about two thirds in the United States. The Great Moderation was brought to an end by the burst of the housing bubble during the second half of the 2000s that led to the Great Recession.

3.4.2 Moderate Luck

3

It has been argued that the Great Moderation has been the outcome of 20 years of plenty of good luck, since only relatively minor shocks have supposedly hit the US economy over the 1985-2005 period. However, this point of view ignores several major financial crises that erupted in the second half of the 1990s and early 2000s, including the burst of the famous dotcom bubble. Two main factors are credited for having contributed to the Great Moderation bonanza, namely structural change in the organization of economic activity within and across developed countries and judicious conduct of monetary policy. On the one hand, structural changes in economic institutions, technology, and business practices have improved the ability of the economy to absorb external shocks. In particular, the increased depth and sophistication of financial markets and openness to trade and international capital flows have helped the economy diversify risks, thus increasing macroeconomic stability. On the other hand, commitment to coherent monetary policy rules has helped to increase economic stability after the stagflation of the 1970s and early 1980s. Before the Great Moderation, monetary policy was set in a discretionary manner, with the aim of fighting recessions, resulting in sudden bursts of inflation that increased economic volatility. The commitment power of the monetary authority was ensured by shielding it from the influence of the fiscal authority, making it independent, and giving the former a mandate to keep inflation at bay following intervention rules, by which monetary policy responds aggressively to deviations of inflation from its target. The adoption of time-consistent monetary policy rules is generally considered a key factor that has helped reduce volatility, thus moderating the business cycle.

3.5 Conclusion

According to real business cycle theory, employment and income fluctuate together as an efficient response to exogenous shocks. With wage rigidity, monetary contractions may give rise to recessions, depressing employment and income. The life-cycle model, unlike the dynastic one, can give rise to fluctuations in employment and income that are generated endogenously by the coordination of the expectations of the traders on negative scenarios that become self-fulfilling.

3.6 Literature

The real business cycle literature originated from the pioneering paper by Finn Kydland and Ed Prescott entitled *Time to Build and Aggregate Fluctuations*. The monetary business cycle literature is often called the new Keynesian literature. The Taylor rule was first proposed by John Taylor in *Discretion versus Policy Rules in Practice*. The overlapping generations model was invented by Paul Samuelson in the paper entitled *An Exact Consumption-Loan Model of Interest wi-*

thout the Social Contrivance of Money. The endogenous cycles literature within the overlapping generations model originated from the paper entitled *On Endogenous Competitive Business Cycles* by Jean-Michel Grandmont. The sunspot literature goes back to the classic paper entitled *Do Sunspot Matter?* written by David Cass and Karl Shell.

Exercises

1. Consider an infinite-horizon model with a representative dynasty that cares about the consumption of a perishable commodity and dislikes work. The dynasty has a time endowment for each period and preferences for sequences of consumption and labor, $(\mathbf{c}, \mathbf{l})$, represented by the life-time utility

$$U(\mathbf{c}, \mathbf{l}) = \sum_{t=1}^{\infty} \beta^{t-1} \left(\frac{c_t^{1-\epsilon}}{1-\epsilon} - l_t \right).$$

There is a representative company that demands labor, ℓ_t, to produce the commodity at each point in time using a technology represented by the production function $y_t = z l_t^{1-\alpha}$ with $\alpha \in [0, 1)$. Suppose that competitive markets for labor and the commodity are open at every point in time. Let the real wage be denoted by w_t.

- Derive the labor supply as a function of the real wage.
- Derive the labor demand as a function of the real wage.
- Compute the competitive equilibrium.
- Compute the Pareto-efficient allocation.
- Determine the effect of a change in z on equilibrium employment and income.

2. In the same setup as in the previous exercise, suppose that there is a government that levies a tax on labor income with a flat marginal rate τ.

- Derive the competitive equilibrium with taxation.
- Determine the effect of a change in the tax rate on employment and income.
- Suppose that taxation is used to finance public expenditures G, which give rise to the utility of the dynasty with the same utility function as consumption.
- Determine the optimal tax rate with and without commitment.

3. In the same setup as in the previous exercise, suppose that the quantity theory equation holds in each period, with a constant stock of money M.

- Determine the price level.
- Suppose that the nominal wage is set by collective bargaining at $\overline{\omega}$. Determine employment and income.

4. Consider an overlapping generations economy in which agents live for two periods. There is one agent in every generation. Agents can work only when young and care about consumption only when old, with preferences represented by the life-time utility function

$$U(c_{t+1}, l_t) = \beta \frac{c_{t+1}^{1-\epsilon}}{1-\epsilon} - l_t,$$

3

where l_t is the labor supply, which generates disutility when the person is young and c_t is the consumption of the only commodity available at every time, which generates utility when the person is old. Suppose that there is money as a means of saving, in constant supply M. There is a company that demands labor, ℓ_t, to produce the commodity with a technology represented by the production function $y_t = \ell_t^{1-\alpha}$, with $\alpha \in [0, 1)$.

- Compute the stationary monetary equilibrium.
- Compute the efficient stationary allocation.
- Compare the equilibrium allocation with the efficient allocation.
- Derive the equilibrium condition that governs the dynamics of the system.

References

Cass D, Shell K (1983), Do Sunspot Matter?, Journal of Political Economy, 91: 193–227

Grandmont JM (1985), On Endogenous Competitive Business Cycles, Econometrica, 53: 995–1045

Kydland F, Prescott E (1982), Time to Build and Aggregate Fluctuations, Econometrica, 50: 1345–1370

Samuelson P (1958), An Exact Consumption-Loan Model of Interest without the Social Contrivance of Money, Journal of Political Economy, 66: 467–482

Taylor J (1993), Discretion versus Policy Rules in Practice, Carneige-Rochester Conference Series on Public Policy, 39: 195–214

Exogenous and Endogenous Growth

L. Ferraris, *Macroeconomic Theory*, Classroom Companion: Economics,
https://doi.org/10.1007/978-3-031-88740-6_4

4.1 Introduction

Many countries have experienced a sustained trend of income growth over the last couple of centuries. In the United States, for example, income per person has increased at an average rate of 2% for the best part of the last century. This is a relatively new phenomenon in human history, inconceivable in earlier times, when prolonged income growth was unknown.

In premodern societies, any temporary increase in living standards was quickly reabsorbed by the ensuing increase in population, leaving income per person unchanged in the long run. This is known as the *Malthusian trap*. The reason there was a trap is that in agricultural societies, the process of economic development is limited by the decreasing returns to scale of the inputs due to the presence of a factor of production, plowable land, that is in limited supply. The shift from agriculture to manufacturing, which occurred during the Industrial Revolution at the end of the eighteenth century, has replaced land with physical capital whose stock can be altered saving resources for the future.

The Industrial Revolution has made possible the escape from the Malthusian trap but, by itself, is not enough to explain prolonged income growth. The key to progress is technological innovation that allows society to overcome the decreasing returns to capital, through the social increasing returns fostered by immaterial, non-rival inputs such as *knowledge and ideas* that are generated by the accumulation of human capital. An item is non-rival if it can be used simultaneously by many people without depleting its stock. Thus, non-rivalry is key to generate the positive externalities and spillovers that sustain prolonged income growth. In this chapter, we examine theories that explain the emergence of long run growth based on technological innovation generated by the growth of scientific knowledge and the development of new research ideas.

4.2 Capital Accumulation

The model has an infinite time horizon. We will first consider a model with a dynasty living forever and then with overlapping generations of traders.

4.2.1 Dynastic Model

Consider a model with an infinite time horizon, in which time is indexed by $t = 1, 2, \dots$ There is a single commodity that can serve both as input, in the form of capital, and as final output. Human labor is also available to serve as input. There is a technology that uses the two inputs, capital and labor, to produce final output and an infinitely lived representative dynasty, endowed with time available for work and preferences for consumption of the final commodity. First, we will determine the efficient allocation and, subsequently, we will see how it can be decentralized with trade in competitive markets. By the second welfare theorem, decentralization is guaranteed.

4.2.1.1 Efficient Allocation

We begin by describing the technology that is available and the characteristics of the dynasty. Then, we derive the efficient allocation of the resources.

The technology uses capital, K_t, and labor, L_t, to produce the final product, Y_t, in each period. The technology is represented by the production function $Y_t = F(K_t, L_t) =$ that meets the requirements of Assumption 3. Due to constant scale returns, as before, we can express output and capital in per capita terms that define $y_t \equiv Y_t/L_t$ and $k_t \equiv K_t/L_t$. Thus, we can rewrite the production function in intensive form $y_t = f(k_t)$. The elasticity of marginal productivity is $\epsilon_{f'}(k_t) \equiv -f''(k_t)k_t/f'(k_t)$. The capital stock depreciates completely in production.

The representative dynasty has a unit amount of time every period that is made available as productive input and preferences for sequences of consumption $\mathbf{c}$ over the infinite time horizon represented by the life-time utility

$$U(\mathbf{c}) = \sum_{t=1}^{\infty} \beta^{t-1} u(c_t), \tag{4.1}$$

with the time discount $\beta < 1$. The function $u(c_t)$ meets the requirements of Assumption 4. The elasticity of marginal utility is $\epsilon_{u'}(c_t) \equiv -u''(c_t)c_t/u'(c_t)$.

The mechanism that determines efficient allocations chooses per capita consumption, capital, and output to maximize the life-time utility of the dynasty (4.1), using the available technology to produce $y_t = f(k_t)$. The resource constraint that the mechanism faces in each period is

$$c_t + k_{t+1} = f(k_t), \tag{4.2}$$

since the output can be used to consume and accumulate capital for the future. The efficient choice of capital accumulation is governed by the first-order condition

$$u'(c_t) = \beta f'(k_{t+1}) u'(c_{t+1}), \tag{4.3}$$

that equates the marginal cost of accumulating an extra unit of capital, that reduces current consumption, to the marginal benefit of future consumption obtained thanks to the additional production generated by the accumulated capital.

The system of two equations (4.2) and (4.3), in the sequences of consumption and capital, together with the amount of capital e initially available and the transversality condition $\lim_{t\to\infty} \beta^{t-1} u'(c_t) k_{t+1} = 0$, which prevents the mechanism from wasting resources in the indefinite future, fully determine the efficient allocation for this economy.

An allocation is stationary if it is time invariant. The efficient stationary allocation features capital $k^* = f'^{-1}(1/\beta)$, by equation (4.3), and consumption $c^* = f(k^*) - k^*$, by equation (4.2). Consumption is positive since, by Assumption 3, the average product is larger than the marginal product of capital for any capital stock, therefore $f(k^*)/k^* > f'(k^*) = 1/\beta > 1$. Notice that the stationary allocation depends on the fundamentals, namely technology through the production function and preferences through the time discount, but does not depend on the initial capital stock. Hence, economies with different initial endowment of resources but the same fundamentals will reach the same long-term income per person, namely the same living standards. Conversely, economies with the same initial endowment of resources but different fundamentals will reach different long-term income per person, namely different living standards. Economies with more patient consumers, that is, with higher β, will save more for the future and, therefore, will end up with larger capital stocks in the long run.

4.2.1.2 Dynamics

Future capital stock and consumption can be expressed as functions of their current values. The resource constraint (4.2) can be written as

$$k_{t+1} = f(k_t) - c_t,$$

and using this condition the capital accumulation equation (4.3) can be written as

$$c_{t+1} = u'^{-1}\left(\frac{u'(c_t)}{\beta f'(f(k_t) - c_t))}\right).$$

This is a two-by-two dynamical system in consumption and capital stock to be solved together with the initial condition on the capital stock and the transversality condition. Here, we are particularly interested in finding the behavior of the system around the long-run equilibrium. Approximating linearly the system around the stationary allocation, one can check that the dynamical system is saddle-path stable close to the stationary equilibrium. The next proposition characterizes the stability of the stationary equilibrium.

Proposition 4.1

The stationary equilibrium (c^*, k^*) is saddle-path stable.

Proof The Jacobian matrix of the dynamical system evaluated at the stationary equilibrium is

$$\begin{bmatrix} \frac{1}{\beta} & -1 \\ -\frac{1}{\beta}\frac{\epsilon_{f'}(k^*)k^*}{\epsilon_{u'}(c^*)c^*} & 1 + \frac{\epsilon_{f'}(k^*)k^*}{\epsilon_{u'}(c^*)c^*} \end{bmatrix},$$

with determinant $D = 1/\beta > 0$ and trace $T = 1/\beta + 1 + [\epsilon_{f'}(k^*)k^*]/[\epsilon_{u'}(c^*)c^*] > 0$. The characteristic equation is $\lambda^2 - T\lambda + D = 0$. Since $[\epsilon_{f'}(k^*)k^*]/[\epsilon_{u'}(c^*)c^*] > 0$, we have $T > 1/\beta + 1$. Thus, $T^2 > (1/\beta + 1)^2 > 4/\beta = 4D$, since $\beta < 1$. Moreover, we have $1 - T + D = -[\epsilon_{f'}(k^*)k^*]/[\epsilon_{u'}(c^*)c^*] < 0$. Therefore, the two eigenvalues of the system are real, positive, and straddle 1. Saddle-path stability follows. □

The long-term stationary equilibrium (c^*, k^*) is determinate and stable in the sense that a unique path of consumption and capital stock pairs leads to it from the initial condition, with all other trajectories ruled out by the transversality condition.

Example 4.1

Assuming that the production function is Cobb-Douglas with $\alpha \in (0, 1)$ and the utility function is logarithmic $u(c_t) = \ln c_t$, we obtain the dynamic equation that governs capital accumulation $k_{t+1} = \alpha\beta k_t^{\alpha}$. The stationary capital stock is $k^* = (\alpha\beta)^{\frac{1}{1-\alpha}}$ and consumption is $c^* = (1 - \alpha\beta)(\alpha\beta)^{\frac{\alpha}{1-\alpha}}$. If the economy begins with a small capital stock $e < k^*$, the economy will accumulate capital at positive but decreasing rates until it reaches the stationary long-term capital stock k^*. The process converges to the stationary equilibrium since the derivative $\frac{dk_{t+1}}{dk_t}|_{k^*} = \alpha < 1$. The growth rate of capital accumulation and income is positive but decreasing in the capital stock until the stationary equilibrium is reached, when the growth process stops.

4.2.1.3 Market Equilibrium

Now, we consider the decentralization of efficient allocation through trade in competitive markets. There is a single representative company that rents capital and hires labor in each period to produce output with the technology represented by the production function $y_t = f(k_t)$. There is also a single representative dynasty with an initial endowment e of a durable commodity that can be rented in each period at a competitive rental rate r_t and time to work for a competitive salary w_t , with preferences represented by the utility of life (4.1). The dynasty has perfect foresight over future prices.

A competitive equilibrium is an allocation of resources for the company and the dynasty, a rental rate, and wage such that no one wants to change their decisions, the rental rate clears the capital market, and the wage clears the labor market.

Since the welfare theorems apply to this economy, the allocation of capital, labor, and consumption is the same as in the efficient allocation. We only need to determine the equilibrium prices. Through the choice of capital, labor, and production, the company aims to maximize real per capita profits $y_t - r_t k_t - w_t$. Inserting $y_t = f(k_t)$ into the profit function and computing the first-order condition for a maximum capital per person, we obtain the condition that equates the marginal product of capital to its rental rate $r_t = f'(k_t)$. Since the technology exhibits constant returns to scale and the markets are competitive, the company's profit is nil every period. Hence, the condition for the labor demand can be obtained from the zero-profit condition, $y_t - r_t k_t = w_t$, which by using the equilibrium rental rate and the production function gives $w_t = f(k_t) - f'(k_t)k_t$.

4.2.1.4 Capital Taxation

A classic question is whether capital returns should be taxed. We can use the dynastic model to answer this question. Consider a benevolent government that needs to finance public expenditures G_t in every period but has access only to distortionary taxation in the form of a flat tax on capital income, τ_t^k, and on labor income, τ_t^l, in every period. Using the zero-profit condition, the budget constraint of the government is

$$f(k_t) - r_t(1 - \tau_t^k)k_t - w_t(1 - \tau_t^l) \geq G_t.$$

Let us assume that the government can commit to determine taxation initially for the entire future to maximize the life-time utility of the dynasty taking as given the functioning of the economy through competitive markets. Rather than solving such a problem, however, we will consider an equivalent problem in which the government determines the optimal choice of capital accumulation that, in turn, indirectly determines the optimal tax rates. The government chooses the capital stock taking as given the optimality of the dynasty, $u'(c_t) = \beta r_{t+1}(1-\tau_t^k)u'(c_{t+1})$, the optimality of the company $r_t = f'(k_t)$ and $w_t = f(k_t) - f'(k_t)k_t$, and the clearing of the market $c_t + k_{t+1} + G_t = f(k_t)$ at all times.

Let us solve the problem by substituting consumption from market clearing into the dynasty's life-time utility and adjoining the budget of the government every period to the utility through the multiplier $\lambda_t \geq 0$. Then, the government chooses k_{t+1} to maximize

$$\sum_{t=1}^{\infty} \beta^{t-1}\{u(f(k_t) - k_{t+1} - G_t) + \lambda_t[f(k_t) - r_t(1-\tau_t^k)k_t - w_t(1-\tau_t^l) - G_t]\}.$$

The first-order condition for the optimal choice of k_{t+1} by the government from the second period onward is

$$u'(c_t) = \beta\{u'(c_{t+1})f'(k_{t+1}) + \lambda_{t+1}[f'(k_{t+1}) - r_{t+1}(1-\tau_{t+1}^k)]\}. \tag{4.4}$$

Using the optimality of the company, $f'(k_{t+1}) = r_{t+1}$ and of the dynasty, $u'(c_t) = \beta r_{t+1}(1-\tau_t^k)u'(c_{t+1})$, the optimality condition of the government, (4.4), becomes

$$\beta f'(k_{t+1})[u'(c_{t+1}) + \lambda_{t+1}]\tau_{t+1}^k = 0.$$

Since $\beta f'(k_{t+1})[u'(c_{t+1}) + \lambda_{t+1}] > 0$, it follows that $\tau_{t+1}^k = 0$ for $t \geq 2$. Thus, the optimal tax on capital income should be nil in all except the two initial periods, and public expenditures should be financed taxing only labor income thereafter. By a basic principle of optimal taxation, it is best to tax primarily income sources whose supply is inelastic, such as the initial capital stock and labor income in the current framework. More generally, with an elastic labor supply, the optimal tax on capital income would not be nil in the short run but would remain nil in the long run. This is because a flat tax on capital income in the stationary state corresponds to an ever-increasing tax on consumption that cannot be beneficial when the dynasty's intertemporal elasticity of substitution remains constant.

4.2.2 Life-Cycle Model

The life-cycle model with capital accumulation has different features relative to the dynastic model, as the market allocation of resources is not necessarily efficient and the equilibrium may not be unique.

There is a single perishable commodity that is used as the unit of account. There is a company that owns a production function, that uses capital k_t as an input in the production of output of the commodity $y_t = f(k_t)$, twice continuously differentiable, strictly increasing and strictly concave that satisfies $f(0) = 0$ and $f'(0) = \infty$. Capital depreciates completely in production. Each period a new generation of consumers is born, living for two periods. Each generation is denoted with the time at which it was born and is made up of one consumer representing a mass of identical consumers. Consumers have a unit-time endowment when young and enjoy consumption in both periods of their life, with c_t and c_{t+1} denoting consumption of the commodity for a generation born at time t in the two periods of their life. The utility function of every generation is

$$U\left(c_t, c_{t+1}\right) = u(c_t) + \beta u(c_{t+1}),$$

where the utility function satisfies Assumption 4, with $\beta < 1$. The initial generation is alive for their second period and cares about consumption only for such a period. The consumers supply entirely their endowment of time when young as labor and have perfect foresight of the prices that will prevail in the future. There is an initial amount of capital $e > 0$ in the hands of the first generation. Consumers use capital to save resources for the future, with k_{t+1} denoting the savings of the generation born at the time t. Capital and labor are traded at competitive rental rate r_t and wage w_t.

4.2.2.1 Competitive Equilibrium

By optimization of the company, the rental rate of capital satisfies $r_t = f'(k_t)$ and the wage $w_t = f(k_t) - f'(k_t)k_t$. The budget constraints of consumers of a generation born in t in the two periods of their life are $c_t + k_{t+1} = w_t$ and $c_{t+1} = r_{t+1}k_{t+1}$. The markets clear at all times. The optimality condition of the consumer and the company gives

$$u'\left(f(k_t) - f'(k_t)k_t - k_{t+1}\right) = \beta f'(k_{t+1}) u'\left(f'(k_{t+1})k_{t+1}\right).$$

This dynamic equation, together with the initial condition on capital, determines the competitive equilibria of this model. The dynamic behavior of the life-cycle model is potentially more complex than the dynastic model, except in special cases. Consider the stationary allocation with $k_t = k$ at all times, that satisfies

$$u'\left(f(k) - f'(k)k - k\right) = \beta f'(k) u'\left(f'(k)k\right). \tag{4.5}$$

Let $\bar{k}$ satisfy $f(\bar{k}) = f'(\bar{k})\bar{k} + \bar{k}$. Under Assumption 4.ii, a stationary competitive equilibrium allocation of capital $\tilde{k} \in (0, \bar{k})$ exists by the usual continuity argument, but is not necessarily unique. Differentiating the equilibrium condition (4.5) with respect to the capital stock and evaluating it in stationary equilibrium, we obtain a condition whose sign depends on the value of the elasticity of the marginal product of capital and the intertemporal substitution of consumption.

Example 4.2

With the Cobb-Douglas production function and logarithmic utility function, the dynamic equation becomes $k_{t+1} = \tilde{\beta}(1-\alpha)k_t^{\alpha}$, with stationary solution $\tilde{k} = \left[\tilde{\beta}(1-\alpha)\right]^{\frac{1}{1-\alpha}}$, where $\tilde{\beta} \equiv \beta(1+\beta)^{-1}$.

4.2.2.2 Efficiency

Let us compute the stationary efficient allocation also known as the *Golden Rule* allocation. The choice of consumption for the two periods of life of every generation and capital maximizes $u(c_1) + \beta u(c_2)$ subject to $c_1 + c_2 = f(k) - k$, giving the golden rule capital stock $k^* = f'^{-1}(1)$, while consumption satisfies the resource constraint and the optimality condition $u'(c_1) = \beta u'(c_2)$. The stationary efficient allocation has perfect smoothing of consumption across the two periods of the life of every generation and a zero net interest rate. By inspection, the golden rule k^* does not necessarily satisfy the equilibrium condition (4.5). Hence, the competitive equilibrium and the efficient stationary allocation do not necessarily coincide.

There may be under- or over-accumulation of capital in a competitive equilibrium relative to the Golden Rule capital stock k^* and consumption may be excessively tilted toward either period of life, depending on assumptions on the fundamentals. With excessive accumulation of capital relative to the golden rule, the equilibrium is Pareto inefficient since lowering $\tilde{k}$ at some point would make everybody better off including the current generation, while with under accumulation relative to the golden rule the equilibrium is efficient since an increase in $\tilde{k}$ at some point would make the current generation worse off.

The following proposition shows that there is a Pareto-inefficient stationary equilibrium under certain conditions on the fundamentals. Define $\hat{\beta} \equiv u'(f(f'^{-1}(1)) - 2f'^{-1}(1))/u'(f'^{-1}(1))$.

Proposition 4.2

Assume $f(f'^{-1}(1)) > 3f'^{-1}(1)$. If $\beta > \hat{\beta}$, there is a stationary equilibrium capital stock that is higher than the golden rule capital stock.

Proof For $k = \bar{k}$, the LHS of the equilibrium condition (4.5) is infinite by the boundary condition, and the RHS is finite. For $k = f'^{-1}(1)$ the LHS of the equilibrium condition (4.5) is smaller than the RHS if $\beta > \hat{\beta}$. By continuity, there is a stationary equilibrium capital $\tilde{k} > k^*$. The assumption $f(f'^{-1}(1)) > 3f'^{-1}(1)$ ensures that $\hat{\beta} < 1$, due to decreasing marginal utility. □

When people are very patient, they accumulate an amount of capital that exceeds the golden rule level. The excess accumulation could be reduced by issuing an alternative saving instrument, such as public debt.

Example 4.3

In the logarithmic example with the Cobb-Douglas production function, comparing the accumulation of stationary equilibrium capital with k^*, we see that the economy over-accumulates capital provided $\beta > \alpha/(1-2\alpha) \equiv \hat{\beta}$ which requires $\alpha < 1/3$.

4.2.2.3 Public Debt

Suppose that the government issues for every period a one-period bond in amount D_t that is reimbursed with gross real interest R_t. The interest payment is financed with lump-sum taxation of the old of every generation, with $T_t = (R_t - 1)D_t$ in each period. The demand for the bond by the young of each generation is d_{t+1}. The budget constraint of each generation in the first period of life is $c_t + d_{t+1} + k_{t+1} = w_t$ and in the second period of life $c_{t+1} = r_{t+1}k_{t+1} + R_{t+1}d_{t+1} - T_{t+1}$. By no-arbitrage, for the traders to hold both capital and the bond, the two interest payments should be the same $R_t = r_t$. Clearing of the bond market requires $d_t = D_t$ for every period. Consider the stationary equilibrium with time-invariant real variables. The equilibrium condition is

$$u'\left(f(k) - f'(k)k - k - D\right) = \alpha\beta k^{\alpha-1}u'\left(f'(k)k + D\right),$$

that leads to a lower long-run capital stock since the marginal utility is decreasing in consumption. When the equilibrium capital stock is excessive relative to the golden rule, the issuance of government bonds helps limit excess capital.

4.3 Growth Theory

The aim of growth theory is to explain the process of sustained income growth over the long run that we have observed in the last two centuries for several countries. The engine of income growth is technical progress. We will examine first a theory in which the technical progress emerges exogenously and then endogenously as the outcome of investment in human capital, the diffusion of scientific knowledge and the development of innovative research ideas.

4.3.1 Exogenous Growth

Before the nineteenth century, some transitory episodes of economic growth were occasionally observed, but the systematic income growth that has characterized modern economies was an unknown phenomenon. To understand why modern economies are fundamentally different from traditional ones, we will start with an agricultural society.

4.3.1.1 Agriculture

The main feature of agriculture is the use of a technology that combines land and labor to produce output. We will assume that the technology is represented by a constant return-to-scale production function. Since land is, in large part, in fixed supply, we normalize its stock to 1 in all periods, obtaining

$$Y_t = L_t^{1-\alpha}.$$

This is a production function that effectively exhibits decreasing return-to-scale. Dividing both sides by the working population, we obtain income per worker as a decreasing function of the working population,

$$y_t = \frac{1}{L_t^\alpha}. \tag{4.6}$$

The negative relationship between income per person and population due to the impossibility of changing the stock of land as the population changes is the key factor that limits economic growth in agricultural societies. Suppose that the growth rate of the population is an increasing function of income per person, as assumed, for instance, by Malthus. An episode that reduces the size of the population, such as the plague or a war, would lead to an increase in income per person, by equation (4.6). However, a higher income per person would lead to an increase in population, which, in turn, would reduce income per person, according to equation (4.6). In sum, any increase in income per person has the tendency to stimulate an increase in population that drives the income per person back toward its long-term value. Hence, economic growth can only be a temporary phenomenon.

4.3.1.2 Industry

Consider now an economy in which the main productive sector is the industry that uses a technology represented by the production function with constant return-to-scale

$$Y_t = K_t^\alpha (zL_t)^{1-\alpha},$$

where a productivity parameter, z, has been introduced to capture labor-augmenting technical progress. The Malthusian logic of the previous model for the agricultural society does not apply any more since the capital input used in manufacturing is not in fixed supply as land, but can be altered through the process of saving and investment. Indeed, the production function can be expressed in intensive form

$$y_t = z^{1-\alpha} k_t^\alpha, \tag{4.7}$$

where income per person depends on capital per worker which can be kept constant over time increasing the capital stock through savings.

However, accumulation of capital is not enough to generate indefinite income growth. As seen in the dynastic and life-cycle models, the economy begins to grow but then eventually settles onto the stationary equilibrium that, by definition, does not feature any further growth of income per person. Adding a growth factor to productivity can generate an indefinite growth in income per capita. Suppose that the production function (4.7) is modified as

$$y_t = z_t^{1-\alpha} k_t^\alpha,$$

where the productivity factor z_t grows at an exogenous gross rate $Z > 1$ in every period due to purely technological reasons

$$z_t = Zz_{t-1}. \tag{4.8}$$

Consider the dynastic model with the logarithmic utility function, where a fraction $\alpha\beta$ of current income y_t is saved in every period as capital k_{t+1}, giving $k_{t+1} = \alpha\beta z_t^{1-\alpha} k_t^{\alpha}$ in every period. Using this condition in two consecutive periods, we obtain

$$\frac{k_{t+1}}{k_t} = \left(\frac{z_t}{z_{t-1}}\right)^{1-\alpha} \left(\frac{k_t}{k_{t-1}}\right)^{\alpha}. \tag{4.9}$$

With productivity growing over time, a stationary equilibrium does not exist anymore. However, we can consider an equilibrium in which capital and income grow at the same constant net rate g over time, known as the *balanced growth path*. Substituting (4.8) into (4.9) with a time-invariant growth rate of capital g, we obtain

$$g = Z - 1,$$

which is positive since $Z > 1$. The growth process is attributed to an exogenous technological parameter that is not influenced by economic choices.

4.3.2 Endogenous Growth

The aim of endogenous growth theory is to explain long-term growth through economic choices rather than exogenous technological factors. There is a simple mechanical way to generate indefinite income growth without exogenous productivity growth that consists in assuming that the production function is linear in capital per capita.

4.3.2.1 The AK Model

Let us begin with a seemingly mechanical way of obtaining long-term growth in the previous model without exogenous productivity growth. Suppose that the production function is

$$y_t = Ak_t,$$

with the scale factor $A > \beta^{-1}$ and the utility function is logarithmic. This is the *AK model* of endogenous growth. Since the welfare theorems apply, we can derive the allocation maximizing the life-time utility subject to the resource constraint, $c_t + k_{t+1} = Ak_t$. Since $u'(c_t) = 1/c_t$ at all times, the optimal accumulation of capital satisfies the condition

$$\frac{1}{\beta}\frac{c_{t+1}}{c_t} = A,$$

that equates the marginal rate of intertemporal substitution of consumption to the marginal product of capital. In the balanced growth path in which consumption, capital stock, and income per person all grow at the same time-invariant rate, g, we have

$$g = \beta A - 1,$$

which is positive since $A > \beta^{-1}$. The linearity of the production function can be attributed to the presence of an externality in production. Suppose that the production function depends not only on the capital rented by a single company, but also on the average stock of capital available in the productive sector, $\mathcal{K}_t$, through the following function $y_t = Ak_t^{\alpha}\mathcal{K}_t^{1-\alpha}$. In a symmetric equilibrium, the individual and the average amount of capital will be the same, that is $k_t = \mathcal{K}_t$, thus obtaining the AK model. The positive externality reflects the indirect benefits that each company exerts on the rest of the productive sector, generating a cumulative process that leads to long-term growth.

The positive externality can be driven by an investment in research and education through public expenditures financed by taxation. Assuming for simplicity a flat tax on income with constant marginal tax rate τ, a Laffer curve would emerge due to the contrasting effects of taxation that, on the one hand, increases the tax revenue, with an increase of public spending, but, on the other hand, discourages savings. The growth rate would be reduced by the combined effects of taxation, requiring a higher value of A to remain positive relative to the scenario with private investment.

The AK model captures part of the mechanics that drives economic growth, but we still do not have an explicit way to model how long-term growth can be generated by economic choices. Next, we will see how endogenous growth can be explicitly incorporated into the model through the process that generates innovative research ideas.

4.3.2.2 Ideas and Research

Consider the same basic model as before, assuming that there are two employment possibilities, either in the productive sector or in research. The total population, which, for simplicity, we assume to be constant over time, is $N > \beta^{-1}$. The number of manual workers is L_t, the rest are researchers. The available technology in every period is represented by the production function

$$Y_t = z_t^{1-\alpha}K_t^{\alpha}L_t^{1-\alpha}.$$

We interpret the parameter z_t as the stock of available ideas at every point in time. Notice that the production function has constant returns to scale in the physical factors, capital and labor, as doubling them together keeping the stock of ideas fixed doubles the output, but has increasing returns in all the factors, including the ideas, since when also the ideas are doubled output more than doubles. The reason why new ideas foster productivity growth is that they are *non-rival* goods. A good is non-rival if it can be used simultaneously by several people without depleting its stock. An idea can be used simultaneously by many producers without reducing its value, while physical capital, being rival, can be used only by a single worker at a time, and its stock depreciates with use. Thus, to double production with rival inputs one needs to double all of them together, while to double output with non-rival inputs, a single new addition may be enough. Thus, ideas are a natural source of increasing returns. Let $\eta_t \equiv L_t/N$ be the share of manual workers in the population. Dividing both sides of the production function by the population, we can express the production function in intensive form as

$$y_t = z_t^{1-\alpha} k_t^{\alpha} \eta_t^{1-\alpha}.$$

Suppose that stock of ideas increases linearly every period with the number of people employed as researchers in the previous period

$$z_t = z_{t-1}[1 + N(1 - \eta_{t-1})]. \tag{4.10}$$

Thus, the model has a linear production function of ideas in the number of researchers, a feature that is reminiscent of the AK model. In sum, the model combines constant returns of people in the production of ideas with increasing social returns of ideas in the production of commodities. The utility function of the dynasty is logarithmic and the resource constraint in every period is $c_t + k_{t+1} = z_t^{1-\alpha} k_t^{\alpha} \eta_t^{1-\alpha}$, with z_t given by (4.10).

The welfare theorems apply to this economy; thus, we can solve for the efficient allocation and then derive the rental rate of capital and the wage from the optimization of the company. In addition to consumption, there are two choices to be made, one concerning the fraction of people who become manual workers or researchers, and another regarding the accumulation of physical capital. The optimal choice of η_t satisfies the condition

$$\frac{1}{c_t}(1 - \alpha)\frac{y_t}{\eta_t} = \frac{\beta}{c_{t+1}} N(1 - \alpha) z_t \frac{y_{t+1}}{z_{t+1}},$$

that equates the marginal utility cost of allocating one additional person to research, reducing current production, to the marginal utility benefit of increasing the stock of ideas that will pay off with increased productivity in the future. The optimality condition can be simplified as follows

$$\frac{1}{\beta}\frac{c_{t+1}}{c_t} = N\eta_t \frac{y_{t+1}}{y_t}\frac{z_t}{z_{t+1}}, \tag{4.11}$$

that equates the marginal rate of intertemporal substitution of consumption to the marginal product research in generating new ideas. The optimal choice of physical capital k_{t+1} satisfies the condition

$$\frac{1}{\beta}\frac{c_{t+1}}{c_t} = \alpha \frac{y_{t+1}}{k_{t+1}},$$

that equates the marginal rate of intertemporal substitution of consumption to the marginal product of capital. Using this optimality condition for capital and the resource constraint, we obtain the dynamic capital accumulation equation in every period

$$k_{t+1} = \alpha\beta z_t^{1-\alpha} k_t^{\alpha} \eta_t^{1-\alpha}.$$

4 Consider the balanced growth path, in which all variables, consumption, capital stock, and production, grow at the same rate, g. Having a balanced growth path requires keeping the split of the population between workers and researchers constant over time $\eta_t = \eta$. Using the optimality condition (4.11) with (4.10), the time-invariant η, the same time-invariant growth rate for consumption and income, we derive the stationary fraction of researchers in the labor force as $1 - \eta = (\beta N - 1)N^{-1}(1 + \beta)^{-1}$. Finally, we plug this into $g = N(1 - \eta)$, obtaining the net growth rate

$$g = \frac{\beta N - 1}{1 + \beta},$$

that is positive since $N > \beta^{-1}$. In competitive equilibrium, capital, labor, and research will all be rewarded for their marginal product.

The model provides an explanation for sustained income growth, as the growth rate is now determined by the endogenous decision to search for new ideas or work in the production process. The engine of growth are the social increasing returns to scale generated by the accumulation of ideas through scientific research. Notice that the growth rate of income per person depends on the population size. There is a scale effect analogous to the AK model due to the non-rivalry of ideas, whereby every new idea becoming available for use simultaneously by multiple producers allows to overcome the decreasing returns of capital per person. The size of the population is a proxy for the size of the research sector. Thus, *ceteris paribus*, larger countries with more researchers will tend to grow faster than smaller ones.

As it stands, the model fails to capture the well-documented fact that truly new ideas are harder to come by as the research process progresses. However, a small variation in which the growth rate of ideas varies inversely with the existing stock of ideas provides a reasonable fit of the empirical evidence. In such a model, the growth rate of income per person is proportional to the population growth rate rather than its size.

The model can be reinterpreted as describing the accumulation of human capital rather than ideas, with η_t representing the difference in time between the formation of human capital and work, replacing the effect of population size N on productivity with a parameter that captures the quality of human capital. As a result, the growth rate of income per person turns out to be an increasing function of the quality of human capital rather than the quantity of ideas measured by the population size.

The model can also be reinterpreted as describing the process in which the number of intermediate inputs used in production increases over time due to research and development of new ideas. Suppose that the production of the final output uses intermediate inputs combined through an aggregator function with the elasticity of substitution ε. The market for final output, capital and labor are perfectly competitive, while for the inputs, that are produced using final output linearly one-for-one, there is monopolistic competition. Let z_t denote the number of intermediate inputs currently available that is altered by the research effort, following the equation (4.10). With this interpretation, the process of growth is driven by the increasing number of intermediate input varieties available over time as a result of the development of new ideas. The scale effect of the population appears for the same reason as before. The economy, however, suffers from a distortion due to monopolistic competition and, as a consequence, the growth rate is altered, reflecting the elasticity of substitution of the inputs and the capital intensity.

4.3.2.3 Creative Destruction

So far, we have considered innovations that increase the total factor productivity as if the process enlarges the set of available technologies without replacing previous technologies. Now, we consider a theory in which improvements in total factor productivity occur due to technological innovations that replace obsolete technologies, through a process known as *creative destruction*.

Consider a technology that uses labor L_t, and an input X_t, to produce the final good, represented by the production function $y_t = z_t^{1-\alpha} X_t^{\alpha} L_t^{1-\alpha}$, where z_t is the labor-augmenting productivity. The input X_t is produced at a linear cost by a monopolist and is sold at a price p_t. Profit maximization of the representative firm that produces the final commodity under competition leads to the inverse demand function of the input in each period as $p_t(X_t) = \alpha z_t^{1-\alpha} L_t^{1-\alpha} X_t^{\alpha-1}$, which can be substituted for the monopolist's profit obtaining $\alpha z_t^{1-\alpha} X_t^{\alpha} L_t^{1-\alpha} - X_t$. The maximization of profit by the monopolist with respect to X_t gives the optimal supply of the input $X_t = \tilde{\alpha} z_t L_t$, where $\tilde{\alpha} \equiv \alpha^{\frac{2}{1-\alpha}}$. Plugging the optimal supply of the factor into the profit of the monopolist, we obtain $\Pi_t = \tilde{\alpha} z_t L_t$. Suppose, for simplicity, that the working population does not grow over time, so $L_t = N$ in each period.

The entrepreneur who produces the input has the opportunity to develop a technological innovation by investing resources in innovative research every period, I_t. The cost of the investment is linear. The investment may be successful, in which case the productivity will increase next period, jumping to $\bar{z}_t = Z z_{t-1}$ with $Z > 1$, or not, in which case the productivity remains unchanged $z_t = z_{t-1}$. Denote by $\varrho_t \equiv I_t / \bar{z}_t$ the research investment divided by the productivity if the innovation is successful. Innovation succeeds with probability $\pi(\varrho_t)$ and fails with complementary probability. The probability of developing a new technology is increasing in research investment, but at decreasing rates, that is, $\pi'(\cdot) > 0 > \pi''(\cdot)$. The probability of successful innovation depends inversely on $\bar{z}_t$ to capture the fact that it is harder to improve more advanced technologies. Creativity is destructive, as old technologies simply become obsolete and are no longer used when an innovative technology becomes available. If the entrepreneur succeeds in developing an innovative technology in a given period, then becomes a monopolist of that technology in that period, enjoying the corresponding profit; otherwise the profit is absorbed by another entrepreneur chosen at random in the population. The choice of how many resources to invest in research is made by the entrepreneur to maximize the expected profit $\pi(\varrho_t)\overline{\Pi}_t - I_t$, where $\overline{\Pi}_t = \tilde{\alpha}N\overline{z}_t$ is the profit if the innovation succeeds, since otherwise the monopolist is replaced. We can write the expected profit of the innovator as $\overline{z}_t[\tilde{\alpha}N\pi(\varrho_t) - \varrho_t]$, whose first-order condition for the optimal choice of ϱ_t gives in every period $\varrho = \pi'^{-1}((\tilde{\alpha}N)^{-1}) \equiv \varrho(N)$, whose first derivative $\varrho'(N) = -\varrho(N)/N[\pi''(\varrho)\varrho/\pi'(\varrho)]^{-1}$ is positive, since the probability is strictly concave in ϱ. Substituting the optimal choice of research investment into the probability, we obtain $\pi(\varrho(N))$, which also represents the long-term frequency of innovations. In the long run, on average the technology improves with frequency $\pi(\varrho(N))$ or remains the same otherwise. Therefore, in a balanced growth path, the expected growth rate of income corresponds to the expected productivity growth

$$g = \pi(\varrho(N))(Z - 1),$$

which is positive since $Z > 1$ and increasing in both the productivity gains generated by technological innovations $Z - 1$ and the population size N since $\pi'(\varrho)\varrho'(N) > 0$. In the long run, the average net growth rate of the economy is equal to the frequency of innovations times the size of innovations. As in the previous model, there is a scale effect, by which an economy with a larger population is more likely to develop innovative technologies that replace older ones.

In this model, scientific and technological innovations revolutionize the production system by eliminating the rents generated by earlier innovations. Maintaining the incentive to innovate rests on a delicate balance between the presence of short-term profits from exploiting a situation of market power, as the innovator is the only one with access to the new technology, and competition among innovators in the medium and long run, which allows new technologies to regularly replace technologies that have become obsolete. In this context, public intervention could play a role in fostering research and innovation by ensuring the protection of intellectual property rights through patents but also by fostering competition among firms so that new innovators are not discouraged from entering the market for innovation by the incumbent.

4.4 Growth in the Very Long Run

Stable growth of income per capita is a recent phenomenon in human history that started in the beginning of the nineteenth century in the United Kingdom and has spread to some but not all countries over the last century.

4.4.1 Hundred Years of Plenitude

In the first millennium AD, world income remained essentially stable with a world population that increased only slightly, leading to a slight decrease in income per capita. Economic performance improved in the second millennium, with a 13-time increase in world income per capita. The second millennium can be divided into two distinct periods, before and after 1820. Until 1820 the pace of change in per capita income was very slow, increasing by 50% over eight centuries, which corresponds to a meager 0.05% annual growth rate. Since 1820, per capita income has increased at a much faster rate; by the end of the second millennium, income per capita was nine times higher than in 1820, with the largest increase occurring during the last century. The annual growth rate of world income per person was 0.5% in the first half of the period and around 3% in the second half. Economic performance varied greatly in different regions of the world. The most dynamic group of countries was the one that comprises western Europe, the United States, Canada, Australia, New Zealand, and Japan. In the period 1000-1820, their average per capita income grew nearly four times faster than the average of the rest of the world. The differential continued after 1820 with per capita income rising 19 times in the first group relative to a 5 times increase for the rest of the world. Toward the end of the second millennium, a group of Asian countries, including South Korea, China, and, more recently, India, have been catching up with the group of developed countries with high growth rates of income per capita.

4.4.2 Convergence vs Divergence

The exogenous growth theory predicts the convergence of living standards between countries with the same fundamentals due to decreasing returns to capital. As economies accumulate more capital, their returns decrease as a result of their decreasing marginal productivity. Capital will flow to countries with a smaller capital stock and higher returns, increasing the stock and lowering the returns until these are equalized across countries. However, a fair amount of divergence in living standards across economies has been observed over a long period of time, without massive capital outflows from rich to poor countries, as one would expect it would happen if the return of capital was a decreasing function of the accumulated stock of capital. Endogenous growth theory can account for such observed divergence of living standards across countries in the post-war period without capital outflows, in a way that exogenous growth theory could not deliver. According to the endogenous growth literature, it is the accumulation of ideas and human capital, mainly through investment in education, that drives the technological advances leading to higher productivity. This exerts a positive social externality that counteracts the decreasing returns to capital at the individual company level, thus generating growth without a corresponding decline in the real returns. Economies that start growing will continue to do so, distancing themselves increasingly over time from economies in which the growth process has not begun, generating divergence of living standards across countries. Since the returns to human capital increase as the economy increases its human capital stock, there will be human capital inflows from countries in which its return is lower, thus increasing inequality between countries.

4.5 Conclusion

The picture that emerges for the long-run growth is that capital accumulation allows to escape the Malthusian trap since it helps by-pass the decreasing returns to scale of agriculture but is not enough to guarantee that the economy will keep growing indefinitely, since the accumulation of capital eventually runs up against its decreasing productivity and the overall constant returns to scale of manufacturing. It is the diffusion of knowledge and the invention of new ideas that fosters the process of technological innovation allowing to overcome the decreasing returns to capital and the constant returns to scale overall. The reason is the non-rivalry of ideas that generate social increasing returns to scale.

4.6 Literature

The dynastic model with capital accumulation is also known as the Ramsey-Cass-Koopmans model. A general overview of the growth literature is contained in Daron Acemoglu's textbook entitled *Introduction to Modern Economic Growth*. In the paper *National Debt in a Neoclassical Growth Model*, Peter Diamond pointed out the role of public debt in reducing excessive capital accumulation in the life-cycle model. The idea that capital returns should not be taxed in the long run goes back to the paper *Optimal Taxation of Capital Income in General Equilibrium with Infinite Lives* by Christopher Chamley. The literature on exogenous growth began with the seminal paper *A Contribution to the Theory of Economic Growth* by Robert Solow. The pioneering contribution of Paul Romer entitled *Endogenous Technological Change* gave rise to the endogenous growth literature. The role of human capital for growth was highlighted in the book *Lectures on Economic Growth* by Robert Lucas. The model with creative destruction, also known as the Schumpeterian model of growth, is a simplified version of the model by Philippe Aghion and Peter Howitt, whose complete version can be found in their book entitled *The Economics of Growth*.

Exercises

1. Consider a competitive economy with an infinite horizon and a representative agent with preferences for consumption of a single commodity that can be consumed or accumulated as capital represented by the life-time utility

$$U(\mathbf{c}) = \sum_{t=1}^{\infty} \beta^{t-1} \ln c_t,$$

where $\beta < 1$. The commodity is initially available in amount $e > 0$. Consumption at time t is denoted by c_t, while capital accumulation for the future is denoted by k_{t+1}. There is a company that produces the final product by renting capital from the consumer at a competitive rate r_t using a technology represented by the production function $y_t = Ak_t^\alpha$ with $\alpha \leq 1$. Capital depreciates at the rate $\delta \in [0, 1]$ in production.

- Find the efficient allocation of resources.
- Find the competitive equilibrium.
- Suppose $\alpha = 1$. For which value of A there is a positive long-run growth rate of capital and income?

2. Consider an overlapping generations model in which agents live for two periods, with a unit time endowment when young and nothing when old. There is one agent in every generation. There is a single commodity that can be consumed or accumulated as capital, with an initial stock $e > 0$. Assume that the agents of all generations have the same utility function for consumption in the two periods of their lives, c_1 when young and c_2 when old, given by

$$U(c_t, c_{t+1}) = \ln c_1 + \beta \ln c_2,$$

with $\beta \leq 1$. There is a company that produces production that rents capital from the consumer at a competitive rate r_t and hires labor at a wage w_t every period, using a technology represented by the production function $y_t = Ak_t^\alpha$ with $\alpha < 1$. Capital depreciates completely in production.

- Find the stationary efficient allocation.
- Find the stationary competitive equilibria.
- Compare the equilibrium and efficient allocations.

References

Acemoglu D (2009), Introduction to Modern Economic Growth, Princeton University Press

Aghion P, Howitt P (2009), The Economics of Growth, MIT Press

Chamley C (1986), Optimal Taxation of Capital Income in General Equilibrium with Infinite Lives, Econometrica, 54: 607–622

Diamond P (1965), National Debt in a Neoclassical Growth Model, American Economic Review, 55: 1126–1150

Lucas R Jr (2001), Lectures on Economic Growth, Harvard University Press

Solow R (1956), A Contribution to the Theory of Economic Growth, Quarterly Journal of Economics, 70: 65–94

Romer P (1990), Endogenous Technological Change, Journal of Political Economy, 98: S71–S102

Asset Prices and Bubbles

L. Ferraris, *Macroeconomic Theory*, Classroom Companion: Economics,
https://doi.org/10.1007/978-3-031-88740-6_5

5.1 Introduction

The model with a representative dynasty living for ever can be used not only to study the business cycle and economic growth but also to price assets and securities of various types that are traded in competitive financial markets. The dynastic model can be used to determine differences in the return of assets or securities with different risk profiles, in particular, between stocks and government bonds. To prevent arbitrage opportunities, that is, unlimited profits obtained selling some securities to buy others, risky assets will have to carry higher returns than riskless securities. This is known as the equity premium. The standard model with risk averse traders generates an equity premium. Surprisingly, though, two empirical anomalies arise. First, an unreasonably large value of risk aversion is needed to replicate the available data for the US economy on the long-term spread of the average annual returns of stocks over the Treasury bills. This anomaly is known as the *equity premium puzzle*. Second, real-world consumption grows too fast to be compatible with the observed long-run risk-free rate and the willingness of the dynasty to smooth consumption over time. This is known as the *risk-free rate puzzle*.

Another peculiar feature of the standard model concerns asset price bubbles. The standard model predicts that the available assets are priced at their fundamental value and speculative bubbles cannot emerge. In particular, fiat assets without fundamental return cannot have value at equilibrium of the dynastic model. In the life-cycle model, instead, some assets can be priced above their fundamental value, giving rise to speculative bubbles. Fiat monetary assets whose price is a pure bubble can have value at equilibrium in the life-cycle model even when competing with other assets that have fundamental value. This occurs when the presence of an asset whose price has a bubble component helps reduce the excessive accumulation of alternative assets relative to efficiency.

5.2 Asset Pricing

We will use the dynastic model to price risky assets, such as equity and risk-less bonds. We will then use their prices to compare the returns of equity and bonds and derive the equity premium.

5.2.1 Dynastic Model

Consider the following scenario. There is a tree that delivers every period a stochastic amount of fruit, z_t, that can be consumed by a dynasty living for ever with preferences for consumption represented by the life-time discounted expected utility function

$$\mathbb{E}U(\mathbf{c}) = \mathbb{E}\sum_{t=1}^{\infty}\beta^{t-1}u(c_t), \tag{5.1}$$

with $\beta < 1$ and the utility function satisfies Assumption 4. The strict concavity in this context corresponds to the risk aversion of the dynasty. The curvature of the utility function and, consequently, risk aversion can be measured in various ways. The most common measures are the absolute risk-aversion index and the relative risk-aversion index. If the utility function is twice differentiable, absolute risk aversion is measured by the negative ratio of the second and first derivatives of the utility function, $a(c) \equiv -u''(c)/u'(c)$. Relative risk aversion is obtained by multiplying absolute risk aversion by consumption, denoted by $\epsilon_u(c) \equiv -u''(c)c/u'(c)$.

Example 5.1

A utility function with constant absolute risk aversion is $u(c) = -e^{-ac}$, where a measures this aversion. A utility function with constant relative risk aversion is $u(c) = (1-\epsilon)^{-1}c^{1-\epsilon}$, where ϵ measures this aversion. With $\epsilon = 0$, utility is linear in consumption, corresponding to risk-neutrality.

5.2.1.1 Equity Demand

In each period, the dynasty can acquire shares of the tree $\theta_{t+1} \in [0, 1]$ at a price ϕ_t. The shares of the acquired tree currently entitle the dynasty to collect the fruit from the tree and, possibly, to sell the shares at the prevailing price in the following period. The budget constraint of the dynasty in every period is given by

$$c_t + \phi_t\theta_{t+1} = (\phi_t + z_t)\theta_t. \tag{5.2}$$

The dynasty chooses consumption and the share holdings of the tree every period to maximize the expected life-time utility (5.1) subject to the budget constraint (5.2). The dynasty has rational expectations for future asset prices. The optimality condition for the choice of the shares by the dynasty is

$$\phi_t u'(c_t) = \beta\mathbb{E}(\phi_{t+1} + z_{t+1})u'(c_{t+1}), \tag{5.3}$$

where the expectation is taken with respect to the information available in the current period. The dynasty determines the optimal demand for the shares, equating the marginal cost of giving up current consumption to the expected marginal gain of increasing future consumption, enjoying the future value of the shares and their dividends.

Example 5.2

Consider the case with constant relative risk aversion $\epsilon = 1$. The optimality condition (5.3) becomes $\phi_t = \mathbb{E}(\phi_{t+1} + z_{t+1})\beta c_t/c_{t+1}$. The price follows a martingale adjusting for the dividend and scaling for consumption growth. Expected discounted returns are unpredictable.

5.2.1.2 Competitive Equilibrium

The market clearing condition for shares is $\theta_t = 1$ at all times and the market clearing for fruit is $c_t = z_t$ at all times. Inserting the market clearing equation for the commodity in the optimality condition (5.3), we obtain a dynamic equation that determines the price of the tree at every point in time as a function of the expected future price of the shares and fruit of the tree

$$\phi_t u'(z_t) = \beta \mathbb{E}(\phi_{t+1} + z_{t+1}) u'(z_{t+1}). \tag{5.4}$$

Since there is a single representative dynasty, there will be no trade at equilibrium. The model serves only the purpose of pricing the shares of the tree, that is, the only asset available so far.

Substituting iteratively equation (5.4) in subsequent periods, we obtain the price of the tree in a generic period t as

5

$$\phi_t = \beta \mathbb{E} \sum_{t=1}^{\infty} \frac{u'(z_{t+t})}{u'(z_t)} z_{t+t}.$$

Thus, the price of the asset reflects the discounted value of all of its future dividends, using the stochastic marginal rates of substitution of the dividends for the dynasty at all future dates as discount factors. In other words, the equilibrium price reflects purely the fundamental value of the asset, without any speculative component.

5.2.1.3 Risk-Free Security

The model can be used to price any type of asset on these principles, including risk-free securities. Suppose that the dynasty can also acquire a one-period government bond that costs $\psi_t \leq 1$ units of fruit currently and delivers one unit of fruit in the next period. The reimbursement is financed with lump-sum taxation, T_t every period. The available stock of the bond is D_t every period. The demand for the bond by the dynasty in each period is denoted by d_{t+1}. The budget constraint of the dynasty becomes

$$c_t + \psi_t d_{t+1} + \phi_t \theta_{t+1} = (\phi_t + z_t)\theta_t + d_t - T_t.$$

The optimality condition for the choice of the bond by the dynasty is

$$\psi_t u'(c_t) = \beta \mathbb{E} u'(c_{t+1}). \tag{5.5}$$

The dynasty determines the optimal demand for the bond equating the marginal cost of giving up current consumption to buy the bond at the current price ψ_t to the expected marginal gain of increasing future consumption, with the reimbursement of the bond. Clearing of the market in the bond market requires $d_t = D_t$ in every period. Using market clearing, $c_t = z_t$, the price of the government bond in a generic period t is

$$\psi_t = \beta \mathbb{E} \frac{u'(z_{t+1})}{u'(z_t)},$$

that reflects the unit risk-free return discounted by the stochastic marginal rate of substitution for the dividends of the dynasty. In other words, the price of the risk-free government bond is directly related to the willingness of the dynasty to transfer consumption to the next period. This is intuitive, since the bond is the risk-free instrument that allows traders to save for the future.

5.2.2 Returns

The term $\phi_{t+1} + z_{t+1}$ in the equation (5.3) is the payoff of equity, which pays the dividend z_{t+1} and can be sold at price ϕ_{t+1} in the next period. Dividing the payoff by its current price, we obtain the gross return of the tree

$$R_{t+1} \equiv \frac{\phi_{t+1} + z_{t+1}}{\phi_t},$$

namely the payoff of equity per unit invested. On the other hand, the payoff of the risk-free one-period bond is 1, since it does not pay dividend and is reimbursed one-for-one in the period following its issuance. Dividing the payoff by its current price, we obtain the return of the bond as the inverse of its price

$$\mathcal{R}_{t+1} = \frac{1}{\psi_t}.$$

This is the risk-free rate. Dividing the future discounted marginal utility of consumption by the current marginal utility of consumption, we obtain the marginal rate of substitution between current and future consumption for the dynasty as

$$S_{t+1} \equiv \beta \frac{u'(c_{t+1})}{u'(c_t)}.$$

This is also known as the discount factor of the dynasty. Notice that both the return of the tree and the discount factor of the dynasty are stochastic, since the dividend, and hence consumption, are stochastic. Using the return of equity and the discount factor, we can write equation (5.3) as

$$1 = \mathbb{E}(R_{t+1} S_{t+1}). \tag{5.6}$$

The dynasty invests resources in equity to the point where its expected return discounted using the marginal rate of intertemporal substitution covers the cost of an additional unit investment. Analogously, using the return of the bond and the marginal rate of intertemporal substitution, we can write equation (5.5) as

$$\mathcal{R}_{t+1} = \frac{1}{\mathbb{E}(S_{t+1})}. \tag{5.7}$$

The dynasty invests in the risk-less bond to smooth consumption over time, therefore only the discount matters. Even if the bond was not available for trade, its shadow return could be determined using the principle of no-arbitrage. Should there be a difference in expected discounted return between two securities, an unlimited profit could be made selling the security with lower expected discounted return while acquiring the other. This activity is known as arbitrage between the two securities. Hence, for the dynasty to be willing to hold both equity and bond, their expected discounted returns should be the same. In other words, there should be no possibility of obtaining any profit arbitraging between the two. Therefore, $\mathbb{E}(\mathcal{R}_{t+1}S_{t+1}) = \mathbb{E}(R_{t+1}S_{t+1}) = 1$. Since the bond is a risk-less one-period security, equation (5.7) follows.

5.2.2.1 Risk Correction

Since the expected value of the product of two random variables is equal to the sum of the product of their expected values and their covariance, we have

$$\mathbb{E}(R_{t+1}S_{t+1}) = \mathbb{E}(R_{t+1})\mathbb{E}(S_{t+1}) + \operatorname{cov}(R_{t+1}S_{t+1}).$$

Thus, we can write equation (5.6) using the risk-free rate (5.7) as

$$\mathbb{E}(R_{t+1}) = \mathcal{R}_{t+1} - \frac{\operatorname{cov}(R_{t+1}S_{t+1})}{\mathbb{E}(S_{t+1})}. \tag{5.8}$$

The expected return of the risky asset is equal to the risk-free return with a correction for risk that depends on the covariance between the return of the asset and the marginal rate of intertemporal substitution of the dynasty. One may have conjectured that an asset with very volatile dividends is particularly risky and therefore should have a large risk correction. Equation (5.8) shows that this conjecture is incorrect. If the return is volatile but uncorrelated with the discount factor, the risk correction is nil. What matters for expected returns is not the variance of the returns, but their covariance with the discount factor. In other words, only systematic risk gives rise to risk corrections, while idiosyncratic risk does not.

5.2.2.2 Equity Premium

Since marginal utility is inversely related to consumption by the strict concavity of the utility function, the discount factor is inversely related to changes in consumption over time. Therefore, the expected return of risky assets is directly related to the covariance of risky returns with consumption growth. Assets whose returns vary in the opposite direction of changes in consumption offer consumption insurance and, hence, can be held by the dynasty even when their expected returns are lower than the risk-free rate. In other words, since asset prices and expected returns are inversely related, the dynasty is prepared to pay dearly for an asset that is expected to produce more fruit when consumption is expected to be small, as it provides insurance.

Conversely, assets whose returns vary in the same direction as consumption growth make consumption more volatile, which the dynasty dislikes when utility is strictly concave, hence, their expected returns should be higher than the risk-free return to induce the dynasty to hold them. In sum, according to the optimality condition (5.8), an *equity premium* on the risk-free return, that is, an excess return of equity over bonds, emerges when the returns on equity vary in the same direction as changes in consumption over time. When equity is a poor hedge against consumption risk, the return on equity should be greater than the return on the risk-free bond if both types of securities are to be held by the dynasty. Notice that without uncertainty, namely with a non-stochastic dividend z every period, the returns would not vary with consumption growth, and hence the return of equity and bond would be the same, implying a nil equity premium. Also, with a linear utility function, that is, with the neutrality of the dynasty toward risk, the discount factor would be β, which does not vary with equity returns, and hence the equity premium would again be nil.

5.2.2.3 Mean-Variance Frontier

Using the fact that the correlation between two random variables is the ratio between their covariance and the product of their standard deviations, namely $\text{corr}(R_{t+1}S_{t+1}) = \text{cov}(R_{t+1}S_{t+1})[\text{sd}(R_{t+1})\text{sd}(S_{t+1})]^{-1}$, and the coefficient of variation of a random variable is the ratio of its standard deviation and mean, namely $\text{cv}(S_{t+1}) = \text{sd}(S_{t+1})/\mathbb{E}(S_{t+1})$, the expected return (5.8) can be written as follows

$$\mathbb{E}(R_{t+1}) = \mathcal{R}_{t+1} - \text{corr}(R_{t+1}S_{t+1})\text{cv}(S_{t+1})\text{sd}(R_{t+1}).$$

Since the correlation between random variables cannot be larger than 1 in absolute value, the previous formula implies that the absolute value of the difference between the expected return of any risky asset with the risk-free rate cannot exceed the product of the coefficient of variation of the discount factor and the standard deviation of the return of the risky asset

$$|\mathbb{E}(R_{t+1}) - \mathcal{R}_{t+1}| \leq \text{cv}(S_{t+1})\text{sd}(R_{t+1}).$$

Taking this condition at equality, we obtain what is known as the portfolio *mean-variance frontier* with slope $\text{cv}(S_{t+1})$. The frontier provides the answer to the question of how much mean return one can get from a portfolio for a given level of variance. Since the frontier has $|\text{corr}(R_{t+1}S_{t+1})| = 1$, all the assets with returns on the frontier are perfectly correlated with the discount factor, either positively, in which case they are maximally risky, or negatively, in which case they provide maximal insurance against consumption risk. All the returns on the frontier are also perfectly correlated with each other. Assets with returns within the frontier are not worse than those on the frontier, since they satisfy the optimality condition of the dynasty.

5.2.2.4 Sharpe Ratio

The ratio between the excess return over the risk-free rate over the standard deviation of the returns is known as the *Sharpe ratio* that, by the previous inequality, is bounded above by the coefficient of variation of the discount factor. The Sharpe ratio provides the answer to the question of how much additional mean return one can get accepting additional volatility. Using the Sharpe ratio and the portfolio mean-variance frontier, we can express the net standardized premium of equity as the slope of the frontier

$$\left|\frac{\mathbb{E}(R_{t+1}) - \mathcal{R}_{t+1}}{\text{sd}(R_{t+1})}\right| = \text{cv}(S_{t+1}). \tag{5.9}$$

Since the discount factor is inversely related to consumption growth over time, using an explicit utility function and data on assets returns and consumption growth, this equation can be used to identify the dynasty's risk aversion.

5.3 Empirical Anomalies

5

The model can be used to fit the available data for real-world financial markets on the spread between the risky returns of the stock market and the risk-free return of the Treasury bills, namely the equity premium. For this purpose, assume that the utility function has constant relative risk aversion ϵ. Equity dividends can assume at least two distinct values with a positive and time-invariant switching probability between any pair of states for every period. The dynasty maximizes its expected life-time utility (5.1), subject to budget constraint (5.2) in every period. Since the utility function has constant relative risk aversion ϵ, the discount rate is $\beta(c_t/c_{t+1})^\epsilon$. Let the net growth rate of consumption between two consecutive time periods be g_t. Using the property of the expectation operator and a logarithmic approximation, the equity premium condition (5.9) equates the Sharpe ratio to the product of the risk-aversion parameter and the coefficient of variation of the growth rate of consumption, $\epsilon \text{cv}(g_{t+1}^{-1})$. In sum, the equity premium is proportional to the dispersion of consumption growth, where the proportionality factor is identified by the risk aversion of the dynasty, captured by the parameter ϵ. We can now check whether the theoretical predictions are consistent with the available data from the real-world financial markets. Two empirical anomalies arise, concerning the equity premium and the risk-free rate.

5.3.1 Equity Premium Puzzle

The average annual return of stocks in the United States during the last century has been around 9% with a standard deviation of about 1.6%, while the average annual return of Treasury bills during the same period has been around 1%. Therefore, the average annual Sharpe ratio during this period was 0.5. During the same period, consumption has grown at an average rate of 1% with a standard deviation of 1%. Using (5.9) with $\text{cv}(S_{t+1}) = \epsilon \text{cv}(g_{t+1}^{-1})$, since $\text{cv}(g^{-1}) \approx 0.01$, the model with constant relative risk aversion requires a value of the relative risk-aversion parameter $\epsilon \approx 50$, which is considered implausibly large, as it flies in the face of other available evidence for risk aversion. The inability of the dynastic model to match the long-term equity premium found in US financial data, unless the risk aversion of the dynasty is implausibly large, is known as the *equity premium puzzle*.

It is worth noting that this is an empirical puzzle, not a theoretical one, since the model has a clear theoretical explanation for why there should be an equity premium, the reason being that equity is a poorer hedge against consumption risk than government bonds. The difficulty consists in matching the real-world equity premium quantitatively when the model is parameterized with the utility function with constant relative risk aversion.

5.3.2 Risk-Free Rate Puzzle

A second related quantitative problem with the model is that the equilibrium saving rate over time generated by the model is lower than the observed saving rate for the US economy over the past century. If the dynasty has constant relative risk aversion ϵ, the optimality condition for the bond is $\beta \mathcal{R}_{t+1}\mathbb{E}(c_t/c_{t+1})^{\epsilon} = 1$. Consumption has been growing on average at a rate of 1% over such a period in the United States. The average annual return of Treasuries over the same period has been around 1%. By the optimality condition, with the average risk-free rate $\mathcal{R} \approx 1.01$ and the average growth rate of consumption $g \approx 0.01$, the time discount is $\beta \approx 1.01^{\epsilon-1}$, which is greater than 1 with $\epsilon > 1$ as required to match the equity premium data. For $\epsilon = 50$, the time discount is $\beta \approx 1.6$. A time discount larger than unity is incompatible with the underlying assumption that the dynasty is relatively impatient, that is, $\beta < 1$. This is known as the *risk-free rate puzzle.*

5.4 Speculative Bubble

In the dynastic model, assets are priced at their fundamental value, represented by the stream of their discounted dividends. Unlike the dynastic model, the life-cycle model with overlapping generations can give rise to asset prices that diverge from their fundamental values, including speculative bubbles. The extreme case is that of an asset that has no intrinsic or fundamental value whose price has only the bubble component, for instance a fiat asset such as money. We will show that these types of assets can have value in the life-cycle model at equilibrium even when there are alternative assets with positive fundamental value.

5.4.1 Life-Cycle Model

Consider an infinite-horizon economy with time indexed by $t = 1, 2....$ There is a company that owns a technology that uses labor to produce output every period, represented by the production function $y_t = z\ell_t$. Maximization of the company implies $w_t = z$. The economy is populated by overlapping generations of workers with a unit-time endowment when young only. The preferences of every generation are represented by the utility function

$$U(c_t, c_{t+1}) = u(c_t) + \beta u(c_{t+1}),$$

which satisfies Assumption 4, with $\beta < 1$. There is an asset without intrinsic return available in unit supply that can be acquired at a price $\phi_t \geq 0$ for every period, whose demand will be denoted with θ_t. The budget constraint of a generation when young is $c_t + \phi_t\theta_{t+1} = w_t l_t$, since the wage income serves to finance the purchase of consumption and the asset. The budget when old is $c_{t+1} = \phi_{t+1}\theta_{t+1}$, since the asset can be liquidated to finance consumption later in life. The maximization of the worker gives

$$\phi_t u'(w_t l_t - \phi_t\theta_{t+1}) = \beta\phi_{t+1}u'(\phi_{t+1}\theta_{t+1}),$$

that equates the return of the asset, given exclusively by its relative price over time, ϕ_{t+1}/ϕ_t, since the asset has no intrinsic return, to the marginal rate of substitution of consumption over time.

5

5.4.1.1 Competitive Equilibrium

The markets for labor, commodity, and asset must all clear in a competitive equilibrium. In particular, since the asset is in unit supply, the condition $\theta_t = 1$ is valid in all periods. With $w_t = z$ and the unit endowment of labor being provided entirely by the worker, we obtain the equilibrium condition

$$\phi_t u'(z - \phi_t) = \beta\phi_{t+1}u'(\phi_{t+1}),$$

that describes the evolution of the price of the asset. We are trying to find out if such a price can be positive in all periods, despite the fact that the asset has no fundamental value. In a stationary equilibrium, the price will have to remain constant over time to grant a time-invariant allocation. Leaving aside the time subscripts, the equilibrium condition becomes

$$u'(z - \phi) = \beta u'(\phi),$$

which has a solution with $\phi \in (0, z)$, by continuity under Assumption 4.ii. The solution is unique because of the strict concavity of the utility function. Thus, an asset without fundamental value has a positive price in equilibrium. The asset can be identified as being a monetary instrument that serves to save income over time, that is, as a store of value, absent any other means of saving.

Example 5.3

Suppose that the utility function is logarithmic. Then, the stationary equilibrium price of the asset is $\phi = \beta z(1 + \beta)^{-1}$.

5.4.2 Bubble with Capital

In the previous model, there were no alternative means of saving, so it may be conjectured that the bubble only emerged because the corresponding asset was the only instrument available to store value over time. Let us now modify the model introducing capital as a productive input to show that this conjecture is incorrect. The production function in per capita terms is $y_t = f(k_t)$. By optimization of the company, the rental rate of capital is equal to its marginal product $r_t = f'(k_t)$ and the wage to the marginal product of labor that is in unit supply $w_t = f(k_t) - f'(k_t)k_t$. The depreciation in production is complete.

The worker can save by accumulating both capital and the asset. The budget for young people is $c_t + k_{t+1} + \phi_t\theta_{t+1} = w_t l_t$, and the budget for old people is $c_{t+1} = r_{t+1}k_{t+1} + \phi_{t+1}\theta_{t+1}$. By no-arbitrage, the capital rental rate and the asset return should be the same in every period; therefore, we obtain the optimality condition

$$r_{t+1} = \frac{\phi_{t+1}}{\phi_t},$$

since the asset does not pay dividend and therefore its return is given by its relative price in two consecutive periods. The other optimality condition is

$$u'(w_t l_t - k_{t+1} - \phi_t\theta_{t+1}) = \beta r_{t+1} u'(r_{t+1}k_{t+1} + \phi_{t+1}\theta_{t+1}),$$

which equates the marginal cost of giving up current consumption to accumulate additional capital that can be rented out next period or, equivalently, equates the capital rental rate to the marginal rate of substitution of consumption over time.

5.4.2.1 Competitive Equilibrium

The markets for capital, labor, commodity, and asset should all be in equilibrium. In particular, since the fiat asset is in unit supply, the condition $\theta_t = 1$ is valid in all periods. With the rental rate, $r_t = f'(k_t)$, the wage, $w_t = f(k_t) - f'(k_t)k_t$ and the unit endowment of labor being supplied entirely by the worker, we obtain the equilibrium condition

$$\phi_{t+1} = f'(k_{t+1})\phi_t, \tag{5.10}$$

that reflects no-arbitrage and the equilibrium

$$u'(f(k_t) - f'(k_t)k_t - k_{t+1} - \phi_t) = \beta f'(k_{t+1})u'(f'(k_{t+1})k_{t+1} + \phi_{t+1}), \tag{5.11}$$

that reflects the portfolio choice. These conditions jointly describe the evolution of the capital stock and the price of the asset. We know from earlier results that competitive equilibrium is not necessarily efficient in the life-cycle model. In particular, when the equilibrium capital stock is larger than the golden rule capital stock $k^* = f'^{-1}(1)$, the equilibrium is Pareto inefficient, since lowering the current capital accumulation would improve its time profile without hurting anybody, not even the young of the current generation. Here, we are interested in the question whether the other asset can have positive value at equilibrium despite the fact that it has no intrinsic, fundamental value and there is an alternative, intrinsically valuable saving instrument..

Consider stationary equilibria with a time-invariant allocation. To sustain a time-invariant allocation, the price of the asset should be constant over time, which requires $f'(k) = 1 \Leftrightarrow k = f'^{-1}(1)$, by the no-arbitrage condition (5.10). This is the Golden Rule capital stock, which we insert into the equilibrium condition (5.11) together with the no-arbitrage condition (5.10), obtaining

$$\Gamma(\phi) \equiv u'(f(f'^{-1}(1)) - 2f'^{-1}(1) - \phi) - \beta u'(f'^{-1}(1) + \phi) = 0.$$

The following proposition provides the condition for the existence of a positive stationary equilibrium price of the fiat asset. Define $\hat{\beta} \equiv u'(f(f'^{-1}(1)) - 2f'^{-1}(1))/u'(f'^{-1}(1))$, which is strictly smaller than 1 if and only if $f(f'^{-1}(1)) > 3f'^{-1}(1)$ by strict concavity of utility.

▪▪ Proposition 5.1

There is a unique positive stationary equilibrium price for the fiat asset if and only if $\beta > \hat{\beta}$.

Proof The function $\Gamma(\phi)$ is continuous in ϕ with $\Gamma(f(f'^{-1}(1)) - 2f'^{-1}(1)) = \infty$ by Assumption 4.ii and $\Gamma(0) < 0$ if and only if $\beta > \hat{\beta}$. By the intermediate value theorem, there exists a price $\phi \in (0, f(f'^{-1}(1)) - 2f'^{-1}(1))$ that satisfies $\Gamma(\phi) = 0$. The derivative $\Gamma'(\phi) > 0$ by strict concavity of the utility function. Therefore, either there is a unique positive stationary equilibrium price of the fiat asset or there is none.

The bubble emerges at equilibrium if the capital accumulation would have been excessive relative to the efficient benchmark without the fiat asset, since in this case the fiat asset helps reduce the stock of capital bringing it down to the efficient level.

5.5 Bubbles and Crashes

A security whose market value deviates from its fundamental value, namely whose price has a bubble component, can contribute to a better allocation of resources by providing liquidity to the economic system. In this sense, speculation is not a negative phenomenon *per se*. However, when markets for income transfer and risk sharing are imperfect or incomplete, speculative bubbles can emerge on any financial asset, sometimes generating recessions when they burst.

The typical evolution of financial phenomena with a speculative bubble is characterized by a phase in which the demand for an asset grows at first slowly and then increasingly rapidly, fueled by optimistic expectations that raise its market price to a peak beyond which there is a sudden collapse in demand and the corresponding market value of the security itself. The consequence is often a market crash, with real effects on income and unemployment.

5.5.1 Dutch Tulipmania and Other Bubbles

The first recorded speculative bubble phenomenon in history originated from the so-called *tulipmania*, which occurred in Holland in the seventeenth century. Beginning in the year 1635, the value of tulip bulbs on the Dutch marketplace began to rise, marking the gradual start of the speculative bubble. The peak in the value of tulip bulbs occurred in early February 1637, when a single bulb came to cost one and a half times the annual salary of a manual worker. A few weeks after the bubble burst, the price of the tulip bulbs returned to the value before the mania had erupted.

Two other famous bubble episodes, the Mississippi bubble and the South Sea bubble, occurred in the beginning of the eighteenth century almost at the same time in France and England, respectively.

The stock price bubble that inflated in the second half of the 1920s and burst in 1929 is considered the beginning and one of the causes of the Great Depression that affected most of the then developed countries and lasted until WWII.

More recent episodes of market euphoria followed by financial panic consist of the computer company bubble in the 1990s, the so-called *dotcom* bubble, and the bubble in US housing market values of the first half of the 2000s whose bursting led to the junk mortgage crisis, the so-called *subprime* mortgages, which in turn spawned the Great Recession of 2008.

5.5.2 House Price Bubble

Beginning in 2000 and continuing through the middle of the decade, housing prices in much of the United States grew steadily, generating a housing price bubble. This dynamic was aided by the expansionary monetary policy of the US central bank, which kept interest rates low for a long time in response to the previous dotcom bubble crisis. Low interest rates ended up stimulating the demand for housing, supported by cheap mortgages, fueling the growth of property values. The mechanism tended to reinforce itself as rising property values made it convenient for banks to grant mortgages even to people who did not provide collateral for repayment because banks, in the event of the borrower's default, believed that they could recover the loan by foreclosing and reselling the home at high prices anyway. In addition to the housing bubble and low interest rates, the growth of unsecured mortgages was fueled by securitization transactions, which allowed banks to remove the risk of default of their borrowers, reducing the incentive to properly assess their creditworthiness.

In the mid-2000s, the US central bank began raising interest rates in response to the recovery of the US economy. Mortgages became increasingly expensive, and defaults increased among people who could no longer repay increasingly onerous installments. The demand for real estate shrank, resulting in a decrease in the value of mortgages securing existing loans. The banks most involved in the provision of *subprime* mortgages recorded heavy losses. The phenomenon continued until September 2008, when the American investment bank Lehman Brothers failed. In a short time, the crisis transferred to the US and European real economy, causing income and employment to drop in several countries. Contributing to this fall was the restriction of bank credit, the collapse of stock markets and housing prices, with a strengthening mechanism that only aggravated the situation, until the US central bank intervened through the so-called *quantitative easing*, aimed at lifting stock values to ease credit restrictions.

5.6 Conclusion

The dynastic model has a representative long-term trader with access to a complete set of financial instruments to diversify all risks. The model can be used to explain the emergence of short-term business cycles, long-term economic growth, and the pricing of assets. Assets are priced at their fundamental value. However, with the representation of preferences with a constant relative risk aversion typically used in macroeconomics, some quantitative anomalies emerge, known as the equity premium and risk-free rate puzzle. Moreover, there are assets that are traded routinely at prices above their fundamental value, most commonly and obviously the monetary assets. Although the latter observation can be rationalized in the life-cycle model, solving the two puzzles requires a new framework. These puzzles point toward a model that breaks at least one of the underlying assumptions of the model, namely the presence of complete markets to diversify risks or the absence of borrowing constraints on asset trading, or possibly both.

5.7 Literature

The seminal paper on asset pricing using the dynastic model is *Asset Prices in an Exchange Economy* by Robert Lucas. The book *Asset Pricing* by John Cochrane covers the essentials of finance and macro-related topics. The existence of an equity premium puzzle was first pointed out by Rajnesh Mehra and Ed Prescott in their famous contribution entitled *The Equity Premium: A Puzzle*. The key paper on bubbles in the life-cycle model is *Asset Bubbles and Overlapping Generations* by Jean Tirole. The book by Charles Kindleberger entitled *Manias, Panics, and Crashes: A History of Financial Crises* examines several bubble episodes that have occurred in modern history.

Exercises

1. Consider the dynastic asset price model with a tree that bears fruit every period. Suppose that the dynasty has preferences over consumption sequences represented by the life-time utility function

$$U(\mathbf{c}) = \sum_{t=1}^{\infty} \beta^{t-1} c_t,$$

i.e. it is risk neutral, and the fruit of the tree has two possible values $z_1 > z_2$ that follow a Markov process with equal probability of remaining in the same state and switching state every period.

- Calculate the equilibrium price of the shares of the tree.
- Suppose that there is a one-period government bond. Calculate its price.
- Calculate the equity premium.

2. Consider the dynastic asset price model with a tree that bears fruit every period. Suppose that the dynasty has preferences over consumption sequences represented by the life-time utility function

$$U(\mathbf{c}) = \sum_{t=1}^{\infty} \beta^{t-1} \frac{c_t^{1-\epsilon}}{1-\epsilon},$$

with $\epsilon > 0$ and the fruit of the tree is the same in both states $z_1 = z_2 = z > 0$ in every period.

- Calculate the equilibrium price of the shares of the tree.
- Suppose that there is a one-period government bond. Calculate its price.
- Calculate the equity premium.

3. Consider the dynastic asset price model with a tree that bears fruit every period. Suppose that the dynasty has preferences over consumption sequences represented by the life-time utility function

$$U(\mathbf{c}) = \sum_{t=1}^{\infty} \beta^{t-1} \ln c_t,$$

and that the fruit of the tree has two possible values $z_1 > z_2$ that follow a Markov process with the same probability of remaining in the same state or switching state every period.

- Calculate the equilibrium price of the shares of the tree.
- Suppose that there is a one-period government bond. Calculate its price.
- Calculate the equity premium.

References

Cochrane J (2005), Asset Pricing, Princeton University Press

Lucas R Jr (1978), Asset Prices in an Exchange Economy, Econometrica, 46: 1429-1445

Kindleberger C (2011), Manias, Panics and Crashes: A History of Financial Crises, Palgrave Macmillan

Mehra R, Prescott E (1985), The Equity Premium: A Puzzle, Journal of Monetary Economics, 15: 145-161

Tirole J (1985), Asset Bubbles and Overlapping Generations, Econometrica, 53: 1499-1528

II

Heaven Can Wait

Although the standard model of the first part represents reasonably well the major economic observations regarding both the short and the long run, the picture is not entirely accurate. For instance, in terms of business cycle analysis, the model responds symmetrically to positive and negative productivity shocks, while, in reality, recessions are deeper and longer than booms. Moreover, contrary to what the model would predict, the available data show that individual consumption profiles are, at least partially, driven by current personal income rather than overall lifetime wealth. Correspondingly, there is evidence that risk sharing is less complete than the theory would predict. Overall, witness also the equity premium puzzle, the markets in the standard model are presumed to work too well relative to what the empirical evidence seems to imply.

In this part, we will modify the model introducing market imperfections that help to make sense of the observations concerning the macroeconomic implications of the functioning of real world financial markets. The normative properties of the model will not survive the introduction of these market imperfections, opening up a role for public intervention to try to restore efficiency. In particular, the lack of instruments to share risk and smooth consumption opens the door to an effect known as the pecuniary externality, whereby choices in the financial realm spill over to the real economy with adverse macroeconomic implications. Unlike in the case with complete markets, public authorities will be able to play a beneficial role as providers of insurance and liquidity when risk-sharing and consumption smoothing instruments are lacking.

We will begin with a simple departure from the benchmark model in which the reimbursement of loans has to be guaranteed by collateral, since the traders cannot commit to honor their promises, and hence unsecured credit is not feasible. Changes in the prices of the assets used as collateral constitute a channel for the propagation of negative shocks. The real business cycle model has an intertemporal transmission mechanism that works symmetrically for positive and negative shocks and does not generate enough persistence to match the available evidence, for instance, on the US economy. Real-world business cycles are characterized by a rather strong degree of persistency over time and are asymmetric, with negative shocks having deeper consequences than positive ones. With collateral constraints, the model can accommodate the observed persistence and asymmetry of business cycles, by which the recession periods are deeper and last longer than the periods of economic boom. Moreover, pecuniary externalities and endogenous business cycles can arise as equilibrium phenomena.

Second, we consider a model in which consumption has to be acquired with cash, by legal requirement. This relatively simple requirement will have far-reaching consequences, as resource allocation will no longer be efficient, and business cycles will emerge endogenously from the coordination of traders' expectations as in the life-cycle model. In the context of this model, we will discuss two famous theories of inflation, the quantity theory and the fiscal theory, respectively. According to the quantity theory, inflation is generated by systematic monetary expansions; according to the fiscal theory, inflation is generated by swelling government budget deficits.

Next, we will examine a model in which the financial markets are incomplete and, hence, the risk-sharing will be less than perfect, creating inefficiencies due to the pecuniary externality. In such a context, the Ricardian equivalence and the proposition that capital income should not be taxed, which were valid in the standard dynastic model, are overturned. With incomplete risk-sharing, traders end up saving excessively relative to efficiency for precautionary reasons.

In the dynastic model, assets are priced reflecting their expected discounted returns. As a consequence, fiat assets without intrinsic returns, such as money, cannot have positive value at any equilibrium of such a model. This is in direct contrast to the everyday observation that real-world monetary assets without intrinsic return are actively traded even without the legal requirement to do so. In the last chapter of this part, we will consider a scenario in which asset prices diverge from their fundamental values, that is, there are speculative bubbles, due to the presence of borrowing limitations. In such a context, the traders will hold liquid assets devoid of intrinsic value such as fiat money to smooth consumption over time, in a way that is reminiscent of the life-cycle model. With uninsured risks about labor income and borrowing limits, an expansion of public liquidity through money creation can be socially beneficial as a partial substitute for missing insurance instruments.

Credit Cycle

L. Ferraris, *Macroeconomic Theory*, Classroom Companion: Economics,
https://doi.org/10.1007/978-3-031-88740-6_6

6.1 Introduction

The standard real business cycle model has a transmission mechanism that is symmetric between economic expansions and recessions. Both positive and negative shocks to productivity give rise to reactions of the endogenous variables, namely income, employment, investment, and consumption, that differ in sign but not in size. However, real-world economic recessions are typically deeper and last longer than the corresponding booms. Moreover, credit fluctuates with income and employment over the business cycle. Credit market imperfections and credit constraints appear to play a major role in the amplification and propagation of economic shocks, generating asymmetries between booms and recessions.

In this chapter, we examine a departure from the benchmark model in which traders cannot borrow freely against their future income because they cannot guarantee the repayment of loans other than by pledging some assets used as collateral. When loan reimbursement is guaranteed by the value of collateral assets, changes in asset prices amplify the effect of aggregate fluctuations. With binding credit restrictions, the prices of collateral assets exceed their fundamental value, including liquidity premia. Changes in the prices of collateral assets amplify or even cause business cycles. Drops in asset prices tighten credit constraints that compress loans that reduce the demand for the asset by production complementarities, which, in turn, further depress the asset price. A similar mechanism was at work at the beginning of the Great Recession when a fire sale of assets used as collateral for loans has caused their price to drop generating a credit crunch. The policy intervention to support the value of collateral assets, now known as quantitative easing, has proven effective in helping the economy recover from the recession.

6.2 Exogenous Credit Cycle

We prepare the stage to discuss the effects of credit constraints and borrowing limits going back to the minimal model with a representative company and consumer that we examined in the second chapter, which we reinterpret as a two-period model with borrowing and lending. Then, we extend the model to the infinite time horizon with a collateral constraint.

6.2.1 Unlimited Borrowing

Suppose that there are two periods, a representative consumer and a representative company. In the first period, the representative consumer autonomously produces a durable commodity with labor using a linear production function with unit marginal productivity. The consumer cares about consumption only in the second period and can store the commodity or lend it at a competitive net real interest rate r. The preferences of the consumer are represented by the utility function $U(c, l) = \beta u(c) - v(l)$ with $\beta \leq 1$ representing the time discount factor, that satisfies Assumption 2. If the interest rate is non-negative, the consumer will lend $l = b$ in the first period, expecting to consume $c = (1 + r)b$ in the second period. The optimality condition for the choice of the loan b by the consumer equates the intertemporal marginal rate of substitution between labor and consumption with the real interest rate

$$\frac{v'(b)}{\beta u'((1 + r)b)} = 1 + r.$$

The optimality condition implicitly gives the supply of the loan $b(r)$ as a function of the interest rate. The supply of loans increases in the interest rate if and only if the intertemporal substitution effect dominates the income effect. The company has no initial resources and needs the commodity to start production in the first period to generate output in the second period with a technology represented by a linear production function with productivity $z \geq 1$. Profits, if any, are used by the owner of the company to consume C in the second period, with utility $\beta u(C)$. In the first period, the company can issue a one-period bond B to be reimbursed with interest in the second period.

6.2.1.1 Competitive Equilibrium

Without imperfections or limits in borrowing, the market interest rate is $r = z - 1$ and the equilibrium loan satisfies condition $\beta z u'(zb) = v'(b)$. A unique competitive equilibrium loan that satisfies this condition exists for any productivity and time-discount value by the usual continuity argument. The allocation is efficient since the welfare theorems apply. A supply shock that decreases z, leads to a contraction of the loan that, in turn, generates a recession with an even greater decrease in income and consumption. A demand shock that lowers β leads to a contraction of the loan that generates a recession with a decrease in income and consumption.

6.2.2 Borrowing Limit

A limited ability to guarantee the repayment of the bond by the company, in which only a fraction $\mu < 1$ of the profit can be pledged for reimbursement, would lead to the binding borrowing constraint $(1 + r)B = \mu z B$, which in turn leads to a contraction in the market interest rate $r = \mu z - 1 \geq 0$. As a consequence, the equilibrium loan would be determined by the condition $\beta \mu z u'(\mu z b) = v'(b)$, with the resulting inefficiency in the allocation. Denote the equilibrium loan as a function of the credit limit as $b(\mu)$, the equilibrium consumption as $c(\mu)$ and the equilibrium employment as $l(\mu)$. The derivative of the loan with respect to the credit limit is

$$b'(\mu) = \frac{b(\mu)}{\mu} \frac{1 - \epsilon_{u'}(c(\mu))}{\epsilon_{u'}(c(\mu)) + \epsilon_{v'}(l(\mu))}.$$

Provided that intertemporal substitution dominates the income effect, that is, $\epsilon_{u'}(c(\mu)) < 1$, a drop in μ, which represents a shock to the credit conditions, perhaps originating from a contraction in the value of the assets used by the company as collateral, could emerge as an independent source of economic recessions or a factor that exacerbates their effects, since it multiplies productivity z and time discount β. Should the tightening of credit conditions be sufficiently severe to induce $\mu < z^{-1}$, the lending market would shut down altogether, the company would remain inactive and consumption would be determined by $\beta u'(c) = v'(l)$ with $c = l$. Thus, credit constraints can cause booms and recessions, amplifying the effects of economic shocks, especially in the downward direction.

6.2.2.1 Incomplete Contract

The reason why the company's ability to guarantee the payment in full is limited may be the difficulty in enforcing contracts. Suppose that the market for corporate loans, instead of being competitive, is bilateral. In the first period, the entrepreneur, without initial resources but with a project that produces y, and the consumer, with the ability to generate resources in the first period, can sign a lending contract that determines the amount of resources that the consumer will lend to the entrepreneur initially and the amount of the reimbursement of the loan to the consumer at the end of the project. The human capital of the entrepreneur is essential to generate value from the project, and the entrepreneur cannot be forced to work on the project. Therefore, in the second period, the entrepreneur can renege on the commitment and force the renegotiation of its terms, threatening the lender to shirk producing nothing. Notice that the renegotiation occurs after the loan has already been extended by the lender, who has no outside option and whose effort is sunk at this point. Assume that the lender has a bargaining power μ in the renegotiation. Let the reimbursement that emerges from the renegotiation be $R = \mu y$, reflecting the lender's ability to obtain a fraction of the value that can be generated in the second period, through his or her bargaining power. This is the outcome that would be obtained with a negotiation that occurs with the Nash protocol. Since $y = zb$, we can now go back to the initial period to determine the amount of the loan initially offered by the consumer who anticipates that the contract will be renegotiated later on. The loan b, which maximizes the utility $U(b) = \beta u(\mu z b) - v(b)$, satisfies the same optimality condition derived above $\beta \mu z u'(\mu z b) = v'(b)$. Thus, contractual incompleteness provides the foundation for the exogenous credit limit considered above.

6.2.2.2 Pecuniary Externality

Suppose that the public authority can impose a lump-sum tax, T, on the consumer in the first period to subsidize the company at a rate s proportional to the issue of bonds, sB, maintaining the balance of the budget, $T = sB$. By the binding credit constraint of the company, we get the interest rate $1 + r = \mu(z + s)$. The resource constraint of the consumer in the first period is $l = b + T$ and in the second period $c = (1 + r)b$. Optimization of the consumer with the equilibrium interest rate and the public budget gives the equilibrium condition for the loan as

$\beta\mu(z+s)u'(\mu(z+s)b) = v'((1+s)b)$. Denote the equilibrium loan as a function of the subsidy as $b(s)$, the equilibrium consumption of the worker as $c(s)$, equilibrium consumption of the owner of the company as $C(s)$, and the equilibrium employment as $l(s)$. The subsidy increases the interest rate that, in turn, boosts the loan provided the intertemporal substitution effect dominates the income effect. A *pecuniary externality* is at work, as a redistribution of resources toward the company increases the interest rate, thus giving the consumer the incentive to lend more resources. In turn, this increases output and income.

It remains to be seen whether the intervention is socially beneficial. This is an economy with two people enjoying final consumption, the consumer, and the owner of the company; thus, we need to decide how to weigh the relative importance of their well-being for societal welfare. Suppose that we give equal weights to the consumer and the owner of the company in social welfare, treating them as if they were part of the same household, obtaining $W(s) = \beta u(c(s))) - v(l(s)) + \beta u(C(s))$, whose derivative with respect to the subsidy, using the equilibrium allocation as function of the subsidy, is

$$W'(s) = \beta b(s)\left[(1-\mu)u'(C(s))\frac{1+\epsilon_{v'}(l(s))}{\epsilon_{u'}(c(s))+\epsilon_{v'}(l(s))} - \mu u'(c(s))(z+s-1)\right].$$

When evaluating this derivative at intervention with $s = 0$, it can be easily seen that there exist parameters values such that $W'(0) > 0$. Hence, there are circumstances in which a small subsidy can be welfare improving relative to no intervention.

Example 1 With constant elasticity of substitution of consumption $\epsilon_{u'}(c) = \epsilon$ and linear disutility of labor, the derivative $W'(0)$ is positive for ϵ sufficiently small.

6.3 Endogenous Credit Cycle

Let us now extend the model to a longer time frame to discuss the role of collateral asset values in the onset and amplification of credit crises. The time horizon is infinite, with the time indexed by $t = 1, 2, \ldots$. There is a representative dynasty endowed with a technology that uses a perishable commodity and an asset in fixed unit supply to produce the consumption good. The dynasty can borrow an amount b_t of perishable commodity at a competitive net interest rate r_t at the beginning of each period and can acquire an amount θ_{t+1} of the asset at a competitive price ϕ_t at the end of each period. Repayment of the loan with interest occurs at the end of each period. The technology is represented by the production function $y_t = b_t^{\alpha}\theta_t^{1-\alpha}$, with $\alpha \in (0,1)$. The dynasty has preferences over consumption sequences $\mathbf{c}$ represented by the life-time utility function

$$U(\mathbf{c}) = \sum_{t=1}^{\infty} \beta^{t-1}u(c_t),$$

where $u(\cdot)$ is differentiable, strictly increasing and strictly concave, and $\beta < 1$ represents time discount. There is an international market for loans in which the interest rate is $r_t = \beta^{-1} - 1$ in every period.

6.3.1 Competitive Equilibrium

The dynasty chooses the loan b_t and the asset holdings θ_{t+1} in each period to maximize its life-time utility subject to the budget constraint $c_t + \phi_t\theta_{t+1} = y_t - (1 + r_t)b_t + \phi_t\theta_t$. The choice of loan is guided by the optimality condition

$$\alpha b_t^{\alpha-1}\theta_t^{1-\alpha} = 1 + r_t, \tag{6.1}$$

which equates its marginal product with the cost of borrowing in each period. The choice of the asset satisfies in each period the optimality condition

$$u'(c_t)\phi_t = \beta u'(c_{t+1})[(1-\alpha)b_{t+1}^{\alpha}\theta_{t+1}^{-\alpha} + \phi_{t+1}], \tag{6.2}$$

that equates the marginal cost of acquiring the asset at its current price in terms of foregone current consumption to the future marginal benefit in terms of higher production and asset market value.

In competitive equilibrium, the market for the asset is cleared with $\theta_t = 1$ in every period. With $1 + r_t = \beta^{-1}$ and $\theta_t = 1$, the optimality condition (6.1) gives $b_t = b^* = (\alpha\beta)^{\frac{1}{1-\alpha}}$ in each period and the budget constraint that reduces to $c_t = b_t^{\alpha} - \beta^{-1}b_t$ in each period gives consumption $c_t = c^* = (1-\alpha)(\alpha\beta)^{\frac{\alpha}{1-\alpha}}$. The competitive price of the asset is determined by the equation (6.2) with $\theta_t = 1$ and the equilibrium allocation, which is given by the linear dynamic equation

$$\phi_{t+1} = \frac{\phi_t}{\beta} - \frac{1-\alpha}{\beta}(\alpha\beta)^{\frac{\alpha}{1-\alpha}}. \tag{6.3}$$

The unique stationary asset price is $\phi^* = (1-\alpha)\alpha^{\frac{\alpha}{1-\alpha}}\beta^{\frac{1}{1-\alpha}}(1-\beta)^{-1}$, that is determinate since the derivative of (6.3) is $\frac{d\phi_{t+1}}{d\phi_t} = \beta^{-1} > 1$. Without imperfections, as usual, competitive equilibrium achieves the efficient allocation of resources.

6.3.2 Collateral Constraint

Next, assume that the dynasty cannot commit to repay the loan. However, the asset can be seized by lenders in case a reimbursement does not occur. Therefore, borrowing can be guaranteed by the value of the asset used as collateral. The dynasty chooses the loan b_t and the assets holdings θ_{t+1} in each period to maximize its life-time utility under the previous budget constraint and the collateral constraint that guarantees reimbursement with the market value of the asset

$$(1 + r_t)b_t \leq \phi_t\theta_t, \tag{6.4}$$

whose multiplier is $\lambda_t \geq 0$. The choice of loan b_t satisfies the optimality condition

$$\beta^{t-1}u'(c_t)[\alpha b_t^{\alpha-1}\theta_t^{1-\alpha} - (1+r_t)] - (1+r_t)\lambda_t = 0, \tag{6.5}$$

as a higher loan increases production at the cost of increasing reimbursement, also tightening the collateral constraint. The choice of asset θ_{t+1} satisfies the optimality condition

$$-\beta^{t-1}u'(c_t)\phi_t + \beta^t u'(c_{t+1})[(1-\alpha)b_{t+1}^{\alpha}\theta_{t+1}^{-\alpha} + \phi_{t+1}] + \phi_{t+1}\lambda_{t+1} = 0, \tag{6.6}$$

as a higher amount of asset increases future production at the cost of reducing current consumption while increasing its availability for future sales and relaxing the collateral constraint in the future. The optimality condition for the asset demand includes the next period multiplier of the collateral constraint since the current price of the asset reflects its future use as input and its future value as collateral in case the credit constraint binds. This reflects the potential liquidity component of the asset price. Using the multiplier from the optimality condition (6.5), obtain the complementary slackness condition for the collateral constraint (6.4)

$$[\alpha b_t^{\alpha-1}\theta_t^{1-\alpha} - (1+r_t)][\phi_t\theta_t - (1+r_t)b_t] = 0,$$

by which either the collateral constraint (6.4) binds or the marginal product of the commodity obtained through the loan equals its cost, given by the interest rate.

6.3.2.1 Unconstrained Region

First, consider the case where the collateral constraint is slack, with $\lambda_t = 0$ in all periods. With $1 + r_t = \beta^{-1}$ and $\theta_t = 1$, the nil multiplier in (6.5) gives $\alpha b_t^{\alpha-1} = \beta^{-1}$ in every period. Therefore, the company borrows the amount $b_t = b^* = (\alpha\beta)^{\frac{1}{1-\alpha}}$ in each period, consumption is $c^* = (1-\alpha)(\alpha\beta)^{\frac{\alpha}{1-\alpha}}$ and the price of the asset is determined by the equation (6.3), whose unique stationary solution is ϕ^*. For the collateral constraint (6.4) to be slack, it must be $\beta\phi^* \geq b^*$, which, substituting the stationary loan and the asset price, gives $\beta \geq \alpha$. Therefore, if the dynasty is sufficiently patient, the collateral constraint is slack, and the allocation is efficient.

6.3.2.2 Constrained Region

Next, consider the case with $\lambda_t > 0$ in all periods. The equilibrium loan is determined in every period by the binding collateral constraint (6.4) with $b_t = \beta\phi_t$. Plugging the multiplier from (6.5) and the loan with $\theta_t = 1$ into the optimality condition (6.6), we obtain the dynamic equation that determines the equilibrium price of the asset is given in every period

$$\phi_t u'(\beta^\alpha\phi_t^\alpha - \phi_t) = \beta u'(\beta^\alpha\phi_{t+1}^\alpha - \phi_{t+1})\beta^\alpha\phi_{t+1}^\alpha,$$

whose non-nil stationary solution is $\hat{\phi} = \beta^{\frac{1+\alpha}{1-\alpha}}$. Using the binding collateral constraint $b_t = \beta\phi_t$, we obtain the equilibrium stationary loan $\hat{b} = \beta^{\frac{2}{1-\alpha}}$ and consumption $\hat{c} = (1-\beta)\beta^{\frac{2\alpha}{1-\alpha}}$. Furthermore, if $u'(0)$ is finite, $\phi_t = 0$ in all periods is also a stationary solution, without loans $b_t = 0$. For the collateral constraint to be binding with $\lambda_t > 0$, the dynasty must be sufficiently impatient, that is, $\beta < \alpha$ is required. Notice that the stationary equilibrium loan and consumption are lower than in the unconstrained equilibrium region, $\hat{b} < b^*$ and $\hat{c} < c^*$, while the price of the asset is higher, $\hat{\phi} > \phi^*$, since it contains a premium for its liquidity service to help relax the collateral constraint.

6.3.2.3 Amplification

The collateral constraint reinforces and amplifies negative shocks to the economy. This can be seen as follows. Suppose that the economy is in stationary equilibrium with the non-binding collateral constraint (6.4), that is, with $\beta \geq \alpha$. Consider now a sudden decrease in the time discount that plunges the economy into the region in which the borrowing constraint is binding. In such a situation, an unexpected shock to the income of the dynasty can set off a spiral in which a decline in the asset price tightens the borrowing constraint, inducing a decline in the loan that breeds a further decline in the asset price since the commodity and the asset are complementary as inputs in the productive technology. In fact, the marginal product of the asset, $(1-\alpha)b_t^{\alpha}$, which contributes to determine its price, increases with the loan; therefore, a credit contraction tends to depress the value of the asset, which in turn tightens the collateral constraint, reinforcing the downward spiral. A policy that supports the price of the asset could help stop the downward spiral. Notice that a positive demand shock that increases β would have no effect, as the economy would remain in the unconstrained region. Thus, the collateral constraint is an asymmetric amplification mechanism.

6.3.2.4 Self-Fulfilling Recession

The collateral constraint is also an independent source of economic instability as it can generate endogenous cycles. Consider the economy with binding collateral constraint (6.4), that is, with $\beta < \alpha$. Approximating linearly the dynamic equation that determines the price of the asset in proximity to the stationary equilibrium with positive loans, we obtain

$$\left.\frac{d\phi_{t+1}}{d\phi_t}\right|_{\hat{\phi}} = \frac{1-\beta-\epsilon_{u'}(\hat{c})(\alpha-\beta)}{\alpha(1-\beta)-\epsilon_{u'}(\hat{c})(\alpha-\beta)},$$

which is equal to -1 if and only if $\epsilon_{u'}(\hat{c}) = \frac{(1+\alpha)(1-\beta)}{2(\alpha-\beta)}$. When the elasticity of substitution of consumption crosses such a value, a two-period cycle emerges in the proximity of the stationary equilibrium with positive loans. The cutoff value for substitution elasticity is higher than 1 as in endogenous business cycle theory based on the overlapping generations model, although it approaches unity when $\alpha \to 1$. Since the loan in every period is given by the binding collateral constraint (6.4) with $b_t = \beta\phi_t$, and consumption is a direct function of the loan, the allocation fluctuates together with the price of the asset.

The cycle can be rationalized as being driven by the self-fulfilling expectations of the dynasty through extrinsic uncertainty that gives rise to a sunspot equilibrium. Suppose that with some probability an adverse event may occur that everyone expects to trigger a drop in the collateral asset price with an ensuing credit crunch, while with the complementary probability the event does not occur. Although such an event does not in itself have any direct link to the fundamentals of the economy, it can lead to a recession simply by acting as a catalyst for the pessimistic expectations of individuals. A sunspot equilibrium is a situation in which such expectations are fulfilled. The sunspot equilibrium close to the stationary equilibrium in the constrained region exists whenever the two-period cycle exists.

6.4 Credit Crunch

The cause of the Great Recession was the burst of the house price bubble in the United States with the rise in delinquencies on subprime mortgages that abruptly ended the credit boom of the first half of the 2000s, plunging the economy into a credit crunch. The drop in the prices of assets commonly used as collateral by businesses and financial institutions worsened the crisis, further tightening borrowing restrictions.

6.4.1 Fire Sale

In the financial realm, a fire sale is the simultaneous liquidation of assets at distressed prices by several companies and financial intermediaries. When investors are urgently in need of funds, they liquidate their assets. If this occurs simultaneously for many investors, security prices decline. These declines, in turn, cause additional liquidation inducing a further decline in asset prices. Self-reinforcing fire sales were a key mechanism in the early stages of the Great Recession. To try to stop the fire sale spiral, the Federal Reserve began to intervene during the fall of 2008, through an unconventional policy tool now known as *quantitative easing*.

6.4.2 Quantitative Easing

The Bank of Japan (BoJ) had used a version of quantitative easing between 2001 and 2006 to try to rescue the Japanese economy from a long period of deflation. Since the short-term nominal interest rate, the conventional policy tool, was at the zero lower bound, the BoJ decided to try an unconventional instrument. Quantitative easing involves an expansion of the central bank's balance sheet. The BoJ had acted through its liability side, altering the amount of bank reserves. The new version of quantitative easing that the then chairman of the Federal Reserve (Fed) Ben Bernanke dubbed *credit easing* used, instead, the asset side of the central bank's balance sheet. The Fed's policy intervention focused on the effect that the acquisition of assets and securities has on credit conditions for the private sector. Following the default of Lehman Brothers in mid-September 2008, the Fed started the quantitative easing program in November, increasing the purchases of private assets throughout the following three years, in three successive rounds of massive operations. At the peak of the program, the Fed held 3 trillion dollars of private assets and securities on its balance sheet. The aim was to support asset prices, especially for those assets used as collateral by the private sector, in order to ease borrowing constraints and help reverse the credit crunch. This intervention is generally credited with successfully containing the damage of the financial crisis. Quantitative easing, initially considered an unconventional monetary policy instrument, is now one of the standard tools of central banking.

6.5 Conclusion

Credit constraints whose tightness depends on asset prices tend to exacerbate the reaction of the economy to negative shocks to productivity, making recession episodes deep and long-lasting. Moreover, endogenous cycles and sunspot equilibria may emerge at equilibrium when the economy is credit-constrained. Sustaining the value of collateral assets through ex-post policy intervention can help the economy recover from a recession. Ex-ante intervention can also be socially beneficial, altering the supply of loans exploiting the presence of pecuniary externalities when borrowing is limited.

6.6 Literature

The point that borrowing constraints may exacerbate recessions with asymmetric effects was originally made by Nobuhiro Kiyotaki and John Moore in their famous paper entitled *Credit Cycles*. The literature on incomplete contracts was initiated by Nobel prize winner Oliver Hart in joint work with John Moore. The paper *Incomplete Contracts and Control* by Oliver Hart contains an overview of the main ideas. In the paper entitled *Creating Business Cycles Through Credit Constraints*, Narayana Kocherlakota has pointed out that the amplification of shocks through collateral constraints is limited when there is more than one input in fixed supply. The modern financial accelerator literature, which describes the process by which adverse shocks to the economy are amplified by worsening financial market conditions, was initiated by Nobel Prize winner Ben Bernanke, chairman of the Federal Reserve during the Great Recession, together with Mark Gertler in the paper entitled *Agency Costs, Net Worth, and Business Fluctuations*.

Exercises

1. Consider an infinite-horizon model with a representative dynasty endowed with a technology that uses a perishable commodity and an asset in fixed unit supply to produce the consumption good. The dynasty can borrow an amount b_t of perishable commodity at a competitive net interest rate r_t at the beginning of each period and can acquire an amount θ_{t+1} of the asset at a competitive price ϕ_t at the end of each period. Repayment of the loan with interest occurs at the end of each period. The technology is represented by the production function $y_t = b_t^{\alpha}\theta_t^{1-\alpha}$, with $\alpha \in (0, 1)$. The dynasty cares about consumption of the perishable commodity and dislikes work. The consumption preferences of the dynasty, c_t , are represented by the life-time utility

$$U(\mathbf{c}) = \sum_{t=1}^{\infty} \beta^{t-1} \frac{c_t^{1-\epsilon}}{1-\epsilon},$$

where $\beta < 1$ represents the discount of time. There is an international market for loans in which the interest rate is $r_t = \beta^{-1} - 1$ in every period.
- Compute the stationary equilibrium.
- Compare the stationary equilibrium allocation with the efficient allocation.

2. In the context of the previous exercise, suppose that the dynasty cannot commit to repay the loan. The asset can be seized by lenders in case a reimbursement does not occur, and hence borrowing can be guaranteed by the value of the asset used as collateral.
- Compute the equilibrium with the collateral constraint.
- Determine the critical value for the emergence of a cycle.

References

Bernanke B, Gertler M (1989), Agency Costs, Net Worth, and Business Fluctuations, American Economic Review, 79: 14–31

Hart O (2017), Incomplete Contracts and Control, American Economic Review, 107: 1731–1752

Kiyotaki N, Moore J (1997), Credit Cycles, Journal of Political Economy, 105: 211–248

Kocherlakota N (2000), Creating Business Cycles through Credit Constraints, Quarterly Review, Federal Reserve Bank of Minneapolis, 24: 2–10

Cash Payment and Inflation

L. Ferraris, *Macroeconomic Theory*, Classroom Companion: Economics,
https://doi.org/10.1007/978-3-031-88740-6_7

7.1 Introduction

One of the counterfactual aspects of the standard dynastic model is the absence of cash payments, which instead occur routinely in real-world transactions. The life-cycle model has a role for cash as a store of value but not as a means of payment. In this chapter, we examine a model in which payment needs to be made in cash, by a legal requirement. We show that this seemingly minor departure from the standard dynastic model is enough to generate endogenous income fluctuations as in the life-cycle model while severing the link with efficiency. The *quantity theory* equation of money emerges as an equilibrium outcome connecting the price level with the quantity of money and inflation with changes in its stock.

The model can be used to discuss the intervention of monetary policy. A systematic monetary expansion generates inflation that reduces the value of currency, which, in turn, distorts the traders' choice, depressing employment, and income. The optimal monetary policy consists in contracting the stock of currency over time to make it more valuable, as required by the *Friedman rule*. Short-run money non-neutrality can emerge when prices do not react fully to market conditions. In this case, a short-run relation between inflation and income known as the Phillips curve may emerge. However, with traders' rational expectations, the attempt to exploit systematically such a relation through monetary policy intervention backfires, giving rise to inflation without income benefits. Well-designed monetary policy adheres to rules, avoiding discretionary intervention.

Since real-world monetary policy is not conducted altering directly the stock of money but rather changing the mix of money and government bonds, through the so-called *open market operations* that allow the monetary authority to control the nominal interest rate, we discuss, in an extension of the cash-in-advance model with government bonds, these policy operations and the ensuing *liquidity effect*, whereby an expansionary open market operation lowers the nominal interest rate and boosts income. Finally, we briefly discuss the so-called fiscal theory of the price level, that attributes the emergence of inflation to increased fiscal deficits rather than monetary expansions.

7.2 Quantity Theory

In the infinite-horizon dynastic model, no asset without intrinsic return can have value at equilibrium. The reason is that consumers exhaust their life-time wealth at equilibrium, with the finite present value of consumption being equal to the present value of the payoffs of all assets in the economy. By definition, an asset whose price has a bubble component has a market value that exceeds the present value of its payoffs, making the present value of consumption exceed the present value of the payoffs of all assets in the economy, hence exceeding the present value of all income in the economy. This is incompatible with equilibrium.

This implies that any asset without intrinsic or fundamental value, such as fiat money, cannot have market value at the equilibrium of the dynastic model. In a previous chapter, we have presented a model in which real cash balances give utility as consumption. Another way to make fiat money valuable consists in assuming that the expenditures on commodities need to be financed with cash on hand. This gives rise to the so-called *cash-in-advance* model that we examine next.

7.2.1 Monetary Equilibrium

Consider for simplicity the case in which the company's production function is linear with unit productivity $y_t = \ell_t$, so that the labor demand is perfectly elastic at the wage $w_t = 1$, and the profit is nil at all times. The dynasty has preferences for consumption and labor sequences, $\mathbf{c}, \mathbf{l}$, represented by life-time utility

$$U(\mathbf{c}, \mathbf{l}) = \sum_{t=1}^{\infty} \beta^{t-1} [u(c_t) - v(l_t)],$$

where the utility function that satisfies Assumption 2, with $\beta < 1$. This is the dynastic model that we have examined in previous chapters. Suppose that we add to this model the requirement that payments have to be made in cash, whose supply is available in time-invariant amount M.

Since the purchases need to be financed with cash on hand, there will be another constraint for the consumer, namely the cash-in-advance constraint

$$c_t \leq m_t, \tag{7.1}$$

in every period, where m_t is the real value of cash held by the consumer at time t, together with the budget constraint

$$c_t + (1 + \rho_{t+1}) m_{t+1} = w_t l_t + m_t, \tag{7.2}$$

in every period, where m_{t+1} is the real demand of cash to be used to finance the expenditures on consumption in the future and $1 + \rho_{t+1} \equiv p_{t+1}/p_t$ is the gross inflation rate. The inflation rate appears in the budget constraint since next period real balances need to be made consistent with current real balances. Denote by $\lambda_t \geq 0$ the Kuhn-Tucker multiplier of the cash-in-advance constraint (7.1).

The purpose of the dynasty is to choose consumption, labor supply, and real cash holdings to maximize utility over a life-time subject to the cash advance restriction (7.1) and the budget restriction (7.2). The dynasty has perfect foresight over future prices. Solve the budget constraint (7.2) for consumption and substitute it into the cash-in-advance constraint (7.1) and the life-time utility function. Now, the problem of the consumer reduces to the choice of labor and real balances to maximize life-time utility subject to the cash-in-advance constraint (7.1).

7.2.1.1 Equilibrium Conditions

Next, we determine the optimal choice of labor supply and cash holdings. The first-order condition for the labor supply is

$$\beta^{t-1} [w_t u'(c_t) - v'(l_t)] = w_t \lambda_t. \tag{7.3}$$

Equation (7.3) contains a potential wedge between the wage and the marginal rate of substitution between labor and consumption, since the wage income cannot be spent immediately on consumption but needs to be converted into cash to finance future consumption expenditures, when the cash-in-advance constraint binds. The first-order condition for cash is

$$\beta^{t-1}(1+\rho_{t+1})u'(c_t) - \beta^t u'(c_{t+1}) = (1+\rho_{t+1})\lambda_t. \tag{7.4}$$

Equation (7.4) governs the decision to accumulate cash over time to finance consumption. Again, a potential wedge appears between the relative price of current and future consumption, given by the gross inflation rate, and the marginal rate of substitution between current and future consumption, since there is a delay in the timing between income receipts and consumption expenditures, due to the assumption that expenditures need to be financed with cash-in-advance when the constraint binds. Using (7.3), the complementary slackness condition for cash-in-advance constraint (7.1) is written as

$$(w_t u'(c_t) - v'(l_t))(m_t - c_t) = 0. \tag{7.5}$$

There are two possibilities. The cash-in-advance constraint may be slack, $c_t \leq m_t$, in which case the complementary slackness condition (7.5) implies $w_t u'(c_t) = v'(l_t)$ that coincides with the one of the model without cash payments. Since the wage is constant, $w_t = 1$, by optimization of the company, it follows that consumption and labor will be time invariant. As a consequence, by the optimality condition (7.4) with constant consumption over time, the inflation rate will have to be $\rho_t = \beta - 1$ at all times. However, this is inconsistent with the budget constraint (7.2) and the equilibrium conditions in the goods, labor, and money market, since the stock of money remains constant over time by assumption.

The other possibility is that the cash-in-advance constraint is binding, with $\lambda_t > 0$ and $c_t = m_t$. Using $w_t = 1$, the optimality condition for labor (7.3), the optimality condition for cash (7.4), the budget constraint (7.2), and the cash-in-advance constraint (7.1), together with market clearing in the goods, labor, and money market, we obtain the single dynamic equation in real money balances that should hold at every point in time

$$m_t v'(m_t) = \beta m_{t+1} u'(m_{t+1}). \tag{7.6}$$

This is exactly the same equilibrium condition that was derived from the life-cycle model. Therefore, these two models have the same equilibria.

7.2.1.2 Competitive Equilibrium

A competitive equilibrium is a sequence of real cash balances m_t that satisfies the equation (7.6). A stationary equilibrium is invariant in time, with $m_t = m$ at all times. The existence of a unique positive m that satisfies $v'(m) = \beta u'(m)$ is proved by the usual continuity argument under Assumption 2. This value determines consumption, income, and employment, since $m = c = y = l$. There is also a stationary equilibrium in which money has no value, with complete unemployment and without production.

Example 7.1

Suppose that the utility of consumption has constant substitution elasticity ϵ and linear disutility of labor. The stationary equilibrium value of the real balances is $m = \beta^{\frac{1}{\epsilon}}$. Employment, income, and consumption are $l = c = y = \beta^{\frac{1}{\epsilon}}$.

7.2.1.3 Inefficiency

The stationary equilibrium is inefficient, since efficiency requires one to equate the marginal rate of substitution between labor and consumption with the marginal productivity of labor which is unitary, that is, $v'(l) = u'(c)$ with $c = l$. The reason why the competitive equilibrium with cash payment is inefficient is that current consumption needs to be financed with money acquired with past income. Since money does not earn interest and people are impatient, the resulting allocation of resources is inefficient. In particular, employment is lower than what efficiency would require, since the labor supply is reduced as the dynasty anticipates that the labor income earned working currently will be spent only later in life without any compensation through interest payments. This inefficiency is reflected in the presence of β as a discount of marginal utility of consumption, since the choice of labor generates disutility in the current period, but the corresponding income can only be spent in the next period.

Example 7.2

Continuing with the previous example, the efficient allocation satisfies the optimality condition $c^{-\epsilon} = 1$, giving $c^* = y^* = l^* = 1$.

7.2.1.4 Cycles and Sunspots

There are plenty of non-stationary equilibria, including cyclical and sunspot equilibria, as in the life-cycle model. In particular, to have a cycle of period two near the stationary state, it has to be that the derivative, calculated from the equilibrium condition (7.6), by implicit differentiation, is

$$\left.\frac{dm_t}{dm_{t+1}}\right|_m = \frac{1 - \epsilon_{u'}(m)}{1 + \epsilon_{v'}(m)} = -1,$$

that is, $\epsilon_{u'}(m) = 2 + \epsilon_{v'}(m)$. A two-state sunspot equilibrium exists in the neighborhood of the deterministic cycle of period two whenever the previous condition holds. Suppose that the dynasty observes a two-state public event. The uncertainty is extrinsic, in the sense that it does not affect the fundamentals, but its realization is public. The dynasty has rational expectations over future prices and believes that the price of the commodity is perfectly correlated with the occurrence of the sunspot event. A sunspot equilibrium is a rational expectations equilibrium in which the dynasty's belief is self-fulfilling and the allocation oscillates between two different values. A continuity argument establishes that a sunspot equilibrium exists whenever a deterministic cycle exists exactly as in the life-cycle model. Although the fundamentals are not hit by shocks, the equilibrium allocations still fluctuate over time. These fluctuations are endogenously driven by the dynasty's beliefs, which become self-fulfilling. These self-fulfilling prophecies give rise to endogenous fluctuations of economic activity, absent any exogenous shock.

7.2.1.5 Quantity Theory of Money

The price level is determined by the binding cash-in-advance constraint (7.1), together with the clearing of the market in the money market $m_t = M/p_t$ and the clearing of the market for the commodity $c_t = y_t$, so that the quantity theory equation

$$p_t = M/y_t,$$

holds in equilibrium. Since income is determined independently of the money stock, the price level is pinned down by the supply of money M. The price level is in direct proportion to the stock of money, with a doubling of the stock doubling the price level. In the stationary equilibrium with positive employment, the price level will remain constant over time and, therefore, inflation will be nil at all times $\rho_t = 0$. There are also non-stationary equilibria in which the inflation rate is not nil.

7

Example 7.3

Continuing with the previous example, the stationary equilibrium price level is $p = M/\beta^{\frac{1}{\epsilon}}$. Since the price level is time invariant, inflation is nil.

7.2.1.6 Money Neutrality

Changes in money stock alter the price level through the quantity theory equation that determines nominal values, but are neutral in terms of allocations, which are determined by the real part of the equilibrium system. However, the evidence shows that while in the long-run money is mostly neutral determining, there is a significant non-neutrality of money in the short run.

Short-run non-neutrality of money can be obtained by modifying the cash-in-advance model as follows. Suppose that there are two separate markets for the exchange of commodities. There is a unit continuum of identical companies that are equally distributed between the two markets every period, and a unit continuum of identical dynasties that, instead, are unequally distributed between the two markets. No one knows which market has the highest proportion of dynasties, and traders observe only the price prevailing in their own market. The money stock may be increased at the beginning of every period or not through a transfer proportional to the real balances held by the dynasties. The transfer is handed out to all the dynasties uniformly, but the companies do not know whether the money injection has occurred or not. Now, in every period, companies that experience a larger than expected demand for their products are uncertain whether this originates from a sudden increase in the money supply or a larger than expected market share. If the money injection was publicly observed, the companies with the largest market share would produce more and the others less than the average, without any aggregate effect. If the prices in the two markets were publicly observed by all traders, the companies would be able to determine whether the higher demand was coming from the money supply or from the market share. In both cases, a money injection would be neutral with only an effect on the price level. When companies cannot disentangle the two possibilities, instead, they will average out over them, increasing production moderately to face a potential increase in their market share. Thus, imperfect information about monetary policy can give rise to money non-neutrality at least as a transitory phenomenon.

An alternative way to generate money non-neutrality in the short run is through price rigidity. Suppose that the price of the commodity is fixed in advance in the first period before trade begins, while in all subsequent periods, the price is flexible and adjusts to clear the market. A contraction of the money stock in the first period, with a fixed commodity price, leads to a contraction in consumption and income through the cash-in-advance constraint. From the following period onward, with a flexible commodity price, the quantity theory of money holds, so that a monetary intervention affects only the price level. Therefore, monetary policy is not neutral in the short term but neutral in the long term.

7.2.1.7 Money Growth

The equilibrium allocation is distorted relative to the efficient benchmark, since the consumers have to use money whose return is not sufficiently high to compensate them for the presence of time discounting. A policy intervention altering relative prices of consumption over consecutive periods of time may help increase the return on money. Suppose that the available stock of the asset can be altered taxing or subsidizing consumers in a non-distortionary way through lump-sum intervention. Let the money stock grow at a constant rate γ over time, that is, $M_{t+1} = (1+\gamma)M_t$. From the clearing condition of the market for money and the binding cash-in-advance constraint, the relative price over two consecutive periods, namely the inflation rate, is equal to $\rho = \gamma$, as inflation is a monetary phenomenon in this environment. As a consequence, the equilibrium condition (7.6) becomes

$$m_t v'(m_t) = \frac{\beta}{1+\gamma} m_{t+1} u'(m_{t+1})$$

The stationary equilibrium with positive employment with time-invariant real balances satisfies the equilibrium condition

$$v'(m) = \frac{\beta}{1+\gamma} u'(m), \tag{7.7}$$

that gives the equilibrium real balances as function of the policy parameter, $m(\gamma)$. The growth rate of the money supply should be restricted to guarantee that the dynasty is willing to spend cash, assuming that $\gamma \geq \beta - 1$. Using the implicit function theorem, we obtain that the equilibrium real balances are decreasing in the growth rate of the stock of the currency

$$m'(\gamma) = -\frac{m(\gamma)}{1+\gamma} \frac{1}{\epsilon_{u'}(m(\gamma)) + \epsilon_{v'}(m(\gamma))} < 0. \tag{7.8}$$

Hence, a systematic expansion of the stock of the asset generates an inflation that distorts the money demand and the labor supply of the dynasty making the asset less valuable over time. In this model, money, while neutral, is not *superneutral*.

Example 7.4
Continuing with the previous example, the stationary equilibrium real balances as a function of policy are $m(\gamma) = \left[\beta/(1+\gamma)\right]^{\frac{1}{\epsilon}}$, whose derivative with respect to γ is $m'(\gamma) = -m(\gamma)[(1+\gamma)\epsilon]^{-1}$.

7.2.1.8 Friedman Rule

If the cash stock is reduced over time at the appropriate rate, so that $\gamma = \beta - 1$, by equation (7.7), we obtain $v'(m) = u'(m)$. Therefore, inducing the appropriate rate of deflation, the stationary equilibrium allocation is efficient.

7

By no-arbitrage, the interest rate of a nominal bond can be determined as the product of the real interest rate and the inflation rate. This gives the Fisher equation $1 + i_t = (1 + r_t)(1 + \rho_t)$ for every period. The real interest rate is $r_t = \beta^{-1} - 1$. In stationary equilibrium, the inflation rate is $\rho_t = \gamma$. Therefore, the stationary nominal interest rate is $i = (1+\gamma)\beta^{-1} - 1$. Since the nominal interest rate is the opportunity cost of holding cash instead of the nominal bond, efficiency is restored when the opportunity cost is nil, that is, $i = 0$, using the Fisher equation. This intervention corresponds to the policy known as the *Friedman rule*.

Example 7.5
Continuing with the previous example, plugging $\gamma = \beta - 1$ into the stationary equilibrium real balances, we obtain $m(\beta - 1) = 1$, which achieves the efficient allocation $c^* = y^* = l^* = 1$.

7.2.1.9 Seignorage

Suppose that the government needs to finance public expenditures G_t in real terms in period t, but cannot issue debt or raise additional taxes. The printing of new money can be used to finance public expenditures through the so-called *seignorage tax*. The government budget can be written as

$$G_t = \frac{M_t}{p_t} - \frac{M_{t-1}}{p_{t-1}} \frac{p_{t-1}}{p_t},$$

since the change in the stock of money in real terms is used to finance public expenditures every period. Using the definition of inflation and real balances, we can rewrite this equation as $G_t = m_t - m_{t-1}(1 + \rho_{t-1})^{-1}$. Focusing on stationary equilibria, with the inflation controlled by the growth rate of the money stock, $\rho = \gamma$, we obtain

$$G(\gamma) = \frac{\gamma}{1+\gamma} m(\gamma),$$

that is positive if and only if the stock of money grows over time at a positive rate, $\gamma > 0$. From the formula above, we see that inflation, controlled by money creation, acts as a tax on income represented by the real balances with marginal rate $\tau(\gamma) \equiv \gamma(1+\gamma)^{-1} < 1$ that serves to finance public expenditures. This is known as the seignorage tax. The derivative of tax revenue with respect to γ is

$$G'(\gamma) = \tau'(\gamma)m(\gamma) + \tau(\gamma)m'(\gamma),$$

where $\tau'(\gamma) = (1+\gamma)^{-2}$ is positive, while the derivative of real balances, (7.8), is negative. Hence, tax revenue may be non-monotonic in γ, since a higher seignorage tax rate discourages the dynasty from holding cash balances.

Example 7.6

Continuing with the previous example, plugging $\gamma = \beta - 1$ into the stationary equilibrium real balances, we obtain $m(\beta - 1) = 1$, which achieves the efficient allocation $c^* = y^* = l^* = 1$.

7.2.1.10 Time Consistency

Suppose that public expenditure G_t has a consumption value for the dynasty, so that the spot utility is modified to $u(c_t) + u(G_t) - v(l_t)$. Both private and public consumption must be financed with cash on hand, so that the cash-in-advance constraint is $c_t + G_t \leq m_t$ at all times.

Consider stationary equilibria in which the monetary authority sets γ optimally from the beginning with the commitment to stick to the initial choice. In stationary equilibrium, public expenditures are given by $G(\gamma) = \tau(\gamma)m(\gamma)$ and private consumption, through the binding cash-in-advance constraint, is given by $c(\gamma) = m(\gamma) - G(\gamma) = (1 - \tau(\gamma))m(\gamma)$. The optimality condition for the choice of γ is

$$u'((1-\tau(\gamma))m(\gamma))\tau'(\gamma)m(\gamma) = u'(\tau(\gamma)m(\gamma))[\tau'(\gamma)m(\gamma) + \tau(\gamma)m'(\gamma)],$$

which has been simplified using the optimality condition of the dynasty for the real balances. Optimal monetary policy takes into account the discouraging effect of inflation on the accumulation of real balances by the dynasty. Since the marginal utility decreases in consumption and $m'(\gamma) < 0$, the optimal monetary policy has $\gamma < 1$.

Consider now the case in which the monetary authority ignores the effect of inflation on the accumulation of real balances, obtaining

$$u'((1-\tau(\gamma))m)\tau'(\gamma)m = u'(\tau(\gamma)m)\tau'(\gamma)m,$$

which gives $\gamma = 1$. This result would be obtained with discretionary intervention from the monetary authority. Thus, discretionary intervention would lead to excessive inflation relative to the time-consistent benchmark, without benefits for the dynasty. If the dynasty anticipates that the monetary authority will intervene in a discretionary manner, it will respond by reducing its money holdings in the first place, thus depressing economic activity. The adoption of credible monetary policy rules can help avoid the time inconsistency problem generated by discretionary intervention.

▪▪ Example 7.7
Continuing with the previous example, plugging $\gamma = \beta - 1$ into the stationary equilibrium real balances, we obtain $m(\beta - 1) = 1$, which achieves the efficient allocation $c^* = y^* = l^* = 1$.

7.2.1.11 Phillips Curve

The Phillips curve is the short-term negative relation between inflation and unemployment or, equivalently, since unemployment and income are negatively related, the short-term positive relation between inflation and income. Assuming that the monetary authority controls inflation ρ through the policy instrument γ, after a logarithmic transformation, the Phillips curve can be written as

7

$$y(\rho) = z + \rho - \mathbb{E}\rho, \tag{7.9}$$

where income depends on productivity while being positively affected by current inflation, due to short-term non-neutrality, but negatively affected by expected future inflation, due to the long-term distortionary effects of inflation.

Suppose that monetary authority has been assigned the dual role of keeping income at a target level $\overline{y} > z$ and inflation at a target rate $\overline{\rho} \geq 0$. Thus, the monetary authority chooses a policy to fix ρ in order to minimize

$$\mathcal{L}(\rho) = \frac{(y(\rho) - \overline{y})^2 + (\rho - \overline{\rho})^2}{2},$$

that represents the loss experienced (perhaps in reputation) from not hitting the prescribed targets. Inserting the Phillips curve (7.9) into the loss function $\mathcal{L}(\rho)$ and computing the optimality condition $\mathcal{L}'(\rho) = 0$, we obtain

$$z - \overline{y} + \rho - \mathbb{E}\rho + \rho - \overline{\rho} = 0. \tag{7.10}$$

Suppose that the monetary authority believes that the private sector has passive expectations with respect to the policy, assuming that the monetary target will be achieved $\mathbb{E}\rho = \overline{\rho}$. Inserting this condition into the optimality condition (7.10), we obtain the inflation rate $\rho = \overline{\rho} + (\overline{y} - z)/2$, which is above the target; and inserting this inflation rate with $\mathbb{E}\rho = \overline{\rho}$ into the Phillips curve (7.9), we obtain the income $y = (\overline{y} + z)/2$, which is below the target but above productivity. The monetary authority would have succeeded in exploiting the Phillips curve, using inflation to boost income. This requires the ability to fool the private sector systematically, since the expectation that the inflation target will be hit remains unfulfilled.

Contrary to the belief of monetary authority, suppose that the private sector has rational expectations of monetary policy with $\mathbb{E}\rho = \rho$. Inserting this condition into the optimality condition (7.10), we obtain the inflation rate

$\rho = \overline{\rho} + \overline{y} - z$, which is higher than the target; and inserting $\mathbb{E}\rho = \rho$ into the Phillips curve (7.9), we obtain the income $y = z$, which remains tied to productivity. Therefore, with rational expectations, the monetary authority is unable to exploit the Phillips curve, generating inflation above the target without any income benefit. This is considered to be the explanation for the Great Inflation. With rational expectations of the private sector, income cannot increase above productivity, so the loss-minimizing choice for monetary authority is to commit to a policy rule that hits exactly the inflation target $\rho = \overline{\rho}$, thus avoiding unnecessary inflation. This is the recipe for combating inflation in a world of rational expectations.

7.2.2 Liquidity Effect

Real-world monetary policy is conducted by altering the relative supply of government bonds and money, namely through open market operations. Open market operations (OMOs) affect the nominal interest rate, which in turn affects private borrowing, with knock-on effects on income. We now use the cash-in-advance model to understand the effect of open market operations on the nominal interest rate. Suppose that the dynasty can acquire a one-period government bond at price $\psi_t \leq 1$ each period. A bond acquired in one period gives the right to a unit payment of money at the beginning of the following period.

7.2.2.1 Government Budget

Let the cash stock at time t be M_t and the bond stock D_t. The consolidated public administration has a budget constraint given every period by

$$M_{t+1} + \psi_t D_{t+1} = M_t + D_t.$$

Assuming the public administration keeps constant the bond-to-money ratio $D_t/M_t \equiv \delta_t = \delta$ at all times, the government budget constraint becomes

$$\frac{M_{t+1}}{M_t} = \frac{1+\delta}{1+\psi_t \delta}. \tag{7.11}$$

Notice that the growth rate of the money stock is in part controlled by the policy parameter δ and in part determined endogenously, since it depends on the price of the bond ψ_t.

7.2.2.2 OMOs Neutrality

Suppose, first, that money and bonds operate as perfect substitute instruments as regards transactions, so that the dynasty can use either instrument to save and finance expenditures. In this case, by no-arbitrage, for the dynasty to hold both instruments, it has to be the case that the price is $\psi_t = 1$, i.e. the interest rate is nil, at all times. By equation (7.11), the liquidity stock will remain constant and any change in the composition of its stock between money and the bond will be irrelevant to the determination of real allocations. Therefore, OMOs are neutral.

7.2.2.3 OMOs Non-Neutrality

Suppose now that the bond has to be acquired with money. The purchase of consumption and bonds occurs at the beginning of the period, before the reimbursement of the previous period bond, whose payment cannot be committed by the dynasty in advance. The dynasty chooses consumption, money, and bond holdings to maximize its life-time utility subject to the budget constraint

$$c_t + (1+\rho_{t+1})(m_{t+1} + \psi_t d_{t+1}) = w_t l_t + m_t + d_t,$$

where d_{t+1} is the dynasty's demand for the bond and the cash-in-advance constraint

$$c_t + (1+\rho_{t+1})\psi_t d_{t+1} \le m_t,$$

with perfect foresight of future prices. The optimality condition for the choice of cash is the same we had before, namely

7

$$w_t^{-1} v'(l_t) = \beta(1+\rho_{t+1})^{-1} u'(c_{t+1}), \tag{7.12}$$

and the optimality condition for the choice of the bond is

$$\psi_t u'(c_t) = \beta(1+\rho_{t+1})^{-1} w_{t+1}^{-1} v'(l_{t+1}), \tag{7.13}$$

where the current purchase of government debt has a cost in terms of foregone current consumption but generates a future benefit as it allows the dynasty to reduce the effort cost of working to acquire cash next period, as the one-period bond acquired currently will be reimbursed in cash in the following period. Moreover, there is the cash-in-advance constraint, which is binding for the same reasons seen above. The markets for commodities, money, and bonds clear at all times. We will consider only stationary equilibria. The equilibrium wage is $w_t = 1$ at all times as before. In a stationary equilibrium, equation (7.11) determines the inflation rate

$$1 + \rho_t = \frac{1+\delta}{1+\psi_t \delta}. \tag{7.14}$$

Combine the equilibrium conditions (7.12) and (7.13) with the inflation rate (7.14), obtaining the quadratic equation that determines the price of the bond

$$\Psi(\psi, \delta) \equiv \beta^2 - [1 + 2(1-\beta^2)\delta + \delta^2]\psi + \beta^2\delta^2\psi^2 = 0, \tag{7.15}$$

with $\psi \le 1$. The next proposition proves that there exists a unique equilibrium nominal interest rate for each policy choice.

Proposition 7.1

There is a unique stationary equilibrium bond price $\psi \in (0,1)$ for every positive δ.

Proof The function $\Psi(\psi, \delta)$ is quadratic in ψ with $\Psi(0, \delta) = \beta^2$ and $\Psi(1, \delta) = (\beta^2 - 1)(1+\delta)^2 < 0$ for any δ. Hence, there is a unique $\psi \in (0,1)$ for each feasible δ that satisfies the equation (7.15).

Therefore, we have the equilibrium bond price function $\psi(\delta)$, whose derivative, by implicit differentiation, is given by

$$\psi'(\delta) = -\frac{\psi(\delta)}{\delta} \frac{2\delta[1-\psi(\delta)][1-\delta^2\psi(\delta)] + \delta^2\psi(\delta)^2}{(1+\delta)^2[1+\delta^2\psi(\delta)^2]}$$

that is negative since $\psi(\delta) < \min\{1, \delta^{-2}\}$. Since the price of the bond and the nominal interest are inversely related, a lower bond-to-money ratio, δ, corresponding to an expansionary open market operation, leads to a lower nominal interest rate.

From the equilibrium condition (7.12) with the inflation rate (7.14), at the stationary equilibrium with $c = y = l$, $w = 1$ and the equilibrium bond price function $\psi(\delta)$, we obtain

$$v'(y) = \frac{1+\psi(\delta)\delta}{1+\delta} \beta u'(y),$$

that defines implicitly income as a function of the open market operations policy parameter, $y(\delta)$. By implicit differentiation, we obtain the effect of an open market operation on income, consumption, and employment as

$$y'(\delta) = -\frac{y(\delta)}{\delta} \frac{\delta[1-\psi(\delta)-\psi'(\delta)\delta(1+\delta)]}{[\epsilon_{u'}(c(\delta)) + \epsilon_{v'}(l(\delta))][1+\psi(\delta)\delta](1+\delta)},$$

that is negative, since $\psi(\delta) < 1$ and $\psi'(\delta) < 0$. Therefore, a decrease of δ increases equilibrium income, consumption, and employment. In short, an expansion of the money stock relative to the bonds stock, namely a decrease in δ, which can be interpreted as an expansionary open market operation, lowers the interest rate and increases employment and income. This is known as the *liquidity effect*.

7.3 Fiscal Theory

The cash-in-advance model gives rise to the quantity theory of money, which determines the price level. As a consequence, inflation emerges as the by-product of expansionary monetary policy. However, when there are also nominal government bonds, the model can also give rise to a different theory of the determination of the price level in which the government deficits generate inflation. This is the gist of the *fiscal theory of the price level.*

7.3.1 Debt Valuation

Consider the following variation of the cash-in-advance model. Public authorities issue at the end of each period a one-year nominal government bond at a price $\psi_t \leq 1$ that is paid in cash one-for-one at the beginning of the following period. Cash is needed to make purchases. The nominal stock of bonds is time invariant

$D_t = D$, which corresponds to the initial stock outstanding. There is a lump-sum taxation invariant in time $T_t = T$ in real terms. The only difference from the previous model is that the dynasty does not have to hold cash overnight.

The optimality conditions for the dynasty in every period are the following. There is the first-order condition for the optimal demand of bonds

$$\psi_t v'(l_t) w_t^{-1} = \beta(1 + \rho_{t+1}) u'(c_{t+1}),$$

since the current cost of acquiring the bond is compensated with the future benefit of additional purchases; the complementary slackness condition for the cash-in-advance constraint $[w_t u'(c_t) - v'(l_t)](d_t - c_t) = 0$; and the budget constraint $c_t + \psi_t d_{t+1}(1 + \rho_{t+1}) = w_t l_t + d_t - T_t$. The optimality condition for the company gives $w_t = 1$ in every period. Market clearing for the commodity requires $c_t = y_t = l_t$ and for the bond $d_t = D/p_t$ in every period.

7 Standard theory assumes that the public authorities need to satisfy their budget constraint every period exactly as the dynasty. This is what we assumed in the previous cash-in-advance model. Therefore, condition $\psi_t D_{t+1}(1 + \rho_{t+1}) = D_t - p_t T_t$ must hold at all times for any value of the price level. In this traditional scenario, there exists a stationary equilibrium without inflation, in which the price of the bond is $\psi_t = \beta$, the cash-in-advance constraint is slack, and the allocation is efficient with $u'(l_t) = v'(l_t)$ at all times. There is a redundancy between the private and public budget conditions in the competitive equilibrium. As a consequence, the price level is indeterminate. The government adjusts taxation T to meet the public budget for the given initial stock of debt.

Fiscal theory, instead, assumes that the government is a special agent that, unlike the private sector, does not have to balance its budget in every period. As a consequence, the private budget constraint is no longer redundant. In this non-standard scenario, the budget of the dynasty with market clearing for the commodity and the bond in the stationary equilibrium without inflation and with $\psi_t = \beta$ gives $D/p = T(1 - \beta)^{-1}$. The cash-in-advance constraint is slack, and the allocation is efficient. Since the stock of debt is given initially, the government, fixing taxation T, can determine the price level p, and, in non-stationary equilibria, the inflation rate. Since the price level emerges as an inverse function of taxation, a fiscal deficit due to a decrease in taxation will have an inflationary effect.

More generally, the fiscal theory implies that the real value of government debt must satisfy at any time t the following bond valuation condition

$$\frac{D_t}{p_t} = \mathbb{E}\sum_{t=0}^{\infty} T_{t+t} S_{t+t}, \tag{7.16}$$

since the real value of the debt stock will have to reflect the future expected value of the government taxation discounted to the present using the intertemporal marginal rate of substitution S_t as the discount factor, as any other security whose current value reflects the expected future value of the dividends discounted using the marginal rate of substitution. In fact, dividends in the case of government bonds are future surpluses raised through taxation. In the absence of public budget balance in every period, the outstanding government stock of debt needs to be consistent with the entire future discounted stream of revenues that can be raised through taxation. If the bond is nominal, the tax profile determines the price level, given the outstanding stock of debt.

7.3.2 Unpleasant Arithmetic

In the cash-in-advance model with government debt in which money and bonds are not perfect substitutes and the dynasty holds money overnight, we considered the monetary and fiscal policy as determined jointly by a consolidated public authority that selected the ratio of bonds to money. Let us take the traditional point of view, in which the government is subject in every period to budget balance, including lump-sum taxation. In reality, monetary and fiscal authorities are not subject to the above consolidated budget constraint, but act independently of each other with different instruments and goals that may be in conflict with each other. This state of affairs may induce competition between the monetary and fiscal authorities through what is sometimes described as a game of chicken that determines who has the control over the public policy. The resolution of the conflict leads to two possible regimes, the monetary and fiscal regimes, respectively. In the monetary regime, the monetary authority chooses the money supply, thus determining the price level through the quantity theory equation, and the fiscal authority adjusts bond issuance and taxation to satisfy the consolidated budget for any given price level. In the fiscal regime, the fiscal authority chooses the debt issuance and taxation, but then the monetary authority has to accommodate the fiscal policy and loses control of the price level leading to inflation. This phenomenon is known as unpleasant monetarist arithmetic.

Fiscal theory offers a way out of this conundrum. Suppose that the fiscal authority is not subject to budget balance but only to the fiscal theory equation (7.16). Now, if the public sector controls at all times the nominal stock of money through the monetary authority and, separately, taxation through the fiscal authority, the price level is overdetermined. This is because, with all other variables determined in the equilibrium, the only remaining variable, that is, the price level, needs to satisfy in every period both the quantity theory equation and the fiscal theory equation (7.16). If neither authority sets the policy, the price level is indeterminate. These two scenarios are not equilibria of the chicken game. Consider the two equilibrium regimes. In the monetary regime, the monetary authority determines the price level to fix the stock of money, and the fiscal authority accommodates the choice of the monetary authority to let taxation satisfy (7.16) at the given price level. In the fiscal regime, the fiscal authority determines the price level using the fiscal theory equation (7.16), and the monetary authority accommodates the choice of the fiscal authority, allowing the money supply to satisfy the quantity theory equation for any given price level. Therefore, the price level is determined and inflation under control in both regimes, eliminating the problem of unpleasant monetarist arithmetic.

7.4 Great Inflation

The Great Inflation was a key macroeconomic event characterized by high inflation and soaring unemployment, the phenomenon known as *stagflation*, that has affected the United States and other developed economies in the period 1965-1985.

7.4.1 Stagflation

In 1964, the inflation rate in the United States was about 1% a year. Inflation began to increase the following year, reaching 15% a year in 1980. By the second half of the 1980s, the inflation rate decreased to about 2% a year, remaining stable thereafter throughout the period of the Great Moderation. In the post-WWII period, monetary policy had been commonly used in many countries to stabilize economic activity, under the assumption that there existed an exploitable negative relationship between unemployment and inflation, known as the *Phillips curve*. However, major inflation hikes in pursuit of lower unemployment did not occur in the 1960s, since most currencies were anchored to the US dollar that, in turn, was anchored to the value of gold by the Bretton Woods agreement established at the end of WWII that fixed the rate of exchange between most world currencies and the US dollar, linking, in turn, the latter to gold. In 1971, President Nixon withdrew the United States from the Bretton Woods agreement ending the linkage between the dollar and gold, thus unhinging monetary policy. In 1973 the oil crisis broke out, leading to a major increase in crude oil prices that led to a burst of inflation accompanied by unemployment, the so-called *stagflation*. Motivated by a mandate to maintain full employment without the anchor of the Bretton Woods agreement, monetary authorities accelerated the expansion of the money supply, raising inflation without reducing unemployment. In 1980, the inflation rate was at 15% and the unemployment at 8%. The existence of a Phillips curve began to be questioned by economists and policy makers. The evidence of a stable trade-off between inflation and unemployment that policy makers had hoped to be able to exploit as a rationale for the use of expansionary monetary policy as an easy recipe for income stabilization turned out to be spurious.

7.4.2 Conquest of Inflation

In the early 1980s, the Fed adopted strong measures to control the growth of the money supply in an attempt to rein in inflation. Over time, tight control of money growth produced the desired slowing of inflation. The Fed continued to press the fight against inflation with a combination of higher interest rates and low money growth. During the 1980s, both inflation and unemployment subsided. By the mid-1980s, the Great Inflation was over. The transformation of macroeconomic theory brought about by the adoption of the rational expectations paradigm was informed by the lesson learned from the Great Inflation. In particular, the key lesson for policy makers was the importance of adopting time-consistent policy rules that help to resist the temptation to sacrifice longer term goals for short-term gains. Conquering inflation requires commitment to monetary policy rules with inflation targets that anchor the value of otherwise unbacked currency.

7.5 Conclusion

When a cash-in-advance requirement is added to the dynastic model, the equilibrium allocation is not efficient anymore due to the presence of a time mismatch between income receipts and cash payments. Monetary intervention that implicitly pays interest on cash helps correct the inefficiency. Open market operations are not neutral and induce a liquidity effect. The cash-in-advance model naturally leads to the determination of the price level through the quantity theory of money. According to quantity theory of money, the price level and inflation are entirely determined by the money stock and its growth rate, while employment and income are determined independently of money that is neutral relative to real allocations. This holds at least in the long run, while in the short-run monetary non-neutrality emerges when there are nominal rigidities or information imperfections. According to fiscal theory of the price level, instead, this is pinned down by the bond valuation condition. In such a regime, a nominal deficit is compensated for by an increase in the price level, giving rise to inflation.

7.6 Literature

The cash-in-advance economy presented above is a simplified version of the model contained in the paper entitled *Money and Interest in a Cash-in-Advance Economy* by Robert Lucas and Nancy Stokey. The short-run and long-run effects of monetary policy are discussed in Lucas' Nobel lecture entitled *Monetary Neutrality*. The liquidity effect is derived in the paper by Robert Lucas entitled *Liquidity and Interest Rates*. The time inconsistency of monetary policy is the subject of *Rules, Discretion and Reputation in a Model of Monetary Policy* by Robert Barro and David Gordon. The fiscal theory of the price level is examined in the book *The Fiscal Theory of the Price Level* by John Cochrane. The issue of unpleasant monetarist arithmetic has been raised by Thomas Sargent and Neil Wallace in the paper entitled *Some Unpleasant Monetarist Arithmetic*.

Exercises

1. Consider a competitive economy with an infinite horizon and a representative dynasty, in which purchases have to be made in cash, as in the cash-in-advance economy. There is a single perishable commodity every period that can be con-

sumed by the dynasty, c_t that can offer labor services, l_t, for a competitive real wage, w_t. There is a constant stock of money, M. The company's production function is linear, $y_t = \ell_t$. The dynasty has preferences over consumption and labor sequences represented by the life-time utility function

$$U(\mathbf{c},\mathbf{l}) = \sum_{t=1}^{\infty} \beta^{t-1} \left(\frac{c_t^{1-\epsilon}}{1-\epsilon} - l_t \right).$$

- Calculate the stationary monetary equilibrium.
- Calculate the efficient allocation.
- Suppose now that the stock of currency grows at a constant rate over time. The currency is injected or withdrawn through lump-sum transfers or taxes at the end of every period. Compute the stationary monetary equilibrium.
- Determine the value of the growth rate of money that allows the economy to achieve an efficient allocation of resources.

2. In the setup of the previous exercise, suppose that the life-time utility of the dynasty is

- Calculate the stationary monetary equilibrium.

$$U(\mathbf{c},\mathbf{l}) = \sum_{t=1}^{\infty} \beta^{t-1} (-e^{-ac_t} - l_t).$$

- Calculate the efficient allocation.
- Derive the dynamic equation that governs the evolution of currency holdings.
- Determine for what value of a there is a cycle of period 2.

References

Barro R, Gordon D (1983), Rules, discretion and reputation in a model of monetary policy, Journal of Monetary Economics, 12: 101–121

Cochrane J (2023), The Fiscal Theory of the Price Level, Princeton University Press

Lucas R Jr (1990), Liquidity and interest rates, Journal of Economic Theory, 50: 237–264

Lucas R Jr (1996), Monetary Neutrality, Journal of Political Economy, 104: 661–682

Lucas R Jr, Stokey N (1987), Money and Interest in a Cash-in-Advance Economy, Econometrica, 55: 491–513

Sargent T, Wallace N (1981), Some Unpleasant Monetarist Arithmetic, Minneapolis Fed Quarterly Review, 531: 1–17

Risk Sharing and Precautionary Saving

L. Ferraris, *Macroeconomic Theory*, Classroom Companion: Economics,
https://doi.org/10.1007/978-3-031-88740-6_8

8.1 Introduction

The real business cycle model represents the economy in the aggregate through the simplifying assumption of the representative consumer. This means that individual and economy-wide consumption fluctuations are indistinguishable. At first sight, the assumption that there is a representative consumer would seem restrictive. However, trade at market prices equates the consumers' marginal rates of substitution, and hence heterogeneous consumers become marginally homogeneous, making the representative agent assumption a harmless simplification in economies in which the welfare theorems apply. In such economies, risk-averse consumers who dislike consumption variability are able to insure fully against personal income shocks. Thus, personal consumption fluctuates only as a consequence of aggregate shocks, not idiosyncratic ones. The representative agent assumption becomes problematic, instead, when the markets are incomplete, as the welfare theorems cease to apply.

According to the available evidence, aggregate and individual consumption are imperfectly correlated. In other words, risk sharing seems to be less than perfect in real-world economies. This suggests that markets may be incomplete, making the assumption of a representative consumer questionable.

In this chapter, we will examine a departure from the complete market benchmark in which the traders cannot share risks being only able to self-insure against adverse shocks to personal income saving for the future. This precautionary motive leads to excessive savings relative not only to Pareto efficiency but also to a more constrained notion of efficiency that considers only the feasible alternative allocations of resources that can be obtained with the existing financial instruments. The key feature of economies with incomplete financial markets is the presence of a *pecuniary externality* that distorts the allocation away from constrained efficiency.

8.2 Full Insurance

Full risk sharing requires access to all insurance possibilities. Thus, we begin with a model that offers full insurance options. Later, we will see what happens when these options are not available.

Consider a two-period model with a single durable commodity that is used as a saving instrument. There is a technology that uses capital and labor to produce output represented by a constant return-to-scale production function, $Y = F(K, L) = K^{\alpha}L^{1-\alpha}$ with $\alpha \in (0, 1)$. Since the production function has constant return-to-scale, we will use income and capital in per capita terms $y = k^{\alpha}$. Capital depreciates completely in production.

There is a mass of ex-ante identical savers with an initial endowment of resources e who face the risk of being unable to work in the future and are interested in consuming both before and after the realization of the uncertainty. There are two states of uncertainty, indexed by $s = 1, 2$ that are realized with probability $\pi \in (0, 1)$ and $1 - \pi$, respectively. Only people in the first state will be able to work, in which case they will supply their entire time endowment as labor. For simplicity, we normalize the labor time in the first state to $l = \pi^{-1}$, so that the aggregate labor supply is unitary by the law of large numbers. The expected utility of the traders is given by

$$\mathbb{E}U(c, c_1, c_2) = u(c) + \beta[\pi u(c_1) + (1 - \pi)u(c_2)],$$

where c is current consumption and c_s future consumption in state $s = 1, 2$, respectively, and $\beta \leq 1$ is the time discount. The utility function is differentiable, strictly increasing and strictly concave in consumption.

8.2.1 Efficient Allocation

The resource constraint in the beginning is given by $c + k = e$, since people can use their initial endowment of resources to consume them immediately or save them for the future, where k denotes savings. In the following period, the resource constraint is

$$\pi c_1 + (1 - \pi)c_2 = y = k^\alpha.$$

The efficient allocation of resources maximizes the ex-ante utility of the traders subject to the resource constraints in the two periods and satisfies the following optimality condition for consumption

$$u'(c_1) = u'(c_2),$$

namely equal consumption in the two risky states with $c_1^* = c_2^* = (k^*)^\alpha$, where k^* satisfies the optimality condition for the savings

$$u'(e - k) = \alpha\beta k^{\alpha-1}u'(k^\alpha), \tag{8.1}$$

that equates the marginal utility cost of giving up current consumption to the marginal benefit of larger future consumption due to the increase in productivity obtained through the extra investment of resources. A unique $k^* \in (0, e)$ that satisfies this equation exists under the boundary conditions and the strict concavity of the utility function. Consumption in the initial period is $c^* = e - k^* > 0$.

Example 8.1

Suppose that the utility function is logarithmic. The condition (8.1) gives the capital stock $k^* = \alpha\beta e(1 + \alpha\beta)^{-1}$, consumption in the initial period $c^* = e - k^*$ and subsequently $c_1^* = c_2^* = (k^*)^\alpha$.

8.2.2 Market Equilibrium

By the second welfare theorem, efficient allocation can be decentralized with trade in competitive markets. Several equivalent market mechanisms can implement the efficient allocation. First, we consider a scheme with insurance and contracts. Then, we will consider trade in financial securities and, finally, in contracts for state and time contingent commodities.

8.2.2.1 Insurance and Saving

There is a company that borrows capital in the initial period at a competitive interest rate r and hires labor in the second period at a competitive real wage w to be used as input in the production function. The company maximizes its profit by equating the capital rental rate to its marginal productivity $r = \alpha k^{\alpha-1}$, and the wage to satisfy the zero-profit condition $w = (1-\alpha)k^{\alpha}$. The profit of the company is nil due to competition with constant returns to scale.

Before the realization of uncertainty, traders can save resources by lending them to the company at a competitive interest rate r. The initial constraint on the resources for savers is $c + k = e$. In addition, traders are able to acquire insurance from competitive insurance companies before the realization of uncertainty. The insurance demand is denoted by a and its competitive price q. The insurance contract stipulates that everybody will pay a premium qa, the people unable to work will receive a payment $(1+q)a$ and the workers will receive nothing. Therefore, the budget constraint for someone who can work is $c_1 = rk + wl - qa$, while the budget constraint for those unable to work is $c_2 = rk + (1+q)a - qa = rk + a$. Substituting consumption from the budget constraints into the expected utility function and maximizing with respect to k, we obtain the optimality condition for the demand of insurance

8

$$q\pi u'(rk + wl - qa) = (1-\pi)u'(rk + a), \tag{8.2}$$

that equates the marginal cost and benefit of giving up some resources in the good state to buy insurance to increase consumption in the bad state and the optimality condition for the savings

$$u'(e-k) = \beta r[\pi u'(rk + wl - qa) + (1-\pi)u'(rk + a)], \tag{8.3}$$

that equates the marginal cost of giving up current consumption to the marginal benefit of a later increase in consumption, obtained saving some resources for the future.

The insurance company collects the premium from the workers and makes payments to those who cannot work, exploiting the law of large numbers. Maximization of the insurance company's profit implies that the insurance supply is perfectly elastic at the fair price $q = (1-\pi)\pi^{-1}$ and the insurance company's profit is nil.

Inserting the price of insurance into the optimality condition (8.2), we obtain equal consumption in the two states as required by efficiency, with $a = w = (1-\alpha)y$ and $c_1 = c_2 = y$. Inserting the rental rate into the optimality condition (8.3), we obtain (8.1). Therefore, the result has full insurance and efficient consumption smoothing over time.

8.2.2.2 Financial Securities

An alternative way in which exchange could be organized is through trade in financial securities. Suppose that consumers can trade, before the realization of uncertainty, in fact even before receiving the endowment of the commodity, a security θ_1 at unit price ϕ_1 that pays one unit of resources in the first state but nothing in the second and a security θ_2 at unit price ϕ_2 that pays one unit of resources in the second state but nothing in the first. These financial instruments are called *Arrow securities*. There is now an extra budget constraint in the initial period

$$\phi_1\theta_1 + \phi_2\theta_2 = 0,$$

that says that the traders can acquire one security selling short the other. The budget constraint in the first state is $c_1 = rk + wl + \theta_1$ and in the second state $c_2 = rk + \theta_2$. By solving the constraint in the initial period for the amount of the first security and defining the relative price of Arrow securities $\phi = \phi_2/\phi_2$, we obtain $\theta_1 = -\phi\theta_2 \equiv -\phi\theta$. Hence, we can rewrite the constraint in the first state as $c_1 = rk + wl - \phi\theta$ and in the second state as $c_2 = rk + \theta$, which are the same constraints of the case with insurance, modulo a relabeling of the variables, namely replacing ϕ for q and θ for a. Therefore, the allocation will be the same. The traders will sell short the first security to buy the second at a fair price $\phi = (1-\pi)\pi^{-1}$, thus obtaining full risk sharing and perfect consumption smoothing.

8.2.2.3 State Contingent Claims

A third equivalent way to obtain full risk sharing consists in trading claims to consumption contingent on the realization of uncertainty in ex-ante idealized markets at competitive prices, obtaining once again the efficient allocation of resources. Consider the insurance model. Solve the budget constraint for the second state, $c_2 = rk + a$, for a and plug it into the budget constraint for the first state, $c_1 = rk + wl - qa$, obtaining the single budget constraint $c_1 + qc_2 = (1+q)rk + wl$. Solve the initial constraint, $c + k = e$, for k and plug it back into the previous condition, obtaining $rc + c_1(1+q)^{-1} + qc_2(1+q)^{-1} = re + wl(1+q)^{-1}$. Define the ex-ante prices of contingent commodity in time and state, $p \equiv r$ for the commodity available initially, $p_1 \equiv (1+q)^{-1}$ for the commodity available later in the first uncertainty state, $p_2 \equiv q(1+q)^{-1}$ for the commodity available later in the second state and the wage $\omega \equiv w(1+q)^{-1}$. Using these prices, we can write the consolidated lifetime budget constraint in ex-ante terms

$$pc + p_1c_1 + p_2c_2 = pe + \omega l.$$

Consumers choose contingent consumption of time and state to maximize their expected utility of life subject to the consolidated budget constraint taking the ex-ante prices as given and the markets for contingent commodities of time and state clear. Since the optimization problem is equivalent to the one with insurance and the market clearing conditions for the commodities are the same, the equilibrium allocation will be the same. Notice that in this ex-ante formulation, the insurance and saving instruments that were part of the sequential formulation of the problem are not explicitly determined.

The equivalence of the ex-ante and sequential formulations implies immediately the *Ricardian equivalence* whereby, for a given program, the alternatives to financing it with immediate outright taxation or issuing public debt to be reimbursed with future taxation are equivalent for both the government and the consumers, since the only relevant aspect is the overall budget to be financed ex-ante. In other words, the public debt is neutral as regards the determination of the equilibrium allocation.

8.3 Lack of Insurance

Diversification of risk requires access to complete insurance possibilities. When these possibilities are lacking, the model has incomplete or missing markets. The rational expectations equilibrium of the model with incomplete markets is not only Pareto inefficient, but also constrained inefficient. An allocation is constrained efficient if it cannot be improved by reallocating existing assets. The reason for constrained inefficiency is the presence of a pecuniary externality that is not internalized by traders.

8.3.1 Absence of Risk Sharing

8

To see how the pecuniary externality affects the allocation of resources, consider the previous model but without insurance possibilities or access to financial securities. In this case, the budget constraint of the traders is $c_1 = rk + wl$ in the first state and $c_2 = rk$ in the second state. Notice that there is only one asset, capital, with non-contingent returns. This severely limits the traders' risk-sharing possibilities. By the consumers' maximization, the following optimality condition holds,

$$u'(e-k) = \beta r[\pi u'(rk+wl) + (1-\pi)u'(rk)]. \tag{8.4}$$

Notice the difference between the optimality condition for savings without insurance (8.4) in which future consumption cannot be equalized across states of uncertainty and the optimality condition (8.3) in which, instead, this is possible thanks to the availability of insurance. By maximization of companies, the rental rate equates to the marginal product of capital $r(k) = \alpha k^{\alpha-1}$ and the real wage is $w(k) = (1-\alpha)k^{\alpha}$.

▪▪ Example 8.2

Continuing with the logarithmic example, define $\varphi \equiv 1 - \pi(1-\alpha)$. The equilibrium capital stock is $\tilde{k} = \varphi\beta e(1+\varphi\beta)^{-1}$, consumption in the initial period is $\tilde{c} = e - \tilde{k}$, consumption in the first state is $\tilde{c}_1 = \tilde{k}^{\alpha}$, while in the second state it is $\tilde{c}_2 = \alpha\tilde{k}^{\alpha}$. The allocation is distorted with respect to efficiency with $\tilde{k} > k^*$ since $\alpha < 1$ and $\pi < 1$.

8.3.1.1 Constrained Inefficiency

The equilibrium is bound to be inefficient relative to the Pareto efficiency benchmark since the insurance is incomplete. Let us examine the question of constrained efficiency. By constrained efficiency, in this context, we mean that not all the Pareto improving reallocations of resources can be achieved but only those that can be obtained reallocating the only available asset in this economy, namely capital.

Suppose that a benevolent authority can alter the allocation of capital before the realization of uncertainty relative to the optimal decentralized choice of the saver. The change has a direct effect on the quantity of the commodity obtained by the saver both before and after the realization of uncertainty. This effect is nil, since the saver has optimized the allocation of capital. However, there are also indirect effects that a change in capital allocation has on the marginal product of labor and capital, which, in turn, alter the wage and rental rate of capital. The indirect effect of such a change on the equilibrium payoff of the traders is given by

$$\mathbb{E}U'(k) = u'(c_1)w'(k) + [\pi u'(c_1) + (1-\pi)u'(c_2)]kr'(k), \tag{8.5}$$

where $w'(k)$ is the derivative of the wage function and $r'(k)$ the derivative of the rental rate with respect to capital. By direct computation from the functions derived above, we obtain

$$kr'(k) = -w'(k) = -\alpha(1-\alpha)k^{\alpha-1},$$

that can be substituted into equation (8.5), obtaining

$$\mathbb{E}U'(k) = -(1-\pi)\alpha(1-\alpha)k^{\alpha-1}[u'(c_2) - u'(c_1)].$$

Since $c_2 = rk < rk + wl = c_1$ and the marginal utility decreases in consumption, we have $\mathbb{E}U'(k) < 0$, implying that there is excessive investment in the asset in competitive equilibrium relative to the efficient benchmark restricted. Hence, the capital accumulation should be reduced.

▪▪ Example 8.3

With the logarithmic utility function, the expected marginal utility evaluated in equilibrium is $\mathbb{E}U'(k) = -(1-\pi)(1-\alpha)^2\tilde{k}^{-1} < 0$.

8.3.1.2 Pecuniary Externality

This inefficiency occurs because traders use capital not only to save for the future but also to self-insure against income risk. Reducing investment increases the rental rate of capital and lowers the wage. These price effects, in turn, induce consumers to move away from risky labor choices in favor of the risk-less return of the asset. This reduces the variability of consumption, which is beneficial for consumers who are risk averse, as manifested in the decreasing marginal utility of consumption. This is the essence of the *pecuniary externality*.

With complete markets, there would be no variability in consumption to begin with, as $c_1 = c_2$ with complete markets, leading to $\mathbb{E}U'(k) = 0$, hence, this pecuniary effect arising from changes in relative prices would be silenced. Thus, a reallocation of the asset cannot improve the situation of the saver when markets are complete. With incomplete markets, there is variability in consumption between states, and the pecuniary externality is at work, so that a reallocation of the asset by the public authorities relative to the market outcome may be beneficial. This reallocation may be achieved by taxing capital income or issuing public debt.

8.3.1.3 Capital Taxation

Suppose that the government taxes capital income at a flat rate τ. The optimality condition of traders is

$$u'(e-k) = \beta(1-\tau)r[\pi u'((1-\tau)rk + w) + (1-\pi)u'((1-\tau)rk)].$$

Since the marginal utility of consumption is a decreasing function, a positive tax rate helps reduce the overaccumulation of capital relative to efficiency. More generally, in a model with a longer time horizon, with incomplete markets, it may be socially beneficial to tax capital income even in the long run, unlike complete markets.

Example 8.4

Continuing with the previous logarithmic example, we get $\bar{k} = \frac{(\varphi-\alpha\tau)\beta e}{1+\varphi\beta-\alpha\tau(1+\beta)}$. The tax rate that induces efficient capital accumulation, k^*, is $\tau^* = \frac{\varphi-\alpha}{\alpha(1-\alpha)}$, which is strictly positive since $\varphi > \alpha$, whenever $\alpha, \pi \in (0, 1)$.

8.3.1.4 Public Debt

Government-issued saving instruments, such as bonds, may help reduce the excessive accumulation of capital. Suppose that the government issues a one-period bond in amount D. By no-arbitrage, the interest payment has to be r, which we assume is financed with lump-sum taxation T in the second period. The government budget is balanced, so that $(r-1)D = T$.

The budget constraint of the traders in the initial period is $c + k + d = e$, while in the second period in the first state it is $c_1 = rk + wl + rd - T$ and in the second state $c_2 = rk + rd - T$, denoting with d the demand for the treasuries. At equilibrium, the optimality condition of the traders with the government budget and market clearing in all the markets including for the government debt, $d = D$, gives

$$u'(e-k-D) = \alpha\beta k^{\alpha-1}[\pi u'(k^\alpha + D) + (1-\pi)u'(\alpha k^\alpha + D)].$$

Since the marginal utility of consumption is a decreasing function of consumption, a positive debt issuance reduces the accumulation of capital, since the government bond provides an alternative saving instrument. This is socially beneficial, as accumulation would otherwise have been excessive relative to efficiency. Notice that this implies that, in general, with incomplete markets, public debt is not neutral and the Ricardian equivalence proposition does not hold.

Example 8.5

Continuing the previous logarithmic example, we can obtain the debt issuance that induces efficient capital accumulation, k^*, as $D^* = \frac{\alpha\beta(k^*)^{\alpha-1}(e-k^*)}{1+\alpha\beta(k^*)^{\alpha-1}}$ which is positive, since $k^* < e$.

8.3.2 Private Information

So far, we have taken the market incompleteness as exogenous. However, the reason markets are incomplete may be that there is some underlying element of private information that makes complete risk-sharing not feasible. To see the point, consider the following small variation of the previous setting. Suppose that whether traders have time to work or not is private information. Moreover, traders who can work may decide to supply the entire time unit as labor at a utility cost $v > 0$ or shirk completely. The rest of the model remains the same.

8.3.2.1 Constrained Efficiency

The determination of the efficient allocation is now subject to the incentive constraint

$$u(c_1) - v \geq u(c_2), \tag{8.6}$$

that makes sure that the traders with time to work find it in their interest to do so. Indeed, if not compensated with higher consumption, the traders with the ability to work would simply pretend to be unable to do so, shirking and enjoying the consumption intended for the traders who are unable to work. Since the information on the ability to work is private, it is always possible to make such a claim without fear of consequences. In sum, the constrained efficient allocation maximizes the expected useful life of traders subject to the resource constraint in the initial period and the resource constraint in the second period, together with the incentive compatibility constraint (8.6).

The optimality conditions that determine the constrained efficient allocation include the complementary slackness condition for the incentive compatibility constraint (8.6), which can be written as

$$[u'(c_2) - u'(c_1)][u(c_1) - v - u(c_2)] = 0,$$

since the incentive constraint is slack and full risk sharing is obtained or risk sharing is limited and the incentive constraint binds. By the incentive condition $u(c_1) \geq u(c_2) + v$, it follows that $c_1 > c_2$, which, in turn, implies $u'(c_2) > u'(c_1)$, since the marginal utility is decreasing. Thus, risk-sharing is incomplete due to the need to discourage traders who can work by shirking. By the complementary slackness condition, we find that inequality (8.6) is binding. In addition, the resource constraint is met in the second period. Together, these conditions give consumption in the two periods as functions of the capital stock, with $c_1 = g(k) > k^\alpha > h(k) = c_2$. Define $\mathbb{E}u'(k) \equiv \pi u'(g(k)) + (1 - \pi)u'(h(k))$. Using the implicit function theorem, we can compute the derivatives

$$g'(k) = \frac{u'(h(k))}{\mathbb{E}u'(k)} \alpha k^{\alpha - 1} = \frac{u'(h(k))}{u'(g(k))} h'(k).$$

The constrained efficient choice of the capital stock is implicitly determined by the first-order condition

$$u'(e - k) = \beta[\pi u'(g(k))g'(k) + (1 - \pi)u'(h(k))h'(k)],$$

so that, plugging into it the derivatives above, we can write

$$u'(e-k) = \alpha\beta k^{\alpha-1} H(k),$$

where $H(k) \equiv u'(g(k))u'(h(k))\mathbb{E}u'(k)^{-1}$. This condition differs from the optimality condition that determines the unconstrained efficient capital stock, (8.1), since $H(k) \neq u'(k^{\alpha})$. Except by fluke, their solutions differ. The provision of incentives for work requires the partial sacrifice not only of risk-sharing but typically also of consumption smoothing. The constrained efficient allocation can be used as a guide for the design of a socially optimal taxation scheme that is incentive compatible. Interestingly, the optimal marginal income tax rates turn out to be regressive, in order to discourage people who are able to work from shirking.

▪▪ Example 8.6

In the logarithmic example, we have $H(k) = [\pi h(k) + (1-\pi)g(k)]^{-1}$. By resource constraint $\pi g(k) + (1-\pi)h(k) = k^{\alpha}$. Hence, the constrained efficient capital stock is equal to k^* for $\pi = 1/2$, larger than k^* for $\pi > 1/2$ and smaller than k^* otherwise.

8

8.4 Precautionary Saving

Next, we extend the model with incomplete markets and saving to the infinite horizon. Consider a unit continuum of ex-ante identical dynasties with initial endowment e and preferences for consumption sequences $\mathbf{c}$ represented by the lifetime utility function

$$U(\mathbf{c}) = \sum_{t=1}^{\infty} \beta^{t-1} u(c_t),$$

where $\beta < 1$ and the function $u(\cdot)$ is differentiable, strictly increasing, strictly concave. Dynasties can save or borrow resources for the future k_{t+1}, at a competitive gross real rate r every period, and have time to work l for a competitively determined wage w every period.

8.4.1 Permanent Income

Suppose that there is no uncertainty and no binding borrowing limit. The budget constraint is $c_t + k_{t+1} = rk_t + wl$. The dynasties determine their choice of k_{t+1} through the optimality condition

$$u'(c_t) = \beta r u'(c_{t+1}).$$

The only case compatible with a stationary equilibrium has $r = \beta^{-1}$, time-invariant savings $k = e$ and consumption $c = (\beta^{-1} - 1)e + wl$ equal to the per-period share of the discounted wealth of the dynasty. This is the so-called *permanent income* theory of consumption.

Suppose now that the dynasties cannot borrow, so that $k_{t+1} \geq 0$. The complementary slackness condition for the borrowing constraint can be written as

$$[u'(c_t) - \beta r u'(c_{t+1})]k_{t+1} = 0. \tag{8.7}$$

In this case, if $r = \beta^{-1}$, nothing changes relative to the previous situation without the binding borrowing limit; the case with $r > \beta^{-1}$ leads to an ever-increasing saving over time that is incompatible with stationary equilibrium; if $r < \beta^{-1}$, for sufficiently small e, the only situation compatible with stationary equilibrium has no savings from any dynasty, that is, $k_{t+1} = 0$ at all times.

8.4.2 Uninsured Risk

Finally, consider the case in which the dynasties are hit by independent and identically distributed shocks to their work time every period. The labor time of the dynasties is distributed over a bounded interval $[\underline{l}, \bar{l}]$ with $\underline{l} > 0$. Should there be complete insurance possibilities, consumption would be insulated from the labor income risk. Suppose that there are no insurance options available other than saving. The life-time utility above becomes an expected life-time utility. To close the model, suppose that there is a representative company with a technology represented by the production function in intensive form $y_t = k_t^{\alpha}$. Capital depreciates completely in production. Normalize the average labor supply to unity. The company chooses capital to maximize its profit $y_t - r_t k_t - w_t$, equating its marginal productivity with its rental rate $\alpha k_t^{\alpha-1} = r_t$. The wage is determined by the zero-profit condition of the company.

As regards dynasties, the complementary slackness condition of their borrowing constraint (8.7) becomes

$$[u'(c_t) - \beta r \mathbb{E} u'(c_{t+1})]k_{t+1} = 0. \tag{8.8}$$

Now, dynasties that are ex-ante identical become ex-post heterogeneous, since dynasties with different histories of shocks to their labor time accumulate different savings. Dynasties with a sufficiently long streak of bad luck will have no savings, while others will have positive savings. Thus, the model gives rise to an endogenous income and wealth distribution.

We consider stationary competitive equilibria. When $r \geq \beta^{-1}$, there is no stationary equilibrium, since the dynasties will accumulate an infinite amount of capital. Consider the case with $r < \beta^{-1}$. Let $k(r)$ be the demand for capital by the company and $\mathcal{K}(r)$ be the stationary average savings of the dynasties, that is, the supply of capital in stationary equilibrium. The equilibrium in the capital market requires $\mathcal{K}(r) = k(r)$. The next proposition shows that an equilibrium exists.

Proposition 8.1

There exists a stationary competitive equilibrium. The interest rate is $\tilde{r} \in (0, \beta^{-1})$ and capital is $\tilde{k} > (\alpha\beta)^{\frac{1}{1-\alpha}}$.

Proof Capital demand is determined by the optimality condition of the company, which is given by $k(r) = (\alpha/r)^{\frac{1}{1-\alpha}}$, which is continuous and strictly decreasing in r, with $k(0) = \infty$ and $k(\beta^{-1}) = (\alpha\beta)^{\frac{1}{1-\alpha}}$. The supply $\mathcal{K}(r)$ is continuous in r, with $\mathcal{K}(0) = 0$ and $\mathcal{K}(\beta^{-1}) = \infty$. In fact, suppose that there are maximum savings $\mathcal{K}(\beta^{-1}) = \overline{\mathcal{K}} < \infty$. Then, we would have $u'(r\bar{k} + w\bar{l}) \geq \mathbb{E}u'(r\bar{k} + wl) > u'(r\bar{k} + w\bar{l})$, where the weak inequality follows from the complementary slackness condition (8.8) and the strict inequality from the strict concavity of utility. By continuity, a stationary equilibrium capital exists with $\tilde{k} > (\alpha\beta)^{\frac{1}{1-\alpha}}$ for $\tilde{r} \in (0, \beta^{-1})$. □

Without uncertainty or, equivalently, with full insurance, the capital supply is nil for $r < \beta^{-1}$, perfectly elastic for $r = \beta^{-1}$ and infinite for $r > \beta^{-1}$. The capital demand is still $k(r) = (\alpha/r)^{\frac{1}{1-\alpha}}$. Therefore, the stationary equilibrium has $k^* = (\alpha\beta)^{\frac{1}{1-\alpha}} < \tilde{k}$ with $r^* = \beta^{-1} > \tilde{r}$. Savings with uninsured risks are higher than without uncertainty or with full insurance, since the dynasties use capital as a buffer against labor income shocks, that is, as precautionary savings. Consequently, the interest rate is lower.

8

8.5 Conclusion

Without insurance, capital may be used to compensate for the lack of instruments to diversify risks, leading to over-saving relative to constrained efficiency, due to the presence of a pecuniary externality. Taxation of capital income or public debt issuance may help reduce the over-accumulation of capital. With private information about the ability to generate income, the optimal allocation trades off risk-sharing and consumption smoothing with the need to provide the incentive to work rather than shirk.

8.6 Literature

The constrained inefficiency of competitive equilibrium with incomplete markets, identified first by Joseph Stiglitz, was formalized by John Geanakoplos and Herakles Polemarchakis in the paper *Existence, Regularity, and Constrained Suboptimality of Competitive Allocations when the Asset Market is Incomplete*. A book-length exposition of the general equilibrium model with incomplete markets is *Theory of Incomplete Markets* by Michael Magill and Martine Quinzii. The infinite-horizon extension of the incomplete markets framework with capital accumulation is contained in the paper *Uninsured Idiosyncratic Risk and Aggregate Saving* by Rao Aiyagari. The private information version is the subject of extensive literature initiated by James Mirrlees in the seminal paper entitled *An Exploration in the Theory of Optimum Income Taxation*.

8.7 Exercises

1. Consider the risk-sharing model with two states of uncertainty and complete markets. The expected utility function of traders who have an initial endowment e of a durable commodity and can work for one time unit only in the first state is

$$\mathbb{E}U(c, c_1, c_2) = \frac{c^{1-\epsilon}}{1-\epsilon} + \left[\pi \frac{c_1^{1-\epsilon}}{1-\epsilon} + (1-\pi)\frac{c_2^{1-\epsilon}}{1-\epsilon}\right].$$

- Calculate the efficient allocation.
- Calculate the equilibrium with insurance.
- Compute the equilibrium with two securities.
- Calculate the equilibrium with claims for contingent commodities.

2. Consider the setup of the previous exercise but with incomplete markets, namely without risk-sharing opportunities.
- Calculate the equilibrium allocation.
- Derive the effect of the reallocation of capital on the ex-ante well-being of the consumers.
- Derive the amount of government debt that would achieve efficient capital accumulation.

References

Aiyagari R (1994), Uninsured Idiosyncratic Risk and Aggregate Saving, Quarterly Journal of Economics, 109: 659–684

Geanakoplos J, Polemarchakis H (1986), Existence, Regularity and Constrained Suboptimality of Competitive Allocations when the Asset Market is Incomplete, in Essays in Honor of Kenneth J. Arrow, edited by Walter P. Heller, Ross M. Starr and David A. Starrett, Cambridge University Press, 65–96

Magill M, Quinzii M (1996), Theory of Incomplete Markets, MIT Press

Mirrlees J (1971), An Exploration in the Theory of Optimum Income Taxation, Review of Economic Studies, 39: 175–208

Borrowing Limits and Liquidity

L. Ferraris, *Macroeconomic Theory*, Classroom Companion: Economics,
https://doi.org/10.1007/978-3-031-88740-6_9

9.1 Introduction

Borrowing limits disrupt the smoothing of the private sector's consumption. Since rational forward-looking and risk-averse traders dislike variability of consumption, with unlimited access to market instruments, they will try to smooth consumption, giving rise to profiles that depend only on life-time wealth, the so-called permanent income. Consumption variability, if any, may be driven by aggregate income shocks, but temporary idiosyncratic income variability would be smoothed out. Liquidity is useless in such circumstances, since all personal wealth is already fully liquid. However, real-world consumption smoothing appears to be less than perfect. Moreover, even casual observation shows that both companies and households routinely hold liquid instruments without low or no intrinsic value, such as fiat money.

In this chapter, we examine a departure from the benchmark model in which heterogeneous traders cannot borrow without limit against their future income. The profile of personal consumption fluctuates over time independently of the variability of aggregate income and consumption. Financial securities can be used as liquid instruments. With short-selling constraints, when the dividends of securities are not sufficiently abundant, liquidity premia emerge together with distortions in the allocation of resources. Publicly provided liquid instruments such as currency can help improve resource allocation. The price of such liquid public instruments diverges from the fundamental value, including a liquidity premium. In other words, bubbles emerge at equilibrium. Public liquidity creation can be socially beneficial by helping people relax their liquidity constraint when most needed, at the cost of creating inflation that erodes the value of currency.

9.2 Heterogeneous Agents

Now, we describe a model economy with heterogeneous consumers who lend and borrow from each other. There are two periods and a single commodity at each date. The economy is populated by two heterogeneous traders with different income profiles over time. The first trader has a unit endowment of time used to work for a competitive wage w_1 in the first period, the second has a unit endowment of time used to work for a competitive wage w_2 in the second period. Both traders care about consumption in both periods, with preferences represented by the same utility function. There is a company that owns a technology represented by a production function that uses labor every period to generate output, $y_t = z\ell_t$. By optimization of the company, $w_t = z$ in both periods.

9.2.1 Borrowing and Lending

We begin with a situation in which there is a market for the exchange of loans and traders can commit to honor their promises. Then, we examine a situation in which such commitment is problematic.

9.2.1.1 Lender

The first trader with a unit time endowment in the first but not in the second period has preferences over consumption of the commodity in the two periods represented by the utility function $U(c_1, c_2) = u(c_1) + \beta u(c_2)$, where the function is differentiable, strictly increasing and strictly concave in consumption, with $\beta < 1$. This trader can lend an amount b of the commodity at a competitively determined net real interest rate r. The budget constraint in the first period is $c_1 + b = w_1 l_1$ and in the second period $c_2 = (1 + r)b$. Thus, the lender can give up in part the opportunity of immediate consumption to be able to enjoy some future consumption. Optimization leads to the condition

$$u'(w_1 l_1 - b) = \beta(1 + r)u'((1 + r)b), \tag{9.1}$$

that expresses, implicitly, lending as a function of the interest rate, $b(r)$. The optimal choice of lending occurs when the marginal cost of giving up current consumption is equated to the marginal gain of increasing future consumption. In other words, the gross interest rate is equal to the marginal rate of substitution for consumption in the two periods.

9.2.1.2 Borrower

The second trader has a unit-time endowment in the second but not in the first period with preferences over consumption of the commodity in the two periods represented by the utility function $U(C_1, C_2) = u(C_1) + \beta u(C_2)$. This trader can borrow an amount B of the commodity at a competitively determined net real interest rate r. The budget constraint in the first period is $C_1 = B$ and in the second period $C_2 = w_2 l_2 - (1 + r)B$. Thus, the borrower can obtain current resources that promise to reimburse them with interest in the future. Optimization leads to the condition

$$u'(B) = \beta(1 + r)u'(w_2 l_2 - (1 + r)B), \tag{9.2}$$

that expresses, implicitly, borrowing as a function of the interest rate, $B(r)$. The optimal choice of the loan is determined by equating the marginal gain of current consumption to the marginal cost of giving up future consumption. In other words, the gross interest rate is equal to the marginal rate of substitution for consumption in the two periods.

9.2.1.3 Competitive Equilibrium

Competitive equilibrium requires traders to choose optimally with perfect foresight of future interest payments and the interest rate to balance the demand and supply of loans. In other words, Eqs. (9.1) and (9.2) should both hold, together with the market clearing condition $b(r) = B(r)$. The labor market clears in all periods. Equations (9.1) and (9.2) together with market clearing give the equilibrium interest rate $r = \beta^{-1} - 1$ and the equilibrium amount of loans $b = B = \beta z(1 + \beta)^{-1}$, which can be substituted into the budget constraints of traders to obtain consumption for the lender in the two periods $c_1 = c_2 = c^* = z(1 + \beta)^{-1}$ and consumption for the borrower in the two periods

$C_1 = C_2 = C^* = \beta z(1+\beta)^{-1}$. Notice that both traders smooth consumption over time, but the lender permanently consumes more than the borrower, since the latter has to compensate the former for the current use of his or her resources in an economy with time discounting, as $c > C$ since $\beta < 1$. This is an example of the theory of *permanent income*, in which traders use their entire wealth throughout their life to finance a smooth consumption profile but without ex-ante insurance.

9.2.1.4 Efficiency

This is an economy with heterogeneous traders, so computing efficient allocations requires one to take into account the preferences of both traders. The efficient mechanism will allocate consumption to maximize the life-time utility of the consumers with weights $\vartheta > 0$ and $1 - \vartheta > 0$, respectively, subject to resource constraints $c_t + C_t = y_t$ with $y_t = zl_t$ and $l_t = 1$ in both periods $t = 1, 2$. Using the resource constraint, the objective is to choose consumption c_t for $t = 1, 2$ to maximize the welfare function

$$W(c_1, c_2) = \vartheta[u(c_1) + \beta u(c_2)] + (1 - \vartheta)[u(z - c_1) + \beta u(z - c_2)].$$

Maximizing $W(c_1, c_2)$ with respect to the consumption of the first trader in the two periods, we obtain the optimality condition

$$\vartheta u'(c_t) = (1 - \vartheta)u'(z - c_t), \tag{9.3}$$

for $t = 1, 2$. These equations imply constant consumption for the first trader and, hence, by the resource constraint, for the second trader as well. Thus, efficiency requires perfect consumption smoothing. Equivalently, efficiency implies the equality of the marginal rates of substitution of consumption across the two types.

Notice that there are many efficient allocations, with time-invariant consumption per person but a different split across the two consumers. By the second welfare theorem, these allocations can all be decentralized through the market system, provided that the initial endowment is redistributed appropriately with lump-sum taxes and transfers. The competitive equilibrium corresponds to the efficient allocation implemented without such taxes and transfers.

The economy with heterogeneous traders can be interpreted as an economy with an average or representative trader, using the proportions of the types in the population as weights in the utility function. The crucial assumption underlying the representation of the economy through a single trader is the presence of complete markets, guaranteeing the applicability of the welfare theorems.

9.2.2 Security Trading

Suppose now that traders cannot borrow resources since they are unable to commit to repay the loans. However, there is a security in unit supply whose shares can be traded in a competitive market in the first period at a price ϕ that provides a dividend payment per share z in units of output in the second period. The potential borrower initially owns all the supply of the asset. The productivity of the technology in the second period is lower than in the first period but is such that the overall amount of resources available in the second period, including security payment, is still z as in the first period. The rest of the model remains the same.

Efficiency requires to equate the marginal rates of substitution of consumption over time between the two types, fulfilling the resource constraint in the first period $c_1 + C_1 = z$ and in the second period $c_2 + C_2 = z$. By the second welfare theorem, without imperfections or trade limitations, efficient allocations can be decentralized by trading shares of the security in competitive market.

9.2.2.1 Short-Selling Constraint

Due to the inability of the traders to honor their promises, security trading is subject to a short-selling constraint. Consider, in particular, the trader who has labor income only in the second period. This trader may have an incentive to sell in the first period more than his or her initial endowment of the security, promising to come up with resources in the second period to honor the promise. Without the short-selling constraint, the trader would effectively be able to borrow resources, which we have assumed to be not feasible. Denote by $\theta \in [0, 1]$ the portfolio choice of the trader type with the early labor income and by $\Theta \in [0, 1]$ the portfolio choice of the other type.

The first type maximizes utility subject to the first period budget constraint $c_1 + \phi\theta = w_1 l_1$, since labor income can be used to purchase consumption or security; and the second period constraint $c_2 = z\theta$, since the security dividend payment is used to consume. The optimality condition for portfolio choice is

$$\phi u'(w_1 l_1 - \phi\theta) = \beta z u'(z\theta), \tag{9.4}$$

which equates the cost of acquiring the security in terms of foregone current consumption to the benefit of using the dividend payment for future consumption.

The second type of trader maximizes utility subject to the first period constraint $C_1 = \phi(1 - \Theta)$, since part of the security unit endowment is sold to purchase consumption; and the second period constraint $C_2 = w_2 l_2 + z\Theta$, since labor income and security dividend payment are used to finance consumption. Moreover, the optimization of the second trader, who may be interested in selling more than the unit endowment of the asset, is also subject to the short sale constraint $\Theta \geq 0$, whose multiplier we denote by $\lambda \geq 0$. The optimality condition for portfolio choice for this trader is

$$\phi u'(\phi(1 - \Theta)) = \beta z u'(w_2 l_2 + z\Theta) + \lambda, \tag{9.5}$$

which equates the benefit of selling the security in terms of current consumption to the cost of foregone dividend payment in terms of future consumption including the tightening of the short sale constraint. There is also the complementary slackness condition $\lambda\Theta = 0$, which using (9.5) we can write as

$$[\phi u'(\phi(1 - \Theta)) - \beta z u'(w_2 l_2 + z\Theta)]\Theta = 0, \tag{9.6}$$

In competitive equilibrium, the asset market should clear, and hence $\theta + \Theta = 1$. The real wage is pinned down by the productivity of the company in each period, and the aggregate labor supply is unitary in each period.

9.2.2.2 Unconstrained Regime

Consider first the case in which the constraint is not binding, with $\lambda = 0$. By the complementary slackness condition (9.6), the short sale constraint is not binding with $\Theta \geq 0$. The optimality condition (9.4) becomes

$$\phi u'(z - \phi\theta) = \beta z u'(z\theta),$$

and the optimality condition (9.5) with $\Theta = 1 - \theta$ becomes

$$\phi u'(\phi\theta) = \beta z u'(z - z\theta).$$

These two equilibrium conditions give the equilibrium price of the security as $\phi^* = \beta z$ and the security demand by the first trader $\theta^* = \frac{z}{z(1+\beta)}$. The rest of the security is held by the second trader. For this security market equilibrium to be feasible, it must be $z \geq \frac{z}{1+\beta}$ such that $\theta^* \leq 1$.

Both traders smooth consumption perfectly over their life-time. The first trader obtains $c_1 = c_2 = c^* = \frac{z}{1+\beta}$ and the second trader $C_1 = C_2 = C^* = \frac{\beta z}{1+\beta}$. This allocation is efficient because it equates the marginal rates of substitutions of the two traders.

9.2.2.3 Constrained Regime

Suppose now that the constraint is binding with $\lambda > 0$. In this case, the equality of the price with the marginal rate of substitution of consumption over time is impeded by the short-selling constraint. By the complementary slackness condition (9.6), the short sale constraint is binding with $\Theta = 0$. Consequently, the first trader holds the entire amount of the security, $\hat{\theta} = 1$. The equilibrium condition is

$$\phi u'(z - \phi) = \beta z u'(z),$$

which gives a unique security price $\hat{\phi} \in (0, z)$ under the boundary condition, $u'(0) = \infty$. The existence of a solution is established by continuity, since the RHS is independent of the asset price, while the LHS is nil when $\phi = 0$ and infinitely large when $\phi = z$ under the boundary condition. Uniqueness holds by the strict concavity of the utility function. For the multiplier to be positive, it must be $z < \frac{z}{1+\beta}$.

The consumption of the first trader is $\hat{c}_1 = z - \hat{\phi} > z = \hat{c}_2$ and the consumption of the second trader is $\hat{C}_1 = \hat{\phi} < z - z = \hat{c}_2$. The allocation no longer equates the marginal rates of substitution of consumption across the two traders anymore; consumption smoothing is disrupted, and hence the market allocation is inefficient. When the short-selling constraint is slack, the asset is priced at fundamental value, when the constraint instead is binding, the price is higher as it contains a liquidity component $\hat{\phi} > \phi^*$. This occurs because the security, whose dividend payment is not sufficiently abundant to guarantee the efficient allocation of resources, plays a key liquidity role and hence carries a liquidity premium. For the security to play a role in this short-term model, its dividend payment z must be positive. In the dynamic extension of the model, this phenomenon will occur even for an asset that has no dividend payment or intrinsic return, such as fiat money.

Example 9.1

Suppose that the utility function is logarithmic. When $z < \frac{z}{1+\beta}$, the short-selling constraint is binding. The price of the asset is $\hat{\phi} = \frac{\beta z}{1+\beta} > \beta z = \phi^*$. Consumption of the first type in the first period is $c_1 = \frac{z}{1+\beta}$ and in the second period $c_2 - z$, while the second type obtains $C_1 = \frac{\beta z}{1+\beta}$ and $C_2 = z - z$.

9.3 Public Liquidity

Let us now extend the framework to the long run. We use the model to study the public provision of liquidity when traders are borrowing constrained. Suppose that the time horizon stretches indefinitely into the future. There are two infinitely lived dynasties with alternating unit labor supply, with the first dynasty being able to work in the beginning. The technology represented by the production function $y_t = zl_t$ is available in all periods. The preferences of the first dynasty over consumption sequences **c** are represented by the life-time utility

$$U(\mathbf{c}) = \sum_{t=1}^{\infty} \beta^{t-1} u(c_t), \tag{9.7}$$

where $\beta < 1$ is the time discount factor. The utility function is differentiable, strictly increasing and strictly concave in consumption. The preferences of the second dynasty are represented by the same life-time utility defined over consumption sequences denoted with uppercase letters. The utility function is differentiable, strictly increasing, and concave.

The efficient allocation still satisfies the same condition (9.3) at every point in time. If there are no limits to the enforcement of contracts, the competitive equilibrium allocation still satisfies the perfect consumption smoothing. To maintain an equilibrium with perfect consumption smoothing, the interest rate should be $1 + r = \beta^{-1}$, at all times. Hence, the consumption profile is still given by $c_t = c^* = \frac{z}{1+\beta}$ and $C_t = C^* = \frac{\beta z}{1+\beta}$ for the two dynasties at all times.

9.3.1 Money as Liquidity

Suppose that borrowing is impossible, but dynasties can save using a monetary asset that is in fixed supply, M. We will focus on the first dynasty. The solution for the second dynasty is symmetric. The dynasty maximizes the life-time utility (9.7) subject to the budget constraint

$$c_t + (1 + \rho_{t+1}) m_{t+1} = w_t l_t + m_t, \tag{9.8}$$

where m_{t+1} represents the savings of the monetary asset in real terms, $1 + \rho_{t+1}$ is the inflation rate and the labor supply alternates between $l = 1$ and $l = 0$. Moreover, there is the liquidity constraint $m_{t+1} \geq 0$, since the dynasty cannot short-sell the asset. Let $\lambda_t \geq 0$ be the multiplier of the liquidity constraint. Solving (9.8) for consumption and plugging it into (9.7), we are left with the problem of determining the optimal savings, $m_{t+1} \geq 0$.

The optimality condition that determines the saving is

$$\lambda_t = \beta^{t-1}[(1 + \rho_{t+1})u'(c_t) - \beta u'(c_{t+1})], \tag{9.9}$$

and the complementary slackness condition for the liquidity constraint is $\lambda_t m_{t+1} = 0$, in every period, that we can write as

$$\left[(1 + \rho_{t+1})u'(c_t) - \beta u'(c_{t+1})\right] m_{t+1} = 0.$$

If the dynasty accumulates money, that is, $m_{t+1} > 0$, it does so at the margin, satisfying the Euler condition for the accumulation of the asset; otherwise if the Euler condition is slack, the constraint binds and the savings are nil, $m_{t+1} = 0$. Thus, there are two possibilities for the dynasty, either it saves optimally or does not save at all.

9

9.3.1.1 Monetary Equilibrium

We will focus on stationary equilibria. Competitive equilibrium requires that the dynasties make optimal choices with perfect foresight of future prices and markets clear. The money market clears in every period, with $m_t = M/p_t$. Optimization of the company implies $w_t = z$ in every period. Since the amount of money is constant, the inflation rate will be zero at all times $\rho_t = 0$.

We guess that the two possibilities for the optimal behavior of the dynasties alternate over time between periods in which the dynasty has the labor income saving an amount m and periods in which it has no income and therefore consumes entirely its past savings m. Therefore, the consumption of the dynasty alternates over time between $c = z - m$ when the dynasty has income and saves part of it and $\hat{c} = m$ when it does not have any income and liquidates its savings to consume.

By (9.9) with $\lambda_t = 0$ and $\rho_{t+1} = 0$, the stationary equilibrium condition that determines m is

$$u'(z - m) = \beta u'(m). \tag{9.10}$$

This condition applies to one dynasty in alternating periods, while in the remaining periods the dynasty does not save. By symmetry, this same condition holds for the other dynasty in the remaining periods. The dynasty that does not accumulate money satisfies the incentive condition $u'(m) \geq \beta u'(z - m)$. Using (9.10), we obtain $(1 - \beta^2)u'(m) \geq 0$, which holds since the utility is strictly increasing and $\beta < 1$. The next proposition shows that there is a unique solution of (9.10) with positive $m < z/2$ so that the smoothing of the consumption is partial.

Proposition 9.1

If $u'(0) > u'(z)\beta^{-1}$, there exists a unique stationary equilibrium with partial consumption smoothing.

Proof From Eq. (9.10), define $\Sigma(m) \equiv u'(z-m) - \beta u'(m)$. The function is continuous in m and has the following properties: $\Sigma(0) < 0 \Leftrightarrow u'(0) > u'(z)\beta^{-1}$, $\Sigma(z/2) = (1-\beta)u'(z/2) > 0$, $\Sigma'(m) > 0$. Therefore, there is a unique value $m \in (0, z/2)$ that satisfies (9.10). Since $c = z - m$ and $\hat{c} - m$, it follows that $0 < \hat{c} < z/2 < c < z$. □

Hence, the dynasties use the saving instrument to partially smooth consumption in a world in which borrowing is impossible. Consumption smoothing is only partial, as the profile of consumption oscillates between two different values over time for both dynasties. Consumption fluctuates less than income, but is not completely smooth as required by efficiency. Since the asset does not pay any return at equilibrium, this can be interpreted as an economy in which people save using a monetary asset, which is why $m_{t+1} \geq 0$ was called a *liquidity constraint*. Since the monetary asset has no fundamental value but is traded at a positive price in equilibrium, it is effectively a speculative bubble. Indeed, by definition, the value of an asset has a bubble component if its price exceeds its fundamental value given by its discounted expected returns. In this case, money helps allocate resources that would not be traded otherwise; hence, the bubble is beneficial. There is always an equilibrium in which money has no value and trade does not occur. This is typical of economies with assets whose price is purely a bubble, without any fundamental value, such as money. Notice that the presence of a market imperfection, in this case the borrowing limitation, is necessary for the fiat asset to have value at the equilibrium of the dynastic model. As we have seen before, in the standard dynastic model with perfectly functioning markets, all assets are priced at their fundamental value.

Example 9.2

Suppose that the utility function is logarithmic. Then, the equilibrium balances are $m = \frac{\beta z}{1+\beta}$. Consumption in good times is $c = \frac{z}{1+\beta}$ and in bad times $\hat{c} = \frac{\beta z}{1+\beta}$.

9.3.1.2 Optimum Quantity of Money

Suppose now that the monetary authorities can alter the stock of money withdrawing or injecting some amount every period through lump-sum taxes or transfers T_t in real terms in every period. Assume that the authority changes the cash stock at a constant rate γ. The growth rate of the money stock should be large enough to guarantee that dynasties have the incentive to spend some cash every period to acquire consumption $\gamma \geq \beta - 1$. The budget constraint of the government is $M_{t+1} = M_t + T_t/p_t$ in every period, which gives $T_t/p_t = \gamma M_t/p_t$ in every period. The budget constraint of the dynasty is $c_t + (1 + \rho_{t+1})m_{t+1} = w_t l_t + m_t + T_t/2$. Clearing of the money market requires $m_t = M_t/p_t$ in each period.

In stationary equilibrium, the inflation rate is equal to the growth rate of money $\rho_t = \gamma$ in each period. The stationary equilibrium condition (9.10) is now written as

$$u'(z - m(1 + \gamma/2)) = \frac{\beta}{1 + \gamma} u'(m(1 + \gamma/2)), \tag{9.11}$$

that gives the equilibrium monetary holdings as a function of monetary policy $m(\gamma)$ and consumption for the two types as $c(\gamma) = z - m(\gamma)(1 + \gamma/2)$ and $\hat{c}(\gamma) = m(\gamma)(1 + \gamma/2)$, respectively. For the other dynasty not to be willing to save, it has to be the case that

$$u'(m(1 + \gamma/2)) \geq \frac{\beta}{1 + \gamma} u'(z - m(1 + \gamma/2)),$$

which, by Eq. (9.11), is always satisfied since the utility function is strictly increasing and $1 + \gamma \geq \beta$. The derivative of money balances with respect to monetary policy is

$$m'(\gamma) = -\frac{m(\gamma)/2}{1 + \gamma/2} - \frac{m(\gamma)}{1 + \gamma} \frac{c(\gamma)}{\hat{c}(\gamma)\epsilon_{u'}(c(\gamma)) + c(\gamma)\epsilon_{u'}(\hat{c}(\gamma))} < 0.$$

9

A higher growth rate of the money stock makes the currency less valuable, which distorts the saving decision of the dynasty, reducing its accumulation of money balances, which in turn worsens consumption smoothing. With the adoption of the Friedman rule, that is, setting $\gamma = \beta - 1$ in Eq. (9.11), consumption becomes constant over time, with equilibrium savings $m = \frac{z}{1+\beta}$ and consumption $c = \hat{c} = z/2$, thus achieving one of the efficient allocations, although not the one that corresponds to the competitive equilibrium allocation seen above. Contractionary monetary policy pays implicit interest on money balances through a deflation, increasing the incentive to save resources for the future. When the contraction of the money stock occurs at the rate that compensates the dynasties for their time discount β, perfect consumption smoothing is restored and efficiency is achieved.

9.3.2 Liquidity Provision

We now examine the question of public liquidity provision as a way to insure the dynasties against income shocks. To do so, we add uncertain labor prospects for the dynasties over time. Adding uncertainty, the model becomes hard to handle, since the liquidity constraint impedes not only the smoothing of consumption but also risk sharing, making insurance possibilities incomplete. This complicates the picture as further pecuniary externality arises with incomplete markets.

9.3.2.1 Markov Equilibrium

Consider the following simple scenario. There are two states of uncertainty, denoted by $s = 1, 2$. In the first state, only the first dynasty can work, while in the second state only the second dynasty can work. The two states alternate randomly over time. In every period, the state changes from the state of the previous period with probability π or remains the same with probability $1 - \pi$. Dynasties offer their unit of time when they have it for a competitive wage paid by a representative company that operates a linear technology that uses labor to produce output with time-invariant productivity z. The dynasties cannot borrow, but they can save using fiat money. The nominal stock of money changes at a constant rate γ over time. The stock is injected or withdrawn through lump-sum transfers or taxes, T_t in every period. We assume that transfers or taxes are the same for the two dynasties, so that they cannot be used directly to redistribute resources. This is consistent with the underlying implicit assumption that the dynasties are anonymous, which accounts for their borrowing inability.

Each dynasty maximizes its expected life-time utility, taking the expectations of (9.7), subject to the budget constraint

$$c_t + (1 + \rho_{t+1})m_{t+1} = w_t l_t + m_t + T_t/2,$$

together with the liquidity constraint $m_{t+1} \geq 0$, in every period. The complementary slackness condition is

$$\left[u'(c_t) - \beta \mathbb{E} \frac{u'(c_{t+1})}{1 + \rho_{t+1}}\right] m_{t+1} = 0,$$

in each period, since either the dynasty accumulates money optimally at the margin or does not save at all. The real wage is $w_t = z$ in each period by optimization of the company. The markets for the commodity and money should both clear in competitive equilibrium.

We consider the extension of stationary equilibrium to this stochastic environment. Suppose that the dynasty that can work accumulates money m, while the unemployed dynasty spends all its income on consumption. There are two possibilities that are compatible with this type of equilibrium. Either there is a change in the state in the current relative to the previous period, in which case the dynasty with money has no labor income and spends all its savings on consumption, or the state remains the same, and the dynasty with savings accumulates money for the future. We call this type of equilibrium the *Markov equilibrium*. Denote by c consumption of the dynasty with labor income but without savings and by $\hat{c}$ consumption of the dynasty with savings but without labor income in the first type of situation; denote by c consumption of the dynasty with labor income and savings and by $\hat{\mathsf{c}}$ consumption of the dynasty with neither labor income nor savings in the second situation. The equilibrium requires $c = \mathsf{c}$, which fixes the relative price between consumption in the two situations. The budget constraints of the dynasties and the monetary authority with market clearing together give $c = z - m(1 + \gamma/2)$ for the dynasty that saves in the first situation, $\hat{c} = m(1 + \gamma/2)$ for the dynasty that spends its savings in the first situation, and $\hat{\mathsf{c}} = m\gamma/2$ for the dynasty that spends the only source of income, namely the money transfer from the authority in the second situation. Defining $\tilde{\beta}(\gamma) \equiv \frac{\beta\pi(1+\gamma)}{1+\gamma-\beta(1-\pi)}$, the complementary slackness condition for the saving dynasty in the former situation gives

$$u'(z - m(1 + \gamma/2)) = \frac{\tilde{\beta}(\gamma)}{1 + \gamma} u'(m(1 + \gamma/2)), \tag{9.12}$$

which is the same as (9.11), modulo the rescaling of time discount. Defining $\hat{\beta}(\gamma) \equiv \frac{\beta(1-\pi)(1+\gamma)[1+\gamma-\beta(1-\pi)]}{1+\gamma-\beta(1-\pi)-\beta^2\pi^2}$, the complementary slackness condition for the dynasty that does not save in the former situation gives $m = 0$ and the inequality

$$u'(m(1 + \gamma/2)) \geq \frac{\hat{\beta}(\gamma)}{1 + \gamma} u'(m\gamma/2). \tag{9.13}$$

The condition that ensures that the dynasty without labor income and savings is not willing to save is satisfied whenever the previous incentive condition (9.13) holds. The next proposition shows that the Markov equilibrium exists close to $\gamma = 0$, that is, without intervention.

▪▪ Proposition 9.2
If $\pi \geq 1/2$ and $u'(z)\tilde{\beta}(0)^{-1} < u'(0) \leq u'(z)\hat{\beta}(0)^{-1}$, the Markov equilibrium exists without intervention.

Proof If $u'(z)\tilde{\beta}(0)^{-1} < u'(0)$, the equilibrium condition (9.12) has a unique solution $m \in (0, z/2)$ for $\gamma = 0$ using the same argument as before, since the equation is the same modulo a relabeling of time discount. If $u'(0) \leq u'(z)\hat{\beta}(0)^{-1}$, the incentive condition (9.13) is satisfied. For $\pi \geq 1/2$, we have $\hat{\beta}(0) < \tilde{\beta}(0)$ and therefore the bounds on $u'(0)$ are compatible. □

9.3.2.2 Expansionary Monetary Policy

Equilibrium money balances are a decreasing function of monetary policy as before $m'(\gamma) < 0$. When $\pi = 1$, the two states alternate every period exactly as in the previous deterministic model; therefore, the optimal policy is the Friedman rule, with $\gamma = \beta - 1$. We now use the model to find out whether the optimal monetary policy remains the Friedman rule when $\pi < 1$. The ex-ante welfare evaluated at equilibrium can be written as

$$W(\gamma) = (1 - \beta)^{-1}\{\pi[u(c(\gamma)) + u(\hat{c}(\gamma))] + (1 - \pi)[u(\mathsf{c}(\gamma)) + u(\hat{\mathsf{c}}(\gamma))]\}.$$

Since $c(\gamma) = \mathsf{c}(\gamma)$ and $\hat{c}'(\gamma) = -c'(\gamma)$, using the equilibrium condition (9.12), we can write the derivative of ex-ante welfare as

$$W'(\gamma) = (1 - \beta)^{-1}\{[1 - \pi\tilde{\beta}(\gamma)]u'(c'(\gamma)c'(\gamma) + (1 - \pi)u'(\hat{\mathsf{c}}(\gamma))\hat{\mathsf{c}}'(\gamma)\}.$$

Evaluating this derivative at the point of no intervention $\gamma = 0$, we find that $W'(0) > 0$ if $1 > \pi\tilde{\beta}(0) \Leftrightarrow \beta \geq (2 - \pi)^{-1}$, since both $c'(0) > 0$ and $\hat{\mathsf{c}}'(0) > 0$. A positive growth rate of the money stock provides the dynasties with the means to consume when they have no labor income and no savings at the cost of lowering the value of money, thus distorting the saving decision of the dynasties when they have the labor income. When the states alternate deterministically, the first effect is absent and only the second effect matters, making money contraction socially beneficial; otherwise, when the dynasties are patient, the first effect can prevail, making money creation socially beneficial. In the model with liquidity constraints and uncertainty, the economy has not only incomplete access to consumption smoothing, but also incomplete access to the instruments that help diversify risks. In such a case, the assets available to smooth consumption over time are used by traders as imperfect substitutes for the missing risk-sharing instruments. Altering the supply of these assets may improve the allocation relative to the constrained efficient benchmark, namely a situation in which the planner can only reallocate the existing asset, rather than all possible claims to consumption at all times and in all contingencies. In particular, issuing additional liquidity may be beneficial in providing a substitute for missing insurance possibilities. Hence, with uncertainty, the optimal monetary policy may sometimes deviate from the Friedman rule.

9.4 Liquidity and Capital

Finally, we examine two models with heterogeneous dynasties in which liquidity is used alongside capital as savings instruments. In the first model, liquidity and capital are substitute instruments in the allocation of resources. In the second model, they complement each other. We go back to the deterministic version of the model.

9.4.1 Substitutability

Consider a model in which there is a technology represented by a production function that uses capital as input $y_t = k_t^\alpha$, with a complete depreciation of capital in production. Suppose that capital can be used as a saving instrument. Denote consumption in the savings period as c and consumption in the spending period as $\hat{c}$. Consider first the economy without money. In a stationary equilibrium, with the two dynasties accumulating capital in alternating periods, the equilibrium condition would be

$$u'(c) = \alpha\beta k^{\alpha-1} u'(\hat{c}),$$

which equates the intertemporal marginal rate of substitution of consumption to the return of capital represented by its marginal product. Since efficiency requires $\alpha\beta k^{\alpha-1} = 1$, but consumption is not smooth over time, capital accumulation is generally inefficient. When the stationary equilibrium capital stock exceeds the efficient stock, $k^* = (\alpha\beta)^{\frac{1}{1-\alpha}}$, having an alternative liquid instrument such as money to transfer resources over time would be beneficial, helping to reduce excessive capital accumulation. This is the same in the life-cycle model with capital. If the stock of money grows or shrinks at the rate γ, for the two instruments to be held simultaneously, by the non-arbitrage principle, the return of money $(1+\gamma)^{-1}$ and the marginal product of capital $\alpha k^{\alpha-1}$ will have to be the same, giving the stationary equilibrium capital stock

$$k(\gamma) = [\alpha(1+\gamma)]^{\frac{1}{1-\alpha}}.$$

Therefore, the equilibrium capital stock is an increasing function of the growth rate of liquidity $k'(\gamma) > 0$, which corresponds to the so-called *Tobin effect*. In short, when capital and money are perfect substitute as saving instruments, making money less valuable fosters capital accumulation, since the dynasties shift their resources from money to capital accumulation, which becomes a more valuable saving instrument. Efficiency, however, requires making money more valuable, setting $\gamma = \beta - 1$, as prescribed by the Friedman rule.

9.4.2 Complementarity

9

Let us now slightly modify the model, assuming that both dynasties can work all the time but that the dynasties have alternating access to the investment opportunity based on the productive technology. Liquidity is also available in the form of fiat money, whose stock grows or shrinks at the net rate γ. In stationary equilibrium, the dynasty that has the opportunity to invest in productive activity will do so, while the other dynasty will acquire money to save for the future. The dynasties alternate over time between money saving and capital investment. Denote consumption in the investment period as c and consumption in the savings period as $\hat{c}$. The optimality condition for the investing dynasty is

$$u'(c) = \alpha\beta k^{\alpha-1} u'(\hat{c}),$$

which equates the intertemporal marginal rate of substitution of consumption between two consecutive periods to the return of capital represented by its marginal product, while the optimality condition for the saving dynasty is

$$u'(\hat{c}) = \frac{\beta}{1+\gamma} u'(c),$$

which equates the intertemporal marginal rate of substitution of consumption between the other two consecutive periods to the return of money represented by the inverse of its growth rate. Notice that, in this case, the return of money and the marginal product of capital need not be equal, given that no-arbitrage does not apply, since the two instruments are not perfect substitutes, as they cannot be used in the same capacity by the dynasties at the same time. Combining these conditions, we obtain the capital stock as a function of the growth rate of the money stock

$$k(\gamma) = \left(\frac{\alpha\beta^2}{1+\gamma}\right)^{\frac{1}{1-\alpha}}.$$

Now, the equilibrium capital stock is a decreasing function of the growth rate of liquidity, $k'(\gamma) < 0$. Hence, making liquidity more valuable fosters capital accumulation. In sum, with complementarity between the two assets, a contraction in the growth rate of the stock of money boosts capital accumulation, inducing an expansionary real effect. This is the opposite of the Tobin effect seen earlier. Efficiency requires setting $\gamma = \beta - 1$, as prescribed by the Friedman rule.

9.5 Conclusion

Borrowing limits impede consumption smoothing, thus making personal consumption respond to individual income fluctuations. In borrowing-constrained economies, asset price bubbles may arise at equilibrium, giving value to instruments that are otherwise worthless, as, for instance, fiat money, which can help people trade when borrowing is severely hampered. Liquidity may be provided equivalently through other publicly issued instruments, such as government bonds, instead of fiat money. The provision of liquidity by public authorities that would otherwise be irrelevant in a frictionless market environment may help relax liquidity constraints. When trade prospects are uncertain, optimal monetary policy faces a trade-off between the provision of the incentive to save, which requires to keep up the value of money restricting its supply, and the provision of additional liquidity for cash-strapped consumers, which requires to enlarge its supply. Money and capital can co-exist playing the same role or complementing each other, with opposite implications for the effect of monetary policy on capital accumulation.

9.6 Literature

The model with the liquidity constraint is essentially the turnpike economy presented by Robert Townsend in the paper entitled *Models of Money with Spatially Separated Agents*, which is a deterministic version of the Bewley model presented in the paper *The Optimum Quantity of Money*. In Townsend's version, the borrowing constraint is justified with a spatial separation story, whereby strangers traveling in opposite directions of a highway stop regularly to trade paying in cash because they are unable to guarantee the repayment of loans. The model with uncertainty in which monetary expansions can be beneficial filling in for missing insurance possibilities has been examined by Timothy Kehoe, David Levine, and Michael Woodford in the paper *The Optimum Quantity of Money Revisited*. The observation that liquidity may play a valuable role in borrowing-constrained economies with capital goes back to the paper by Michael Woodford entitled *Public Debt as Private Liquidity*. The Tobin effect was first identified by James Tobin in the paper *Money and Economic Growth*.

9.7 Exercises

1. Consider a competitive economy with an infinite horizon. There is a single perishable commodity that can be consumed in all periods. There are equal numbers of two types of traders with alternating unit-time endowment so that type 1 has a unit of time in odd periods and type 2 in even periods. The production function is linear, $y_t = \ell_t$. Both types order consumption sequences with the life-time utility function

$$U(\mathbf{c}) = \sum_{t=1}^{\infty} \beta^{t-1} \frac{c_t^{1-\epsilon}}{1-\epsilon},$$

with $\beta < 1$. Lowercase letters denote the choices of the first type, and uppercase letters of the second type.
- Find the efficient allocation of resources.
- Find the competitive equilibrium with complete markets in contingent claims.
- Suppose that unrestricted borrowing and lending is possible through a competitive loan market. Calculate the equilibrium amount of the loans.

9

2. Consider the same setting as in the previous but suppose that borrowing is impossible and contingent claims are unavailable. However, there is a constant supply monetary asset, M, without intrinsic value or return, that cannot be sold short but can be used as a savings instrument.
- Find the stationary competitive equilibrium.
- Compare the allocation of this equilibrium with the efficient allocation.
- Suppose that the supply of the asset can be altered and its stock has a constant growth rate over time γ. Calculate the equilibrium and determine the growth rate that implements an efficient allocation of resources.

References

Bewley T (1980), The Optimum Quantity of Money, in Models of Monetary Economies, Kareken J, Wallace N (ed), Federal Reserve Bank of Minneapolis

Kehoe T, Levine D, Woodford M (1992), The Optimum Quantity of Money Revisited, in The Economic Analysis of Markets and Games: Essays in Honor of Frank Hahn, Dasgupta P, Gale D, Hart O, Maskin E (ed), MIT Press

Tobin J (1965), Money and Economic Growth, Econometrica, 33: 671–684

Townsend R (1980), Models with Spatially Separated Agents, in Models of Monetary Economies, Kareken J, Wallace N (ed), Federal Reserve Bank of Minneapolis

Woodford M (1990), Public Debt as Private Liquidity, American Economic Review, Papers & Proceedings, 80: 382–388

House of Games

It is a common observation that the private sector not only holds routinely liquid assets with low returns, but also, at times, suddenly builds up extra liquidity holdings. Supposedly, this phenomenon, which sometimes turns into a fully fledged liquidity dry-up, has been at the root of the financial panic that has caused the Great Recession.

The dynastic model has a hard time making sense of sudden liquidity needs, as the entire wealth of the private sector is always liquid since the private sector is assumed to be able to transfer income smoothly over time and across states of uncertainty through well functioning financial markets. We have shown, in the previous part, that liquidity may have a role to play when financial markets are not working properly, but without identifying the causes of the market imperfections.

In the last part of the book, we examine models in which markets do not function properly or are absent because of fundamental reasons related to informational asymmetry or strategic interaction. In such models, trade does not occur through anonymous markets, but through contracts offered to the traders by intermediaries or through direct bilateral deals between the traders, due to the presence of elements of private information and obstacles to enforcement that make market trade infeasible. In these circumstances, distortions in the allocation of resources relative to full and even constrained efficiency may arise at equilibrium.

In the first chapter of this part, we examine optimal financial contracts in the presence of private information and limited contractual enforcement. With asymmetric information, the best societal arrangements trade off the need to provide insurance with the need to provide the incentive to reveal the private information that is relevant for the allocation of resources. Markets may be endogenously incomplete when traders have private information. In turn, contracts may be endogenously incomplete when the ability to enforce their provisions is limited.

In the second chapter, we examine the role of banks as liquidity providers. When liquidity needs are private information, deposit contracts offered by banks help provide liquidity insurance in a way that is compatible with the incentive to reveal private information truthfully by letting people withdraw their deposits at will. Unfortunately, the very feature that makes the deposit contract useful, namely the option to withdraw liquidity when needed, makes the liability side of the balance sheet of the banks fragile, potentially exposing them to runs on the deposits by their clientele. Bank runs emerge as equilibrium phenomena from the coordination of the traders' expectations on scenarios of mutual distrust. With incomplete information, the bank run is triggered by a change in fundamentals that induces a regime change, plunging the economy into a financial crisis. We use the model presented in this chapter to advance a theory of liquidity and financial crises originating from bank runs, in which the private sector coordinates its expectations on boom or bust outcomes using arbitrary non-fundamental signals or slightly imprecise signals about unknown fundamentals. Public policy intervention through deposit insurance can help prevent the crisis; alternatively, once the crisis has erupted, public liquidity provision can help prevent or at least reduce the negative spillover on the rest of the economy.

In the final chapter, we examine a scenario in which both markets and contracts are absent and trade happens on a bilateral basis. When trade is not mediated by the market mechanism, strategic externalities emerge that distort the allocation of resources. When even contracts are unavailable, strategic externalities fail to be internalized by traders. In these circumstances, fiat money can have value in equilibrium. Monetary policy has distributive effects that work to protect traders who are short of liquidity when it is most needed. A sudden monetary expansion can have positive real effects in the short run while having inflationary effects in the long run. When transactions happen on the basis of bilateral random encounters, as is often the case in the labor market, thick market and congestion externalities that are not internalized through the adjustment of the wage distort the allocations generating equilibrium unemployment.

Endogenously Incomplete Markets

L. Ferraris, *Macroeconomic Theory*, Classroom Companion: Economics,
https://doi.org/10.1007/978-3-031-88740-6_10

10.1 Introduction

We have examined several models in which risk sharing and consumption smoothing are hindered primarily for exogenous reasons. In this chapter, we examine models in which the limitations to risk-sharing and consumption smoothing emerge endogenously from deeper informational imperfections. We will examine three classes of models, with credit contracts offered by intermediaries arising as optimal responses to private information about income realizations, with endogenous incomplete markets arising from the possibility that the traders may hide their income from the risk-sharing mechanism, and with endogenous incomplete contracts arising from contractual enforcement limitations. The common thread running through these models is that either risk-sharing or consumption smoothing, or both, are limited when the credit markets do not function properly due to asymmetric information or difficulties in contractual enforcement, leading to individual profiles of consumption that follow the vagaries of current personal income.

With private information over personal income, the optimal contractual arrangement limits risk sharing and consumption smoothing relative to the fully efficient benchmark to induce the disclosure of private information. With private information about savings, risk-sharing becomes impossible, while consumption smoothing may still be viable. With limited enforcement, the contracts become endogenously incomplete, possibly disrupting also consumption smoothing.

10 In this chapter, we adopt the point of view of mechanism design, considering the best institutions to deal with information asymmetries and enforcement limitations. The institutional arrangements that emerge are the constrained efficient response of the environment to the presence of private information and the limitations of the enforcement. Hence, no further external intervention is required to help improve the situation.

10.2 Efficient Allocation

We begin with a model in which ex-ante identical traders share risks and smooth consumption over time through an optimal insurance contract when information is publicly available. The presence of private information or limited contractual enforcement will constrain efficient allocation.

10.2.1 Public Information

Consider the two-period model examined before with two types of traders, with the possibility to work one unit of time either early or late for a wage w_t in either period $t = 1, 2$. Suppose that the traders are ex-ante identical and they may be of either type with probability π and $1 - \pi$, respectively, which we assume equal for simplicity. The two types of traders have identical consumption preferences in the two periods represented by the utility function $U(c_1, c_2) = u(c_1) + \beta u(c_2)$, where the function is differentiable, strictly increasing and strictly concave, with $\beta \leq 1$.

We will denote the consumption of the first type with lowercase letters and those of the second type with uppercase letters. The traders can save resources through a technology that returns $1 + r$ units of consumption for each unit invested. For simplicity, we assume that $1 + r = \beta^{-1}$. There is a technology represented by a production function that converts labor into production each period $y_t = zl_t$.

10.2.2 Efficiency

Consider, first, the efficient allocation of resources. The aim is to choose consumption for the two types of traders in the two periods to maximize expected utility

$$\mathbb{E}U(c_1, c_2, C_1, C_2) = \pi[u(c_1) + \beta u(c_2)] + (1 - \pi)[u(C_1) + \beta u(C_2)], \tag{10.1}$$

subject to the resource constraint

$$\pi\left(c_1 + \frac{c_2}{1+r}\right) + (1 - \pi)\left(C_1 + \frac{C_2}{1+r}\right) = \pi y_1 + (1 - \pi)\frac{y_2}{1+r}, \tag{10.2}$$

where we have used $1 + r$ to discount the resources from the second to the first period. By assumption, $1 + r = \beta^{-1}$. Since traders are equally likely to be of either type $\pi = 1/2$. Since traders have a unit endowment of time, using the production function, we have $y_t = z$ for $t = 1, 2$. The optimality conditions are $u'(c_1) = u'(c_2)$, $u'(C_1) = u'(C_2)$, and $u'(c_t) = u'(C_t)$ for $t = 1, 2$. Thus, efficient allocation features constant consumption over time with an equal split of the output between the two types, namely $c_1 = c_2 = C_1 = C_2 = c^* = z/2$. The efficient allocation features full consumption smoothing for each trader and perfect risk sharing among traders. The decentralization of such an allocation may happen through market trade in securities market trade in contingent commodities or through an insurance scheme. As a consequence of the second welfare theorem, decentralization through a market system is always possible.

10.3 Credit Contract

We now modify the initial model with two periods and two ex-ante identical types of traders who become heterogeneous ex-post as regards their labor income possibilities arising either in the first or in the second period, assuming that the information concerning their ability to generate income is private. We identify the best incentive compatible contract.

10.3.1 Private Information

Suppose that the realization of uncertainty is private information of the traders, so that each trader knows whether he or she is an early or late income type, but nobody else does.

This complicates the problem of efficiently allocating resources. The allocation with complete smoothing of consumption and perfect risk sharing $c^* = z/2$ cannot be implemented with private information, since the early income types have the incentive to claim to be of the late income type, thus being able to consume both their income and efficient allocation. This, in turn, makes the allocation impossible to implement. For instance, with insurance, everybody will claim that they are of the type with late income so as to avoid having to pay the premium to the insurance. Since the insurance company anticipates that no one will pay the premium, the insurance scheme unravels.

10.3.2 Constrained Efficiency

Consider the constrained efficient allocation that takes into account that traders need to be given the incentive to reveal truthfully their private information, that is, their type. By the Revelation Principle, with private information about the realization of the state of uncertainty, the efficient allocation of resources needs to take into account not only the physical resource constraint, but also the following incentive constraint for the first type

$$u(c_1) + \beta u(c_2) \geq u(z + C_1) + \beta u(C_2), \tag{10.3}$$

since the type with the early income could pretend to be the late income type, thus, benefiting from the allocation meant for such a type while still consuming the early income. This constraint requires the allocation to be designed so as to make the early income type traders reveal truthfully their private information. The late income type traders cannot misrepresent their type because they have no income in the first period. Participation in the scheme is guaranteed since the alternative consists of consuming the current income. Therefore, the efficiency criterion that we are considering is constrained by the requirement of truthful disclosure of private information by the participants in the scheme. In other words, we are trying to determine the constrained efficient allocation, where the constraint is the revelation of private information.

Hence, we are looking for the allocation of resources among traders that maximizes the expected utility function (10.1), subject to the resource constraint (10.2) and the incentive constraint (10.3), under the maintained assumptions.

Denote by $\lambda \geq 0$ the multiplier of the incentive constraint (10.3) scaled by half to simplify the algebra. Solve the resource constraint (10.2) for $C_2 = [z(1+\beta) - c_1 - \beta c_2 - C_1]\beta^{-1}$ and substitute it into the expected utility function (10.1). The optimality condition for the consumption of the first type in the first state is

$$(1+\lambda)u'(c_1) = (1-\lambda)u'(C_2), \tag{10.4}$$

and in the second state

$$(1+\lambda)u'(c_2) = (1-\lambda)u'(C_2). \tag{10.5}$$

The optimality condition for the consumption of the second type in the first state is

$$u'(C_1) - \lambda u'(z + C_1) = (1 - \lambda)u'(C_2). \tag{10.6}$$

The consumption of the second type in the second state is determined by $C_2 = [z(1 + \beta) - c_1 - \beta c_2 - C_1]\beta^{-1}$. Finally, there is the complementary slackness condition for the incentive constraint (10.3). The following proposition characterizes the constrained efficient allocation.

Proposition 10.1
Constrained efficiency has $c_1 = c_2 > C_1 > C_2$.

Proof By (10.4) and (10.5), $c_1 = c_2 \equiv c$. From (10.6), we obtain

$$\lambda = \frac{u'(C_2) - u'(C_1)}{u'(C_2) - u'(z + C_1)},$$

that is strictly positive since the incentive constraint must be binding, otherwise the efficient allocation would be implementable. Since $C_2 < z + C_1$ and the marginal utility decreases in consumption, it has to be $C_2 < C_1$, to have $\lambda > 0$. Notice also that $\lambda < 1$, since $C_1 < z + C_1$ and the marginal utility is decreasing in consumption. Combining the optimality conditions (10.4) and (10.6), we immediately have $u'(C_1) > u'(c)$. Since the marginal utility decreases with consumption, $c > C_1$ follows. □

In sum, the constrained efficient allocation features both imperfect risk sharing and imperfect consumption smoothing for the type with the late income, while the early income type enjoys perfect consumption smoothing. These distortions relative to the fully efficient benchmark are designed to discourage the early income type of traders from selecting the allocation meant for the other type of traders, while misrepresenting their private information.

The allocation has the qualitative properties associated with financial intermediation, since the late income types are effectively paying interest for borrowing resources, while accepting limited insurance. Decentralization can be obtained assuming that there are competitive financial intermediaries offering incentive compatible credit contracts to their clients.

10.4 Incomplete Markets

We now consider an economy in which the insurance possibilities are missing, first exogenously and then endogenously.

10.4.1 Exogenous Incomplete Markets

Suppose that there are no insurance instruments to share the risk of becoming a person without early income, but there is an asset that allows one to transfer income over time without any borrowing limit, paying interest r. As seen earlier, traders will be able to smooth out consumption over time. The first type, with an early endowment, will get $c_1 = c_2 = c = z(1+\beta)^{-1}$, while the other type will get $C_1 = C_2 = C = \beta z(1+\beta)^{-1}$. Notice that $c > z > C$ whenever $\beta < 1$. The equilibrium interest of the security is $1 + r = \beta^{-1}$.

10.4.2 Endogenous Incomplete Markets

Suppose now that there exists a financial scheme offered by a competitive intermediary that allows the traders to share the risk of not having an early income, but the traders can hide their resources from the intermediary saving them secretly and privately through the market. This is a model with hidden action in which the financial contract is nonexclusive in the sense that traders can take up other investment opportunities unbeknownst to the intermediary that has offered the original contract.

In this case, risk sharing becomes impossible, as traders with early resources would simply save them privately, instead of making them available through the risk-sharing mechanism. Suppose that traders can borrow without limits. The type of traders with an early endowment will be able to save their resources privately, so, denoting the saving with s, their budget constraints will be $c_1 + s = w_1 l_1$ for the first period and $c_2 = (1+\hat{r})s$ for the second period, where
10 $\hat{r}$ is the market interest rate. By no-arbitrage, the net interest rate will have to be $\hat{r} = r$. Combining these constraints with the no-arbitrage condition, we obtain the life-time budget constraint for traders with early endowment $c_1 + \beta c_2 = w_1 l_1$. By optimization of the company, $w_t = z$ in both periods. The objective of this type of traders is to choose consumption in the two periods of life to maximize the utility function $u(c_1) + \beta u(c_2)$, subject to the previous life-time budget constraint. The first-order condition for the optimum is

$$u'(c_1) = u'(c_2),$$

that is, equal consumption, $c_1 = c_2$. Thus, traders with an early endowment can guarantee themselves an amount of consumption that is constant over time and, by the life-time budget constraint, at least equal to $z(1+\beta)^{-1}$ in the second period. Consequently, traders with the late endowment will receive at most $\beta z(1+\beta)^{-1}$ in the second period. The constrained efficient allocation will have to offer at least these quantities while satisfying the resource constraint in order to be implementable; otherwise, the traders with the early income would save their resources privately through the market. Since these quantities are distorted relative to the full efficiency benchmark and satisfy the feasibility, there is no reason to distort them further. Thus, the constrained efficient allocation boils down to $c_1 = c_2 = c = z(1+\beta)^{-1}$ for the types with early endowment and $C_1 = C_2 = C = \beta z(1+\beta)^{-1}$ for the types with late endowment. Once again, $c > z > C$ whenever $\beta < 1$. In other words, traders can perfectly smooth consumption, but they cannot insure themselves against income risks. This is the same allocation obtained in the exogenous incomplete market case, with instruments to transfer income over time, such as loans, but without financial instruments to transfer income across states of uncertainty. In sum, the model features endogenous incomplete markets that arise from the problem of hidden action. The profile of consumption follows the prediction of the permanent income hypothesis, whereby consumption should be unaffected by variations in current income, being determined by life-time wealth.

10.5 Incomplete Contracts

Next, we will examine contractual enforcement limitations that will make contracts incomplete, first in an exogenous sense, then in an endogenous sense.

10.5.1 Exogenous Incomplete Contracts

Suppose now that traders can hide a fraction $\chi \in [0, 1]$ of their labor income and consume it privately. Consider the efficient allocation with limited commitment restriction for the first type of trader, $c_1 \geq \chi z$, and for the second type of trader, $C_2 \geq \chi z$. If the fraction of the endowment that the traders can hide is sufficiently small, so that $\chi \leq 1/2$, an efficient allocation can still be achieved, as the limited commitment constraints are not binding. If the fraction of the endowment that the traders can hide is large enough, namely $\chi > 1/2$, instead, the efficient allocation cannot be achieved. The constrained efficient allocation has early consumption $c_1 = \chi z$ for the first type of trader and $C_1 = (1 - \chi)z$ for the second type of trader in the first period, and vice versa in the second period. Should commitment be impossible, that is, $\chi = 1$, the only implementable allocation would be autarky. Constrained efficiency requires that the allocations fluctuate and alternate over time for the two traders, partially following the personal income fluctuations.

10.5.2 Endogenous Incomplete Contracts

Suppose now that the traders cannot keep their commitments. Society can punish people for not delivering on their promises, but only excluding them from future trading possibilities. In other words, the enforcement of contracts is limited. Should the time horizon be finite, the threat of exclusion from trade on the last date would be empty, and any consumption smoothing scheme would unravel starting from the end.

Consider the infinite-horizon extension of the previous model. There are two infinitely lived dynasties with alternating unit labor supply, with the first dynasty being able to work in the beginning. The dynasties are ex-ante identical, turning out to be of either type from the beginning with equal probability. The technology represented by the production function $y_t = zl_t$ is available in all periods. The preferences of the dynasties over consumption sequences **c** are represented by the life-time utility

$$U(\mathbf{c}) = \sum_{t=1}^{\infty} \beta^{t-1} u(c_t),$$

where $\beta < 1$ is the time discount factor. The utility function is differentiable, strictly increasing and strictly concave, with $u'(0) = \infty$.

The efficient allocation is still $c^* = z/2$. If there are no limits to the enforcement of contracts, the competitive equilibrium allocation still satisfies the perfect risk-sharing and consumption smoothing among the traders.

10.5.2.1 Limited Enforcement

Let's consider the model with limited enforcement and examine whether the threat of excluding people who do not meet their commitments to market trade may help when there are indefinite future trading possibilities. First, let us check whether the efficient allocation is compatible with the participation of traders in the risk-sharing and consumption smoothing scheme. The tighter participation constraint occurs when the traders have the labor income, namely

$$u(c^*) + \beta u(c^*) \geq u(z) + \beta u(0). \tag{10.7}$$

10 The LHS of inequality (10.7) reflects the benefit of remaining in the arrangement enjoying efficient allocation, while the RHS reflects the payment that the trader would receive if he or she fails to stick to the contract, which would entail the immediate consumption of the entire income, but also the permanent exclusion from thearrangement henceforth. This condition can be written as

$$\beta \geq \frac{u(z) - u(z/2)}{u(z/2) - u(0)} \equiv \hat{\beta},$$

where $\hat{\beta} < 1$, by the strict concavity of the utility function. Hence, if $\beta \geq \hat{\beta}$, efficient allocation can be achieved, but not otherwise. Therefore, when traders are sufficiently patient, efficiency can be achieved.

Consider now the case in which the traders are impatient with $\beta < \hat{\beta}$. The closest we can get to consumption smoothing in this case is an allocation that alternates between two values, say, c and $\hat{c} = z - c$, for both traders over time in opposite periods. This allocation is determined so as to make them indifferent between participating in the consumption smoothing scheme, making sure that they have the incentive to stick to it, and getting out of the scheme. The relevant equilibrium condition is

$$u(c) + \beta u(z - c) = u(z) + \beta u(0), \tag{10.8}$$

since the alternative to participating in the trading arrangement with alternating consumption consists in the immediate consumption of the entire current endowment followed by the exclusion from market trade for ever, with a profile of consumption that alternates indefinitely between starvation and the consumption of the entire endowment. Since the allocation alternates every two periods for the two options, both sides of (10.8) are discounted by the same factor $1-\beta^2$, which we have removed from the notation.

Clearly, a solution of Eq. (10.8) is autarky with $c = z$. Thus, no trade is still an equilibrium, even in the model with the infinite horizon. The next proposition shows that there is also an equilibrium with trade, even when the traders are impatient.

Proposition 10.2

If $\beta \geq \hat{\beta}$, full consumption smoothing is an equilibrium. If $\beta < \hat{\beta}$, there are two stationary equilibria, an equilibrium without consumption smoothing and an equilibrium with partial consumption smoothing.

Proof The first part of the statement follows from previous considerations. The second part can be shown as follows. From Eq. (10.8), define the function $\Delta(c) \equiv u(c) + \beta u(z-c) - u(z) - \beta u(0)$, which is continuous in c. The function has the following properties: $\Delta(e) = 0$, $\Delta(z/2) < 0$ if $\beta < \hat{\beta}$, $\Delta'(z) = -\infty$ and $\Delta''(c) < 0$. Hence, $c = z$ is an equilibrium and an equilibrium with $c \in (z/2, z)$ exists and is unique. □

With an infinite horizon, traders have an indefinite future of trading opportunities. The threat of taking away such opportunities if people renege on their commitments makes it possible to sustain an efficient allocation with consumption smoothing if the traders are sufficiently patient. Otherwise, it is still possible to sustain an allocation with trade, but only with partial risk-sharing and consumption smoothing. In such an equilibrium, personal consumption fluctuates in a way that partially reflects the fluctuations in personal income, absent any shock to aggregate income. Notice that, taking into account that enforcement is limited, the allocation is constrained efficient, in the sense that it could not be improved by external intervention.

Consumption is smoother in this economy with the endogenous borrowing constraint than in the economy with the liquidity constraint and the monetary asset examined earlier in the book. The reason is that in this economy, a deviation from the equilibrium allocation is punished severely with the exclusion from trade rather than at the margin, as it happens when trade occurs using fiat money. Hence, better allocation can be sustained with smoother consumption.

Example 10.1

Suppose the utility function has a constant substitution elasticity with $\epsilon = 1/2$. The cutoff value $\hat{\beta} = \sqrt{2} - 1$. For $\beta \geq \sqrt{2} - 1$, there is perfect consumption smoothing with $c^* = z/2$ for both types at all times. For $\beta < \sqrt{2} - 1$, the equilibrium features the autarkic allocation, with $c = z$ and $\hat{c} = 0$, as well as the allocation with trade $c = \frac{(1-\beta^2)^2}{4\beta^2+(1-\beta^2)^2} z \in (z/2, z)$ and $\hat{c} = \frac{4\beta^2}{4\beta^2+(1-\beta^2)^2} z \in (0, z/2)$.

10.5.2.2 Uncertainty

The model can be extended to encompass uncertainty. Consider a model in which the availability of time for work changes over time in a random rather than deterministic fashion. Suppose that there are two possible states of uncertainty in each period. In the first state, the first dynasty has the time endowment, while in the second state the second dynasty has the time endowment. The state changes every period with probability π, while it remains the same with probability $1-\pi$. Denote by c the consumption in the state where the dynasty has time to work and by $z-c$ otherwise. We need to check that the dynasty with time for work has the incentive to stick to the arrangement. The incentive condition that determines c is

$$u(c)+\beta[\pi u(z-c)+(1-\pi)u(c)]=u(z)+\beta[\pi u(0)+(1-\pi)u(z)],$$

since, if in the current period the dynasty in question has income, in the next period its status may change with probability π leading to different consumption, while with probability $1-\pi$ the status will not change and consumption will remain the same as in the current period. Redefining the time discount as $\tilde{\beta}\equiv\frac{\beta\pi}{1+\beta(1-\pi)}$, we can rewrite the equation above as the condition without uncertainty (10.8). Hence, the solution is the same.

10.6 Conclusion

The standard model has no role for financial intermediaries, as the efficient allocation can be decentralized through market trade by the second welfare theorem. When some relevant piece of information is private, efficient allocation may no longer be decentralized through market trade. To decentralize the constrained efficient allocation that typically features distortions in the risk sharing and consumption smoothing offered to the traders in order to make them reveal their private information, contracts provided by intermediaries are often needed. The allocation entailed by the contract is distorted in relation to the efficiency to induce the disclosure of private information. In particular, some risk sharing is sacrificed to extract private information.

Hidden action problems give rise to an endogenous market incompleteness that prevents risk-sharing but allows consumption smoothing, while contractual enforcement problems give rise to an endogenous contractual incompleteness that distorts consumption smoothing, preserving some risk-sharing. The combination of these imperfections would further distort the allocations away from the efficient benchmark.

10.7 Literature

The classic model with private information about income shocks is contained in the paper entitled *Lending and the Smoothing of Uninsurable Income* by Edward Green. The model with hidden savings is contained in the paper entitled *Ef-*

ficient Allocations with Hidden Income and Hidden Storage, by Harold Cole and Narayana Kocherlakota. The model with the endogenous borrowing constraint is a simplified version of the model presented by Timothy Kehoe and David Levine in their paper entitled *Debt Constrained Asset Markets.* A comparison of debt-constrained and liquidity-constrained economies can be found in the paper entitled *Liquidity Constrained Markets versus Debt Constrained Markets* by Timothy Kehoe and David Levine.

Exercises

1. Consider an economy with an infinite horizon. There is a single perishable commodity that can be consumed in all periods. There is a continuum of ex-ante identical traders with preferences over consumption sequences represented by the life-time utility function

$$U(\mathbf{c}) = \sum_{t=1}^{\infty} \beta^{t-1} \frac{c_t^{1-\epsilon}}{1-\epsilon},$$

with $\beta < 1$. Ex-ante identical traders are equally likely to become of two types, with the possibility of working one unit of time in even or odd periods for a wage w_t. There is a company that has a technology represented by the production function $y_t = \ell_t$.

- Find the efficient allocation of resources.
- Suppose that agents can secretly save their resources through an opaque but competitive savings market. Compute the constrained efficient allocation.

2. Consider the same setting as in the previous exercise. Suppose that competitive markets are available for the exchange of commodities, but agents cannot commit to keep their promises. The punishment for failing to keep a commitment is exclusion from market trade.

- Find the stationary competitive equilibrium.
- Compare the allocation of this equilibrium with the efficient allocation.

References

Cole H, Kocherlakota N (2001), Efficient Allocations with Hidden Income and Hidden Storage, Review of Economic Studies, 68: 523–542

Green E (1987), Lending and the Smoothing of Uninsurable Income, in Contractual Arrangements for Intertemporal Trade, Prescott E, Wallace N (ed), University of Minnesota Press, 3–25

Kehoe T, Levine D (1993), Debt Constrained Asset Markets, Review of Economic Studies, 60: 865–888

Kehoe T, Levine D (2001), Liquidity Constrained Markets Versus Debt Constrained Markets, Econometrica, 69: 575–598

Bank Runs and Liquidity Crises

L. Ferraris, *Macroeconomic Theory*, Classroom Companion: Economics,
https://doi.org/10.1007/978-3-031-88740-6_11

11.1 Introduction

Banks routinely provide liquidity services to their customers. In the benchmark complete markets model without imperfections, the entire life-time wealth of the individuals is fully liquid and available for use at any time. Hence, banks do not have a role to play. Instead, with imperfections due to private information, banks may be able to play a key role in the provision of liquidity.

In this chapter, we will consider the role of deposit contracts offered by banks as tools to provide liquidity for the private sector, when liquidity needs are private information. The flexibility of the deposit contract allows the efficient allocation of liquidity, but at the cost of making the banks potentially exposed to runs on their deposits. A *bank run* occurs when most or all depositors decide to withdraw their deposits at the same time. Since banks only keep a small fraction of their deposits as reserves, investing the rest in productive activities, such an event typically triggers the bank default. This fragility of the banking system is at the root of the events that caused the liquidity crisis that contributed to the Great Recession of the late 2000s. In fact, the recession began with the failure of an investment bank and a phenomenon similar to a run on the *repo* market.

At the end of the chapter, we will show that behind the bank run model there is a *coordination failure* that is responsible for the existence of multiple Pareto-ordered equilibria. According to this point of view, a bank run is the result of the coordination of the expectations of the depositors on a crisis scenario. We will also show that, with a small amount of incomplete information, it is possible to attribute the emergence of the bank run and the ensuing liquidity crisis to a change in the regime induced by fundamental reasons, due for instance to a decline in the value of the asset side of the balance sheet of the bank, rather than the arbitrary shift in the expectations of the traders.

11.2 Bank Deposits

The next model features liquidity needs that cannot be insured through market trade when these needs are the private information of traders. Deposit contracts offered by banks are the instrument that allows one to decentralize efficient allocation with private information, but they are fragile to banking panics. We begin with the benchmark scenario in which the liquidity needs are public information.

11.2.1 Public Information

The are two time periods after the current time. There is a technology represented by the production function $y = zl$ that uses labor to produce output in the current period. There is a continuum of people who are currently uncertain about their future liquidity needs. There are two possible types of traders, those who will have urgent liquidity needs in the next period, denoted with $t = 1$, and those who can wait longer, until $t = 2$. The traders are ex-ante identical and may be of either type with probability π and $1 - \pi$, respectively. Traders with urgent liquidity needs only enjoy consumption at time $t = 1$, with preferences represented by the utility function $u(c_1)$, while traders without urgent liquidity needs can wait until the second period to consume, with preferences represented by the utility function $\beta u(c_1 + c_2)$, discounting the future at rate $\beta < 1$ and evaluating consumption in the two periods as perfect substitutes. The utility function is differentiable, strictly increasing and strictly concave.

The traders have an initial unit endowment of time supplied as labor earning a competitive wage $w = z$ that can be invested in a productive activity that returns $1 + r$ units of consumption for each invested unit if the investor waits until time $t = 2$, but returns only one unit if the investor withdraws the resources at time $t = 1$. For simplicity, we will assume that $1 + r = \beta^{-1}$. In sum, traders can obtain a high return from their investment in the long run if they can wait, but may only get back the initial investment if they have to liquidate it to satisfy their urgent liquidity needs in the short run.

Individually, traders would simply invest the initial endowment, liquidating it if they find that they have urgent liquidity needs at $t = 1$ and obtain only the initial investment z, while obtaining z/β, instead, at time $t = 2$, if they do not have any urgent liquidity needs in the short run.

11.2.1.1 Efficient Risk Sharing

Suppose now that risk sharing among traders is possible. Consider, first, the efficient allocation of resources. Clearly, late consumption should not be assigned to early consumers and early consumption should not be assigned to late consumers. The aim is to choose consumption for the traders in the two periods to maximize their expected utility

$$\mathbb{E}U(c_1, c_2) = \pi u(c_1) + (1 - \pi)\beta u(c_2),$$

subject to the resource constraint

$$\pi c_1 + (1 - \pi)\beta c_2 = z, \tag{11.1}$$

where we have used $\beta = (1 + r)^{-1}$ to discount the resources from the second to the first period. Write the resource constraint (11.1) as $c_1 = \pi^{-1}[z - (1 - \pi)\beta c_2]$ and substitute it into the expected utility to be maximized with respect to c_2. The optimality condition is $u'(c_1) = u'(c_2)$, which is equivalent to $c_1 = c_2$, namely equal consumption for the two types. Inserting this condition back into the resource constraint, we obtain

$$c_1 = c_2 = c^* = \frac{z}{\pi + \beta(1 - \pi)}. \tag{11.2}$$

Notice that, since $\beta < 1$, the efficient consumption $c^* \in (z, z/\beta)$ is larger than the initial endowment and smaller than the full return, hence, the efficient allocation provides insurance for the traders against liquidity shocks.

The efficient allocation can be decentralized through a market system, using financial instruments or with a competitive fringe of insurance companies.

11.2.2 Private Information

Suppose now that the realization of uncertainty about the liquidity needs of the traders is their private information. In such a case, the decentralization of efficient allocation c^* through the insurance schemes provided with market means becomes impossible, as traders of the late type without urgent liquidity needs will have the incentive to pretend to be of the early type with urgent liquidity needs so as to avoid paying the premium and receiving the reimbursement instead. Since all late-type consumers would behave in this way, any market insurance scheme would break down.

However, notice that consumption in efficient allocation is the same for the two types, $c_1 = c_2 = c^*$. Hence, if we can find a scheme that allows its decentralization, the efficient allocation does not create any incentive to misrepresent the private information, since the late consumers would not obtain any benefit from pretending to be the early type had the efficient allocation been offered to them. The only problem is to find an incentive feasible way to offer traders the efficient allocation.

11.2.2.1 Deposit Contract

11

This can be done by competitive banks that offer deposit contracts to their clients. The deposit contract works as follows. A person deposits resources with the bank, maintaining the right to withdraw his or her deposit at any time, possibly earning an interest on the deposit. In the meantime, the bank invests the deposits in the productive technology. Should the depositors decide to withdraw their deposit, they will be served by the bank sequentially as they appear at the counter. Thus, there is a *sequential service constraint*, which prevents the bank, in the event of a run, from being able to spread the available resources among all depositors. This is the source of the fragility of the liability side of the balance sheet of the banks.

Setting the interest on the deposits so that $i = c^*/z - 1$, an efficient allocation would be achieved, since late consumers would have no incentive to withdraw their resources, provided they expect everybody else to behave accordingly. Substituting (11.2) into $i = c^*/z - 1$, we obtain the interest on the deposits

$$i^* = \frac{(1-\beta)(1-\pi)}{\pi + \beta(1-\pi)},$$

that is strictly positive, since $\beta < 1$. Thus, a competitive banking system that offers deposit contracts at the interest rate i^* can help achieve efficient allocation of resources, using the fact that, by the law of large numbers, there will be some people who are more patient than the rest, whose resources can be used to provide liquidity for impatient people with urgent liquidity needs.

11.2.2.2 Bank Run

The potential problem with this arrangement is that the depositors may have different expectations about the behavior of the other depositors. The successful implementation of efficient allocation through the banking system relies on the late-type depositors to expect all other depositors to behave according to their type, so that all early-type depositors withdraw their resources in the first period, while all late-type depositors wait until the second period.

However, nothing prevents a late-type depositor from having reasonable doubts about the reliability of the scheme. In fact, should all other depositors decide to withdraw simultaneously in the first period, the bank would have to start liquidating the investment early, obtaining only the initial capital without any return. Since the deposit contract pays positive interest i^* even to those depositors who withdraw early and the depositors need to be served sequentially, the bank would quickly run out of resources before being able to reimburse all depositors who attempt to withdraw. The conclusion that the depositor would draw is that his or her bank account would be wiped out if he or she decided to wait until later, while rushing to the bank to withdraw immediately, there would still be some hope of being able to withdraw the deposit before the bank goes bust.

Thus, if a depositor expects all other depositors to run to the bank to withdraw in the first period, it is rational for him or her to run to the bank as well. Since this is true for every depositor, a bank run, defined as a situation in which all depositors try to withdraw their deposits in the first period, is an equilibrium.

Thus, we have a situation with two equilibria. In the first case, everything goes according to plan and an efficient allocation is reached. In the second, the depositors have pessimistic expectations about each other, these expectations become self-fulfilling, and the bank run occurs. The consequence is that the bank will disinvest the entire amount of resources from the productive project and a fraction of the depositors will get nothing. A rational panic would have erupted, destroying economic value.

11.2.2.3 Suspension of Convertibility

There are two widely adopted schemes to try to prevent banking panics. The first is called the *suspension of convertibility*. If the bank can commit to stop serving clients after a fraction π of them has withdrawn, then the rest of the depositors would have nothing to fear, knowing that the rest of the deposits would remain safe at the bank. This scheme requires that the bank knows the overall fraction of early-type depositors, something we have assumed so far, but may not hold in reality.

When π is not common knowledge, the optimal contract is more complicated than the simple deposit contract we observe in reality. The reason is that the stream of withdrawals in the first period reveals information to the bank about the unknown fraction of the early types. The optimal payment scheme should depend on this information. To see the point, consider the following thought experiment. Suppose that first a group of depositors shows up at the bank in the first period with known proportions of the two types. The payments to these guys are the same as in the model above. Then, a second group of depositors showing up is either all early or late. When the first depositor of this group shows up to withdraw their resources, a lot of information is revealed to the bank. In any efficient arrangement, the payment offered to this group cannot be the same as the payment offered to the previous group. In other words, the payments of any efficient arrangement have to depend on the sequence of withdrawals, as this reveals information about the unknown proportion of early and late types.

Moreover, even when such a proportion is known, the suspension of convertibility is a blunt instrument that is supposed to work as a threat to prevent bank runs but may suffer from time inconsistency. Should a bank run occur anyway, since the suspension of convertibility is not optimal ex-post because several customers of the early type would still attempt to withdraw, the bank may have the incentive to flout the commitment to stop payments and continue serving the depositors at least for a while even after having served a fraction π of them. However, this time inconsistency problem of the bank could make the bank run more likely in the first place, as the depositors anticipate that the bank may not suspend the convertibility when needed after all.

11.2.2.4 Deposit Insurance

The other tool to prevent bank runs is the *deposit insurance* provided by the public authorities through general taxation or the banking system through a fund financed by individual banks that guarantees deposits up to a certain value. In particular, suppose that the government can tax the people who have withdrawn their deposit early. Unlike the bank that is subject to the sequential service restriction, the government can base the tax on the total amount withdrawn at the end of the first period. With this extra freedom relative to the banking system, the government can always set the tax so as to achieve efficient allocation in any case, discouraging unnecessary early withdrawals and making it a dominant strategy for traders without urgent liquidity needs to wait until the second period. Deposit insurance is a valid instrument to reassure depositors who do not need liquidity that even in the case of a bank run, their resources will be preserved, thus eliminating the incentive to run to the bank in the first place. The problem with this scheme is that it may generate a moral-hazard problem on the asset side of the balance sheet of the bank, since there would be an incentive for the banks to invest in riskier assets, knowing that their liability side is insured.

11.2.2.5 Banks and Markets

Paradoxically, the presence of well-functioning markets can impede the functioning of the banking system. Suppose that the depositors have access to market trade after discovering their types. In particular, depositors can borrow and lend resources at the market rate. Assume that trade among depositors is inscrutable to their bank. The market rate must be equal to the technological return $1 + r = \beta^{-1}$, to avoid arbitrage opportunities. For the traders to be willing to deposit their resources at the bank and participate in such transactions revealing truthfully their types it has to be that

$$u(\beta c_2) \geq u(c_1). \tag{11.3}$$

Thus, early consumption cannot be larger than discounted late consumption, otherwise, the patient depositors would pretend to be impatient. The incentive condition (11.3), and the resource constraint, (11.1), that can be written as $c_1 = \pi^{-1}[z - (1-\pi)\beta c_2]$, together imply $c_2 \geq z/\beta$ and therefore $c_1 \leq z$. Since traders can always obtain at least the allocation $c_1 = z$ and $c_2 = z/\beta$ by investing on their own in the productive technology without depositing their resources in the bank, it follows that autarky is the only equilibrium. In other words, liquidity insurance becomes impossible. Therefore, the possibility for agents to engage in opaque market transactions after having deposited their resources may hinder the provision of liquidity by the banking system.

Public authorities may help rescue the situation by introducing a regulation that imposes a liquidity floor on banks. Setting the minimum liquidity requirement appropriately, at the level that guarantees consumption c^* for those depositors who withdraw early, could help restore efficiency. With more liquidity around in the first period, the market interest rate would be lower, thus discouraging trade in the market. If the liquidity requirement is set at the right level, the interest rate would be so low that no one would have the incentive to trade on the side of the market. Thus, imposing the liquidity floor, the authorities would exploit the presence of a pecuniary externality to restore efficiency.

11.3 Bank Liquidity

Banks offer liquidity services, issuing demand deposits to their clients, and use the funds thus collected to finance illiquid entrepreneurial projects. The activity is inherently fragile, since the depositors can withdraw their funds at any time, while the funds are tied up in productive ventures that require time to pay off. The question is whether this combination of short-term and long-term activities is the result of a historical accident or there is a deeper rationale that binds the two.

11.3.1 Limited Commitment

Consider the following scenario. There is an entrepreneur and some investors. The entrepreneur can develop a project that needs a unit investment in the present to generate a positive net return in the future but does not have the resources to start it. Investors have the resources, but not the know-how to activate the project. The initial resources of the investors are durable. Both sides enjoy linear utility of consumption without discounting. There is no private information. The entrepreneur can sign a debt contract with investors, promising a payment at the end of the project. If the repayment does not happen, the investors can liquidate the project. Suppose that the entrepreneur cannot commit to providing the human capital that is necessary for the project to generate the future return, because the human capital of a person is inalienable. Without the contribution of the entrepreneur, the project cannot generate any return, and dispersed investors have no ability to extract any value from the entrepreneur in renegotiation. In this situation, investors anticipate that after signing the contract and obtaining financial resources, the entrepreneur will try to renegotiate any contract that gives him less than the full return of the project. As a consequence, investors refuse to finance the entrepreneur and keep the resources until the final date for personal consumption. Thus, a project with positive net present value is not financed.

Suppose now that there is a financial intermediary who has no initial resources but can extract a fraction of the return from the entrepreneur being able to reassign the project to somebody who can produce a smaller but still positive return from the project. Thus, in a renegotiation with the entrepreneur, the intermediary can obtain a positive fraction of the return of the project. However, the intermediary has liquidity needs of its own that arise before the completion of the project. To satisfy these liquidity needs, the intermediary tries to obtain a loan from investors through a debt contract. Unfortunately, the intermediary has the same problem with respect to the investors as the entrepreneur, being unable to commit to provide the human capital necessary to extract the payment from the entrepreneur. The prospect of a renegotiation with the intermediary discourages investors who do not provide their funds, and the valuable project remains inactive.

11.3.2 Bank Fragility

Suppose that the intermediary can issue demand deposit contracts to investors, thus effectively becoming a banker. Then, should the banker try to renegotiate the initial contract, investors would threaten to withdraw their deposits. Since a bank run would completely destroy the rent of the banker, the incentive of the banker to renegotiate down the reimbursement to the investors disappears. Hence, the contractual arrangement involving a demand deposit contract allows the project to get off the ground. This occurs not despite the fragility of the arrangement, but precisely because the demand deposit contract is fragile being exposed to potential runs. The lesson is that, in a world with contractual incompleteness, demand deposit contracts may turn out to be optimal to finance illiquid investments since the fragility inherent in the contract provides the investors with a bargaining chip should renegotiation occur, and this assuages their ex-ante fear of being extorted ex-post.

11.4 Liquidity Crisis

Coordination failures arise in environments characterized by the presence of a strategic complementarity, that is, a situation in which the decisions of the agents mutually reinforce each other. We will illustrate the point in a simplified version of the bank-run model.

11.4.1 Coordination Failure

Consider a static model with a continuum of people who have a unit of resources deposited in a bank. People can withdraw, obtaining their unit back, with zero net interest, or leave their resources in the bank invested in an activity whose net profit depends positively on the productivity of the underlying investment technology but negatively on the fraction n of those who decide to withdraw, $z - n$, with $z \in (0, 1)$ being the net productivity of thc investment. The latter option is potentially more rewarding but depends on the others' decisions, while the former option is not rewarding but safer. There is a *strategic complementarity* at work, since the incentive to keep the resources at the bank decreases with the fraction of the population that withdraws the deposits, hence increasing in the fraction of those that keep the resources at the bank.

People make their decisions simultaneously and independently. A Nash equilibrium is a combination of choices by people so that no one has the incentive to unilaterally change choice. The game has three Nash equilibria. In the first equilibrium, all the people keep the resources in the bank, in the second all the people liquidate the investment and withdraw their resources, in the third a random fraction z of the people liquidates while the others keep the investment.

Due to the continuum assumption, single-agent deviations do not alter the aggregates. A unilateral deviation from the first situation reduces the payoff for the deviating person, since $z > 0$; deviating unilaterally from the second situation also lowers the payoff for the deviating person, since $z < 1$; finally, a deviation from the third situation does not improve the payoff according to the continuum assumption. Notice that the first equilibrium dominates the other two equilibria in the sense of Pareto, since people get strictly higher benefits in the first equilibrium than in the other two, since $z > 0$.

This is a coordination game in which the outcome depends on the expectation that every player has on the behavior of the others. The players may end up coordinating their expectations on the inefficient outcome as in the banking model seen earlier. The situation in which everybody liquidates the investment and withdraws the resources from the bank corresponds to the bank run equilibrium. Extrinsic events, such as sunspots, may help the players coordinate their actions on the different scenarios.

11.4.2 Regime Change

Suppose now that the productivity z is unknown to the depositors, being a random variable normally distributed with a mean in the unit interval and a positive variance. The value of the productivity is determined before the beginning of the game, but its realization is not revealed to the depositors, who receive, before playing the game, different and slightly disturbed signals of such a realization with an error term that is distributed normally with zero mean and positive variance. The inverse of the variance represents the precision of the signal.

After receiving the signals, the depositors update their beliefs about the value of productivity and the possible signals received by others. Based on this information, depositors calculate their expected payoff and decide whether to keep their resources invested or not. Assume that, when indifferent to withdrawing or not, the depositors withdraw their deposit. A strategy is a function that maps each realization of the signal into a choice of action. A strategy profile for all depositors is an equilibrium if no one has incentive to change choice unilaterally given the available information.

Since random variables are normally distributed, the posterior probability of productivity after observing a certain signal, denoted by ζ, is a convex combination of the mean of the prior of productivity and the signal received using the relative precision of the two random variables as weight. Next, after updating the belief about the value of the productivity, the depositor will try to figure out the posterior probabilities of the others. Denote by $n(\zeta)$ the fraction of depositors with a posterior smaller than ζ. By the assumption of normality on the error term, the function $n(\zeta)$ is differentiable in ζ and behaves well at least for small noise. In particular, if the signal is sufficiently precise relative to the prior, namely, its variance is sufficiently small relative to the prior variance, $n'(\zeta) < 1$ in the relevant range of ζ. This follows from the properties of the cumulative distribution function of the normal distribution. Thus, we obtain the following result.

Proposition 11.1

If the signal is sufficiently precise relative to the prior, there is a *unique equilibrium* in which all depositors withdraw their deposit if $\zeta \leq \zeta^*$, while no one withdraws if $\zeta > \zeta^*$.

Proof Suppose that the signal is sufficiently precise and consider a depositor who gets a signal reporting that the productivity is strictly negative. For such a depositor, keeping the investment is strictly dominated no matter what the others will do, and hence the deposit is withdrawn. Consider now a depositor with a signal reporting that productivity is nil. If the signal is sufficiently precise, this depositor is virtually certain that the productivity of the investment is nil and believes that a positive fraction of the population, $n(0) > 0$, has received a signal reporting a negative productivity value. Facing a negative expected payoff, the depositor will liquidate the investment, withdrawing the deposit from the bank. This reasoning can be extended to strictly positive values of the signal. Indeed, consider someone with a signal that is only slightly positive, who believes that a significant fraction of the population is either indifferent or unwilling to keep the investment. By continuity, this depositor still has a negative expected payoff, and hence withdraws the deposit. Consider now a depositor who has received a signal reporting a productivity value larger than 1. People with such signals have a strict incentive to keep their investment no matter what others do. A depositor with a signal that reports a unit productivity value believes that less than the entire population has a smaller signal $n(1) < 1$. Such a depositor obtains a strictly positive payoff from keeping the investment and hence will not withdraw the deposit. By continuity, also a depositor who has received a signal reporting a slightly smaller value of productivity still has a positive payoff and, hence, keeps the resources at the bank. Since the payoff $U(\zeta) \equiv \zeta - n(\zeta)$ is continuous in ζ with $U(0) < 0$, $U(1) > 0$, and $U'(\zeta) = 1 - n'(\zeta) > 0$ when the signal is sufficiently precise, there is a unique value ζ^* such that $U(\zeta) = 0$, that is, the cutoff dividing the two regions.

In other words, with a small amount of incomplete information, so that the value of the prior is almost certain for all depositors but is not common knowledge among them, the equilibrium of the game is unique and depends on the value of the prior on the productivity of the investment, namely its fundamental value, since the posterior is extremely close to the true value of the productivity, $\zeta \approx z$. The equilibrium features a bank run when the investment is not sufficiently productive, but not otherwise. Hence, a crisis can be attributed to a sudden change of fundamentals, like a drop in productivity, rather than the coordination of the expectations in a negative scenario, as in the previous coordination failure story. Thus, this is a theory of financial crises based on fundamental tipping points that induce regime changes.

Notice that, when the prior is more precise than the signal, the function $n(\zeta)$ is non-monotonic and multiple equilibria reemerge, thus recovering the result of the game with complete information about the productivity.

11.5 Great Recession

According to most observers, the Great Recession of the years 2008–2012 was caused by a liquidity crisis. At the origin of the liquidity crisis there was a phenomenon akin to a bank run. The prequel of the crisis was the bursting of the house price bubble that had been inflating in the mid-2000s. This contributed to the induction of the financial turmoil and exacerbated its effects.

11.5.1 Repo Market

The crisis began in the United States in mid-September 2008 when the investment bank Lehman Brothers went bust. Due to financial regulation that forbade commercial banks from taking on too risky positions, by the early 2000s, the investment banks had become the center of the American banking system as they were able to pay the higher returns associated with higher risks that commercial banks could not offer. Investment banks and other large financial institutions were routinely exchanging liquidity in the *repo* market, a market for short-term liquidity where collateral, typically in the form of government bonds and other safe assets, is required to secure the loans. During the summer of 2008, investors lost confidence in the ability of some investment banks, such as Lehman Brothers, to redeem their short-term loans. As many financial institutions were simultaneously looking for liquidity to be able to meet the demand of their customers who were asking to liquidate their positions, the liquidity provided through the repo market began to dry up. At the same time, investment banks, scrambling for liquidity, were selling their assets at fire sale prices, including the safe assets used to secure loans in the repo market. The drop in asset prices worsened the liquidity crisis, tightening borrowing constraints and leading to a severe downturn with a major contraction of GDP that lasted for a few years, eventually moving on to affect most developed economies around the world. The situation can be seen as a systemic bank run of the type described in this chapter combined with the burst of a bubble that led to a drop in asset prices, which in turn made secured borrowing harder.

11.5.2 Policy Intervention

During the crisis, the US Federal Reserve intervened to provide fresh liquidity, which helped rescue some of the financial institutions from bankruptcy, but the intervention occurred too late to prevent the crisis from spilling over to the real sector. The Fed and subsequently other central banks, including the European Central Bank, came up with an unconventional policy instrument called *quantitative easing*, whereby the monetary authorities acquire private assets and securities to protect asset and security prices during a liquidity crisis, thus trying to ease the private sector borrowing restrictions. Moreover, after the crisis, new legislation was established to try to prevent the onset of a financial crisis by imposing the so-called *macroprudential* regulations, aimed at preventing the behavior that may lead to systemic financial crises of the type seen during the Great Recession. The key instruments of macroprudential policy are the liquidity, capital, and reserve requirement ratios of financial institutions. The aim of macroprudential policy is to prevent the build-up of the crisis and the pecuniary externalities that go with it.

In sum, there are two main policy approaches to a liquidity crisis. On the one hand, there is the view that favors ex-post intervention to provide liquidity when most needed after the crisis has occurred. This may be done through conventional or unconventional policy instruments and may occur on the equilibrium path or off-path as in the case of deposit insurance. On the other hand, there is the view that favors ex-ante intervention to try to avoid the crises altogether by limiting the risk-taking behavior of financial institutions, imposing minimum liquidity standards even in normal times.

11.6 Conclusion

When liquidity is at stake, banks that offer deposit contracts make it possible to achieve even efficient allocation of resources while inducing the disclosure of the depositors' private information about liquidity needs as they withdraw their deposits. However, the deposit contract is fragile, exposing the bank to rational panics that may lead to bank runs based on the self-fulfilling expectation that a run will occur. These phenomena, typical of coordination failures, are at the root of liquidity crises. The crisis may be triggered by the pessimistic expectations of the private sector or by exogenous shocks to the fundamentals that cause a regime change. The combination of this type of endogenous mechanism that generates liquidity crises with the amplification mechanism through borrowing constraints examined earlier in the book may give a fairly accurate picture of what happened at the onset of the Great Recession.

11.7 Literature

The model with the demand deposit contract is a simplified version of the model of Douglas Diamond and Phillip Dybvig in their pioneering paper entitled *Bank Runs, Deposit Insurance, and Liquidity*. The book by Bengt Holmstrom and Jean Tirole entitled *Inside and Outside Liquidity* examines related models with informational imperfections. The point that private equity markets may destroy the insurance offered by banks was originally made by Charles Jacklin in the paper *Demand Deposits, Trading Restrictions, and Risk Sharing*. The issue has been examined again in the paper *A Theory of Liquidity and Regulation of Financial Intermediation* by Fahri, Golosov and Tsyvinski. The argument that there may be strength in the fragility of the demand deposit contract has been put forth by Douglas Diamond and Raghuram Rajan in the paper entitled *Liquidity Risk, Liquidity Creation, and Financial Fragility: A Theory of Banking*. Coordination games are the subject of the book *Coordination Games: Complementarities and Macroeconomics* by Russell Cooper. The regime change model is a simplified version of the framework examined by Stephen Morris and Hyun Song Shin in the paper *Rethinking Multiple Equilibria in Macroeconomic Modeling*. The techniques of regime change games can be applied to a wide range of phenomena, including currency crises, the pricing of debt, and political turmoil. The paper *Liquidity Crises* by Robert Lucas and Nancy Stokey provides a theoretical framework to interpret the Great Recession as a kind of bank run, with key policy implications to cope with liquidity crises.

Exercises

1. Consider the banking model with two time periods, $t = 1, 2$, beyond the initial planning period. Suppose that there is a continuum of traders who may turn out to be impatient, i.e. in need of resources to consume in the first period, with probability π or patient, i.e. willing to consume in any of the two periods, with probability $1 - \pi$. Suppose that the preferences for consumption of the agents are represented by the expected discounted utility.

$$EU(c_1, c_2) = \pi \frac{c_1^{1-\epsilon}}{1-\epsilon} + \beta(1-\pi)\frac{c_2^{1-\epsilon}}{1-\epsilon},$$

with $\beta < 1$, where c_t is the consumption at time t. There is a technology that allows to produce $1 + r \geq \beta^{-1}$ units of the commodity in the second period per unit invested initially, but returns only one unit if disinvested in the first period. All traders initially have one unit of resources and have access to this technology.

- Calculate the efficient allocation.
- Verify that the efficient allocation can be decentralized even with private information about the traders' types.
- Determine under which condition the equilibrium allocation features insurance.
- Calculate the interest rate that the bank can offer on deposits to implement efficient allocation.
- Check that agents have the incentive to withdraw if they think everyone else is withdrawing the deposit.

References

Cooper R (1999), Coordination Games: Complementarities and Macroeconomics, Cambridge University Press

Diamond D, Dybvig P (1983), Bank Runs, Deposit Insurance, and Liquidity, Journal of Political Economy, 91: 401–419

Diamond D, Rajan R (2001), Liquidity Risk, Liquidity Creation, and Financial Fragility: A Theory of Banking, Journal of Political Economy, 109: 287–327

Farhi E, Golosov M, Tsyvinski A (2009), A Theory of Liquidity and Regulation of Financial Intermediation, Review of Economic Studies, 76: 973–992

Holmstrom B, Tirole J (2011), Inside and Outside Liquidity, MIT Press

Jacklin C (1987), Demand Deposits, Trading Restrictions and Risk Sharing, in Contractual Arrangements for Intertemporal Trade, Prescott E, Wallace N (ed), University of Minnesota Press, 26–47

Lucas R Jr, Stokey N (2011), Liquidity Crises, Economic Policy Paper, Federal Reserve Bank of Minneapolis, 11, 3

Morris S, Shin HS (2001), Rethinking Multiple Equilibria in Macroeconomic Modeling, NBER Macroeconomics Annual 2000, 15: 139–182

Search Model: Money and Unemployment

L. Ferraris, *Macroeconomic Theory*, Classroom Companion: Economics,
https://doi.org/10.1007/978-3-031-88740-6_12

12.1 Introduction

The models examined so far had either well-functioning competitive markets or contracts offered by financial intermediaries. In this chapter, we will examine situations in which markets and contracts are not available and trade happens in a bilateral and haphazard manner, over-the-counter as it were, making the interaction genuinely strategic. In this strategic environment, known as the *search-and-matching model*, a situation is an equilibrium if no one wants to unilaterally change behavior, as dictated by the Nash equilibrium concept. Strategic interaction generates externalities among traders that make resource allocation inefficient, leading to unemployment. Moreover, coordination failures can emerge, giving rise to multiple Pareto-ordered equilibria with different levels of economic activity. Interestingly, coordination failures can provide a rationale for the use of fiat money as a payment instrument that helps overcome the difficulty created by the absence of well-functioning markets when both barter and credit transactions are hindered.

We use the search-and-matching model to discuss the only major phenomenon that has been left out of the picture so far, namely unemployment. By definition, unemployment is involuntary; therefore, the decline in employment obtained in the benchmark model due to a drop in the wage cannot be interpreted as unemployment. For a long time, unemployment has been considered a phenomenon incompatible with equilibrium, since it requires the absence of market clearing in the labor market. In the search-and-matching model, unemployment emerges due to the frictional nature of the labor market in which companies and workers meet bilaterally at random, negotiating the wage on the spot to divide the bilateral gains from trade. In this setting, the wage has no equilibrating role to play for labor market aggregates, opening the door to unemployment.

12.2 Barter

We will begin with a model of barter in which people trade commodities in bilateral meetings with strangers. Multiple, Pareto-ordered equilibria emerge in this setting. The coordination among equilibria may happen through sunspot events or incomplete information as in the literature on global games and the so-called sentiments.

12.2.1 Multiple Equilibria

Suppose that there is a continuum of traders living on an island. Each trader has a coconut tree at home. The traders can pick up a coconut at night from their tree, but there is a taboo that prevents them from eating it. However, traders can exchange their coconut for someone else's coconut the next morning and eat it. Coconuts are durable only if they remain in the hands of the original owner; otherwise, they must be consumed immediately. Islanders do not trust each other, so trade has to happen through barter, coconut for coconut. People can pick and carry one coconut at a time. Coconut picking happens at night; barter happens the next day. Picking a coconut costs $v > 0$, and eating a coconut provides utility $u > v$. People interact indefinitely over time, but always with different trading partners, discounting the future at a rate $\beta < 1$. When two traders with coconuts meet, they inspect their trading partner item and announce simultaneously whether they want to trade or not, and if they both agree to trade, they swap their coconuts; otherwise nothing happens, and the two traders return home.

If traders do not expect anyone else to pick coconuts, they should not pick coconuts, so starvation is always an equilibrium. We now check whether picking a coconut and trading it may be an equilibrium. For the situation in which every time the traders pick coconuts at night and trade them the next morning to be an equilibrium, no one should be willing to unilaterally deviate from such a situation. Notice that, since $u > 0$, traders are certainly willing to trade their coconut for another coconut, once they have picked it, since the cost is sunk. We only need to check whether the traders are willing to pick up a coconut tonight to trade it the next day rather than staying home and getting nothing, namely $-v + \beta u \geq 0$. This incentive condition is satisfied if and only if $\beta \geq v/u$. Therefore, the Pareto dominant situation in which people pick coconuts and trade them is an equilibrium if they are sufficiently patient. There is also a mixed strategy equilibrium when the inequality above is strict. Thus, we have a coordination game with multiple Pareto-ordered equilibria in which there may be full employment, partial, or complete unemployment. The equilibrium with full employment is efficient, since trade should always occur, with $u > v$. In the other equilibria, trade is inefficiently low. The multiplicity arises from coordination failures among the traders. Thus, economic fluctuations may be interpreted as arising endogenously from the coordination of the traders' expectations across equilibria with and without unemployment, perhaps guided by sunspot events.

12.2.2 Sentiments

Suppose now that coconuts are divisible. Picking y coconuts costs $v(y) = y/z^{\epsilon}$ where z is a productivity parameter and consumption of y units gives utility $u(y) = (1-\epsilon)^{-1}y^{1-\epsilon}$ with $1 - \epsilon = \beta$. When two traders meet, they simultaneously announce a quantity of coconuts to be traded. If the announcements coincide trade occurs, otherwise nothing happens. There is a continuum of equilibrium quantities $y \in [0, z]$. The highest production corresponds to efficiency. Fluctuations may occur due to the coordination of the traders on different equilibria over time. Rather than relying on the coordination of the traders' expectations among multiple equilibria, the literature on market *sentiments* generates endogenous fluctuations that arise from the failure of coordination of their beliefs around the unique equilibrium. For example, suppose that the efficient equilibrium with $y = z$ is selected through a competitive trading scheme, but the productivity z of each trader is subject to shocks. The shock is realized during the evening, and remains the traders' private information. Suppose that traders receive private signals about the productivity of their trading partners that are not fully informative with limited precision. In addition, traders receive a second signal about the precision of the signal of their trading partners, which, in turn, has limited precision that is common to all signals and uncorrelated with productivity. This common element reflects the sentiment of the market that affects the beliefs about the beliefs of others without affecting the productivity or the beliefs about productivity. Following a negative realization of the sentiment shock the traders reduce production because of their pessimistic beliefs about the other traders' beliefs about their beliefs about productivity. Fluctuations are driven by market sentiments.

12.3 Money

Consider a situation in which barter is not possible, since there is specialization in both production and consumption. There are several (at least three) varieties of commodities and several (at least three) types of people. Each type produces a variety and consumes a different one. This pattern of specialization is known as *absence of double coincidence of wants*. Trade occurs in bilateral meetings. Credit is impossible since the same two traders do not meet each other more than once in their life-time, and actions are not observable by people who are not present in the trade meeting. Commodities are perishable and indivisible. Production and consumption happen simultaneously on the spot rather than sequentially as in the previous coconut model. The rest is the same as in the coconut model. Since trade has been completely hampered by imperfections, the only equilibrium is autarky.

12.3.1 Monetary Trade

Suppose that we add a durable object without intrinsic value, namely fiat money. Money is indivisible, and people cannot hold more than one unit of it. Initially, a fraction $m \in (0, 1)$ of each type has a unit of money, while the remaining fraction $1 - m$ does not have money. Since people will have no incentive to throw money away if it is valuable, these fractions remain the same over time, assuming that people cannot accumulate more than one unit of money.

If accepted by traders, money can function as a means of payment. Suppose that the traders are matched in such a way that potential buyers are always matched with potential sellers. Each trader is equally likely to be a potential buyer or seller in every period. The only situation in which there will be trade is one in which the potential buyer of the commodity has a unit of money and the seller has no money. In such meetings, the potential buyer will offer a unit of money in exchange for a unit of the commodity, and the potential seller will decide whether to accept, in which case the trade occurs, or reject, in which case nothing happens. The other meetings will remain unproductive, since a buyer without money has no way to pay for his or her purchases, and a seller with money will not trade being unable to accumulate an additional unit of money. Hence, the number of meetings in which trade occurs is at most $m(1 - m)$.

12.3.1.1 Equilibrium

No trade is always an equilibrium, since acquiring money requires a production that is costly and it is not worth for traders to undergo such a cost if they expect to be unable to spend it to acquire consumption in the future. We now check whether there is an equilibrium with monetary trade. Assuming that people trade money for commodities whenever possible, the expected value of the buyers with money is

$$V = (1 - m)(u + \beta U) + m\beta V,$$

since they will meet sellers without money with probability $1 - m$ spend the money and consume, but with probability m will be unable to spend the money and consume, remaining in the same state until next period. The sellers without money, in turn, expect the following value

$$U = m(-v + \beta V) + (1 - m)\beta U,$$

since they will meet buyers with money with probability m and produce for them thus acquiring money, but with the complementary probability meet a buyer without money, remaining in the same state until next period. Since traders have the same probability of being buyers or sellers, we have absorbed the corresponding factor of 1/2 into the payoffs.

Clearly, there is an incentive to spend money wherever possible, since $V > 0$. Note also that there is no incentive to dispose of money once acquired, since $V - U = (1 - m)u + mv > 0$. For monetary trade to be an equilibrium, it has to be that the sellers are willing to accept money rather than reject the offer; therefore, we need to check that $U \geq 0$.

Solving the conditions above simultaneously, we obtain the expected value for the sellers without money

$$U = (1 - \beta)^{-1} m\{-v + \beta[u - m(u - v)]\}, \tag{12.1}$$

that needs to be non-negative. Therefore, monetary trade is an equilibrium if and only if the traders are sufficiently patient, namely

$$\beta \geq \frac{v}{u - m(u - v)}.$$

The lower bound on discounting is tighter than the one obtained in the barter model v/u, because the uncertainty about trade arising from monetary exchange requires people to be more patient in order to be willing to accept money as payment. The lower bound increases with m, as sellers anticipate that spending money will be less likely in the future if there are more money holders around. There is also a mixed strategy equilibrium when the inequality above is strict.

12.3.1.2 Welfare

Efficiency would require that trade occurs in all meetings between buyers and sellers. In the monetary equilibrium, however, this does not occur since money is badly distributed relative to the needs of trade because some buyers who would need money to acquire consumption do not have it, while some sellers who do not need it have it. The ex-ante welfare of the traders in the monetary equilibrium is given by

$$W \equiv mV + (1-m)U = (1-\beta)^{-1}m(1-m)(u-v),$$

where the number of meetings in which trade occurs is $m(1-m) < 1$. There are two contrasting effects of m on the number of productive meetings. On the one hand, with a larger fraction of money holders, the number of buyers who will be able to spend money to consume is larger, but, on the other hand, the number of sellers with money is also larger, which crowds out trade as they will refuse to produce. The best scenario that maximizes ex-ante welfare is a compromise between these two opposing forces in which half of the traders have money, since $m(1-m)$ is maximal for $m = 1/2$.

12.3.1.3 Intensive Margin

Let us now introduce the intensive margin. Suppose that commodities are divisible. Production occurs with the technology represented by the function $y = l$. Labor has utility costs $v(l)$ with $v'(l) > 0$ and $v''(l) \geq 0$ for every $l \geq 0$ and consumption c generates utility $u(c)$ with $u'(c) > 0 > u''(c)$ for every $c \geq 0$. Assume $u(0) = v(0) = 0$ and the existence of a unique positive $\bar{y}$ such that $u(\bar{y}) = v(\bar{y})$. Trade occurs in bilateral meetings; hence, $c = y = l$. The efficient amount y^* is such that $u'(y^*) = v'(y^*)$. To compute the new expected value, in particular for the sellers with money, simply replace the parameters u and v with the corresponding functions in the condition (12.1) above, obtaining the function

12

$$U(y) = (1-\beta)^{-1}m[\beta(1-m)u(y) - (1-\beta m)v(y)].$$

Next, we determine the quantity produced, traded, and consumed in the bilateral meetings. Since traders, when they meet bilaterally, are locked in a situation that is essentially a bilateral monopoly because each party has something the other wants, the outcome of the negotiation over the amount to be traded is indeterminate. To determine the amount traded in a meeting in which the buyer has money and the seller does not have any, we will assume that the former makes a take-it-or-leave-it offer to the latter, extracting all the surplus generated by trade. In other words, we assume that the buyer with money has all the bargaining power in the bilateral meeting. Thus, the quantity y is determined by the condition that makes the sellers without money indifferent between accepting or rejecting the offer of the buyers, namely $U(y) = 0$. Since $u(0) = v(0) = 0$, it follows that no trade is an equilibrium. The next proposition proves that there exists also a monetary equilibrium with trade.

Proposition 12.1

There is a unique stationary monetary equilibrium quantity $\hat{y} \in (0, \bar{y})$ for any m.

Proof Since $U(\bar{y}) < 0$, $U(0) = 0$ and $U'(0) = \infty$, by the continuity of $U(y)$ in y there is a $\hat{y} \in (0, \bar{y})$ such that $U(\hat{y}) = 0$ for any $m \in (0, 1)$. Since $U''(y) < 0$ for all $y \geq 0$, $\hat{y}$ is unique.

Denote by $y(m)$ the equilibrium amount of trade as a function of the fraction of money holders, implicitly identified by equation $U(y) = 0$. Its derivative evaluated in monetary equilibrium, using the implicit function theorem, is

$$y'(m) = \frac{1-\beta}{\beta(1-m)^2} \frac{v(\hat{y})}{v'(\hat{y})} \left[\frac{u'(\hat{y})}{v'(\hat{y})} - \frac{u(\hat{y})/\hat{y}}{v(\hat{y})/\hat{y}} \right]^{-1},$$

which is negative since $u'(y) < u(y)/y$ for all $y \geq 0$ due to the strict concavity of $u(\cdot)$ with $u(0) = 0$ and $v'(y) \geq v(y)/y$ for all $y \geq 0$ due to the convexity of $v(\cdot)$ with $v(0) = 0$. Hence, in the equilibrium with trade, the quantity produced in each meeting is decreasing in the fraction of money holders. This occurs because the trading prospects of the sellers worsen when there are more people with money, as the presence of a larger fraction of money holders makes future spending opportunities less likely. As a consequence, the incentive to produce for money is reduced, and the amount produced at each meeting decreases when m is larger. Since one unit of money buys y units of consumption, the price of a transaction, which is also the price level, is the inverse of the quantity traded. Hence, an increase in m increases the price level.

Example 12.1

Suppose that the utility function is $u(y) = (1-\epsilon)^{-1} y^{1-\epsilon}$ with $\epsilon < 1$ and the cost function is $v(y) = y$. Using these functions in the equilibrium condition, $U(y) = 0$, we obtain the equilibrium production at each meeting $y(m) = [\beta(1-m)]^{\frac{1}{\epsilon}} [(1-\epsilon)(1-\beta m)]^{-\frac{1}{\epsilon}}$.

12.3.1.4 Efficiency

Efficiency requires that trade occurs in all meetings with the amount y^* produced in each meeting. The monetary equilibrium is inefficient on both dimensions, since trade occurs only in a fraction $m(1-m)$ of meetings, and production within meetings in general differs from y^*, since the bargaining power of buyers distorts the allocation within meetings relative to efficiency.

Example 12.2

Continuing with the previous example, the efficient amount is $y^* = 1$. Therefore, there is efficient production within meetings if and only if $\beta = (1-\epsilon)(1-\epsilon m)^{-1}$, while there is under-production for lower values and over-production for higher values of β relative to efficiency.

12.3.2 Monetary Policy

Suppose that the monetary authority can alter the fraction of money holders m by distributing cash to people who do not currently hold it or taking cash from those who currently hold it. Let us see how this affects total output and welfare.

12.3.2.1 Output

Monetary policy has two potentially contrasting effects, arising from the extensive and the intensive margin, respectively, on aggregate output, defined as the amount of trade in each productive meeting times the fraction of meetings in which trade occurs, namely

$$Y(m) \equiv m(1-m)y(m).$$

This can be seen computing its derivative with respect to the fraction of money holders, obtaining

$$Y'(m) = (1-2m)y(m) + m(1-m)y'(m),$$

where the first term is positive if and only if less than half of the people have money, $m < 1/2$, while the second term is unambiguously negative, since $y'(m) < 0$. When less than half of the people hold money, a monetary expansion increases the overall amount of trade, improving the extensive margin, but at the expense of the amount traded in each meeting, worsening the intensive margin. When more than half of people have money, an additional increase unambiguously reduces total output. Expansionary monetary policy has an insurance effect up to the crowding out value when half of the people have money, since it provides some buyers with the means to acquire consumption, but has a disincentive effect on the sellers since it makes it less likely for them to be able to spend their
12
money to acquire consumption in the future.

Example 12.3

Continuing with the previous example, $Y(m)$ increases in m if and only if $m < \hat{m}$ where $\hat{m}$ is the smallest root of $\epsilon - [\epsilon(2+\beta) + 1 - \beta]m + \epsilon\beta m^2 = 0$.

12.3.2.2 Welfare

Consider now the effect of m on the welfare of the traders. Using the equilibrium condition $U(y) = 0$, we can express the ex-ante welfare in the monetary equilibrium as

$$W(m) \equiv mV(y(m)) + (1-m)U(y(m)) = \beta^{-1}mv(y(m)),$$

whose derivative with respect to m is

$$W'(m) = \beta^{-1}[v(y(m)) + mv'(y(m))y'(m)].$$

The first term in parentheses is positive, reflecting the extensive margin, while the second term is negative, reflecting the intensive margin. Whether a monetary expansion increases welfare or not depends on the relative strength of these two effects. In general, the overall effect on welfare is ambiguous.

Example 12.4

Continuing with the previous example, we obtain $W(m) = \beta^{-1} m y(m)$ that increases in m if and only if $m < \tilde{m}$ where $\tilde{m}$ is the smallest root of $\epsilon - [\epsilon(1+\beta) + 1 - \beta]m + \epsilon\beta m^2 = 0$.

12.3.2.3 Short Run Vs Long Run

Suppose now that the monetary authority, at some point, increases the fraction of traders holding money giving one unit of money to some people who don't currently have it. The traders know that there may be an injection or not with equal probability, but they do not initially know its realization that is publicly revealed only in the following period. Assume that less than half of the people have money to begin with and, even with the injection, the fraction of money holders remains below half. We need to check that the traders are willing to exchange money for the commodities both in the initial period and subsequently after the value of the injection has been revealed. When injection becomes common knowledge, the equilibrium is the same as the one described above. In the initial period, buyers who have received money and those who do not have different posterior beliefs about the completion of the injection. To ensure that both types of traders are willing to spend their money, assume that the injection is sufficiently small.

The policy injection has its full effect on the extensive margin in the aftermath of the intervention without affecting the intensive margin and the price level, since the traders do not know the realization of the injection. In particular, producers, whose outside value determines the price, will only be able to use the expected value of the injection to calculate their payoffs. Instead, after the intervention is publicly revealed, the traders will factor in the realized value of the injection, which will be reflected in the intensive margin, generating an increase in the price level that is larger the larger the realization of the injection. Therefore, a sudden expansion of monetary policy boosts income in the short run through the extensive margin effect that makes the economy more liquid but has an inflationary effect in the long run through the intensive margin effect that lowers the incentive to produce and increases the price level.

12.4 Payment

Cash is increasingly replaced by intangible devices as means of payment. However, as the economy becomes cash-less, it may still remain monetary. The key feature of money is that the payment is *quod pro quo*, occurring at the same time as the corresponding delivery of the good or service by the counterpart. Since monetary payments, being final, do not generate any future obligations, the parties involved in the transaction do not need to share any personal information or even reveal their names to each other, as they have no further business to accomplish after the transaction has been completed. As is well known, monetary payments guarantee privacy and anonymity, so that complete strangers can trade while remaining complete strangers. The down side is that monetary purchases are constrained by the traders' past history, as reflected in their current money holdings, which may be insufficient to finance the desired level of expenditures. This is the limitation of monetary payments captured by the cash-in-advance model. Moreover, if the trading process is bilateral and haphazard, unlike in the cash-in-advance but as in the search model, money sometimes happens to be in the hands of people who do not currently need it, while some of those who would urgently need it are cash-strapped. If trading prospects are uncertain and market possibilities to acquire liquidity at short notice are absent, the distribution of money at any time matters for the allocation of resources. This is the reason why monetary expansions may be beneficial with uninsurable liquidity shocks. However, the key feature of credit is that it allows people to delay payments with respect to the time of the delivery of goods and services, using future income to pay for current purchases. This requires a willingness to give up some privacy and anonymity for the benefit of better risk sharing and smoothing of consumption. Credit-based payment systems are more information-intensive than money-based ones, requiring a more elaborate memory of transactions. Correspondingly, credit-based systems are less sensitive to distributional issues than money-based ones, at least as regards the needs of trade.

12.4.1 Memory

Consider the monetary search model with bilateral random meetings, indivisible goods, and the absence of double coincidence of wants. Suppose that there is a technology that allows monitoring of the transactions of the traders within the bilateral meetings. The records are kept in a publicly available memory that can be accessed by anyone at any time at no cost. Next, we show that money can be seen as a rudimentary form of memory.

12.4.1.1 Money as Rudimentary Memory

Fix an allocation with monetary trade. Now, take money out of the system and replace it with a system of gifts as follows. At any time, let every seller, who was in a position to trade the good for money with a buyer in the corresponding monetary economy, give a unit of the good as a gift to the trading partner. Correspondingly, let the technology register on the public record a positive score for the sellers who give gifts and a negative score for the buyers who receive gifts, while in all other situations, no change is made to the record. By construction, this replicates exactly the pattern of trade generated by the monetary economy through a network of gifts and a simple accounting system that updates the public record of scores gained for giving the gifts or lost for receiving them. Therefore, money is just a physical device for achieving trade that can be obtained alternatively using a publicly accessible technology that keeps the record of the transactions constantly updated. The conclusion is that money is a form of memory of past transactions.

However, not all memory-based allocations can be obtained with money. Consider efficient allocations that involve trade in all meetings. These allocations can be achieved with the record-keeping technology when the traders are sufficiently patient, excluding from the exchange system the traders who refuse to give gifts when in a position to produce for a trading partner. However, efficient allocations cannot be achieved as a monetary equilibrium, since traders who acquire money need to be rewarded with better options than traders who do not hold money; otherwise, no one would have the incentive to acquire money in the first place. In other words, in a monetary economy, trade cannot happen in a way that is independent of the money holdings of the traders; otherwise having money would not matter and the incentive to acquire it would vanish. Since some equilibria that can be supported with memory cannot be supported with money, while all equilibria that can be supported with money can also be supported with memory, we conclude that money is an imperfect form of memory.

12.4.1.2 Money and Credit

The record-keeping technology that undergirds public memory can be used to implement a credit-based trading system. Suppose that the traders arrange to adhere to the following societal agreement. Every trader who is in a position to produce does so for the trading partner unless a deviation from the agreement has been detected, in which case nobody ever produces for anyone anymore. Basically, people produce for strangers hoping to be rewarded in the future. This social credit scheme is supported by the threat to end up in autarky if anyone who is in a position to produce refuses to do so at any time. The threat is credible since the information used to trigger the collective punishment for non-compliance is made publicly available through the record-keeping memory technology. For traders to have an incentive to stick to the arrangement, they must be sufficiently patient $\beta \geq v/u$. Since trade occurs in all meetings, ex-ante welfare is given by $W^* = (1-\beta)^{-1}(u-c)$. Clearly, if the public memory is available, cash is not essential to perform transactions, in the sense that its use would only make matters worse since trade would happen only in the fraction of meetings in which the buyer has money. When technology is not available, instead, money is essential to perform at least some transactions, since the economy would otherwise collapse to autarky. Consider the best-case scenario where half of the people are initially endowed with money. In this case, the incentive condition is $\beta \geq 2v/(u+v)$. Since trade occurs in a fourth of the meetings, the ex-ante welfare is $W^*/4$. If money and memory are both available, but the technology sometimes malfunctions so that the public record fails to be updated with some probability, then a continuity argument shows that there are values of the probability with which the public record is updated such that the optimal trading arrangement features a mix of money and credit. Money serves to trade when record-keeping malfunctions. However, technological improvements in the credit system that eliminate malfunctions will eventually drive out money.

12.4.2 Digital Currency

The view that money is a rudimentary form of memory implies an idea of substitution between money and credit, which in turn leads to the conclusion that technical advances that improve the functioning of credit will eventually wipe out money. However, technical advances in payment systems seem to evolve in a different direction, toward payments based on digital currency. This type of currency is more information-intensive than cash because its flows and balances can be recorded and kept in a potentially accessible memory, but the information about the corresponding transactions of goods and services remains private. The payment is still quid pro quo and final, so the digital currency is a monetary instrument, not a credit instrument. This type of technological improvement may not make the economy money-less even as it makes it cash-less. However, additional information available on digital currency flows can be used to improve the distribution issue that affects monetary economies without expanding the currency stock.

12.4.2.1 Trade Mechanism

Suppose that in the search model the payment system is based, instead of cash, on a digital currency whose holdings and flows can be recorded and traced. We take this as the key difference between a digital instrument and physical cash, which can be hidden, and hence its holdings and flows cannot be traced. This additional information can help reallocate digital currency in meetings in which trade would not occur because the currency is held by the seller rather than the buyer. If a short-term currency loan could be arranged within these meetings, more trade would occur. In principle, this currency reallocation is beneficial, provided that it does not destroy the incentive to acquire currency. To check whether this is true, we adopt the point of view of mechanism design. Suppose that in meetings in which the digital currency is in the account of the potential seller instead of the buyer, the digital currency is transferred by the seller to the buyer, who then returns it to the seller to acquire consumption. In these meetings, the commodity is produced and transferred with probability $\pi \in [0, 1]$. To support this trade, the record-keeping system threatens to take away the currency from the account should it find out that it had remained idle in the account during the period. In the other meetings, everything happens as before. For simplicity, we assume that half the traders are initially endowed with currency. Given this arrangement, the expected value of a currency holder at the beginning of any period is

$$V(\pi) = \frac{u - \pi v + \beta[V(\pi) + U(\pi)]}{2},$$

since the trader is currently either in a position to spend currency or lend it having to produce with probability π and, then, in the future will continue participating in the trading system either as a currency holder or not; the expected value of a trader who starts a period without currency is

$$U(\pi) = \frac{\pi u - v + \beta[V(\pi) + U(\pi)]}{2},$$

since the trader is currently either in a position to acquire money or borrow it to consume with probability π and, then, in the future will continue participating in the trading system either as a currency holder or not. The difference in these expected values gives the net value of the currency as a function of π

$$\mathcal{V}(\pi) \equiv V(\pi) - U(\pi) = \frac{(1-\pi)(u+v)}{2},$$

which decreases in π and is positive if and only if $\pi < 1$, since if traders knew that consumption could certainly occur even without holding currency, they would have no reason to acquire it, causing the value of the currency to completely depreciate. Note that the digital currency system is equivalent to the traditional cash-based system for $\pi = 0$.

12.4.2.2 Incentive Compatible Mechanisms

We now define incentive-compatible mechanisms π. There are five incentives to be checked. First, the buyer with digital currency should be willing to spend it rather than waiting for future trade opportunities, $u \geq \beta\mathcal{V}(\pi)$. This incentive condition is satisfied since $u > v$. Second, the seller without digital currency should be willing to acquire it, $\beta\mathcal{V}(\pi) \geq v$. This requires that the probability with which trade occurs in meetings in which there is a currency loan is not too large

$$\pi \leq \frac{\beta(u+v) - 2v}{\beta(u+v)} \equiv \hat{\pi},$$

where $\hat{\pi} \geq 0 \Leftrightarrow \beta \geq 2v/(u+v)$, which coincides with the condition that would prevail in the corresponding cash economy with half of the traders holding money. Hence, the trade equilibrium with digital currency exists precisely when the trade equilibrium with traditional cash does. Third, a buyer without digital currency who receives the transfer should be willing to spend it, as the money would be taken away if it is not spent at the end of the period. This requires $\pi u \geq 0$ which is satisfied since $u > 0$ and $\pi \geq 0$. Fourth, a seller with currency should agree to transfer it to the buyer $\beta\mathcal{V}(\pi) \geq \pi v$, which is implied by the incentive condition for the seller with electronic money, since $\pi \leq 1$. Fifth, we should make sure that buyers with money do not have the incentive to dispose of their currency to receive currency loans and consumption with probability π from sellers with currency, that is, $\beta\mathcal{V}(\pi) \geq \pi u$. This requires that the probability of trade with the loan is not too large

$$\pi \leq \frac{\beta(u+v)}{\beta(u+v) + 2u} \equiv \tilde{\pi}.$$

Finally, when two traders with currency meet, they swap it to avoid being taken away. This is incentive compatible if $\beta\mathcal{V}(\pi) \geq 0$, which is true since $\pi \leq 1$. Therefore, a mechanism is incentive compatible if and only if $\pi \le \min\{\hat{\pi}, \tilde{\pi}\} \equiv \overline{\pi} < 1$, to maintain the incentive to acquire, hold, lend, and spend currency.

12.4.2.3 Optimal Mechanism

The aim is to identify the best incentive compatible mechanism, namely a $\pi \le \overline{\pi}$ that maximizes ex-ante welfare of the traders. The ex-ante welfare is given by the expected value of starting with or without digital currency, which happens with equal probability

$$\mathcal{W}(\pi) \equiv \frac{V(\pi) + U(\pi)}{2} = \frac{1+\pi}{4} \frac{u-v}{1-\beta}.$$

Since $\mathcal{W}(\pi)$ is strictly increasing in π, the best incentive compatible mechanism sets the probability to the upper bound, that is, $\pi = \overline{\pi}$. In meetings in which currency is in wrong hands, trade occurs with less than certainty to maintain the incentive to acquire currency. Should traders expect to be able to consume in any case whether they hold currency or not, the incentive to acquire it would vanish. The lower probability of trade can be interpreted as a lower quantity traded in these meetings, giving rise to an implicit interest rate for these transactions that involve a short-term currency loan.

Since the digital currency system can always replicate cash simply ignoring the information about the currency flows, the ex-ante welfare in the economy with digital currency is at least as high as the ex-ante welfare in the economy with cash. For $\beta > 2v/(u+v)$, the digital currency system strictly improves on cash-based systems, since liquidity is reallocated according to trading needs in meetings in which the currency is present but in wrong hands with $\overline{\pi} > 0$. Compared to the memory-based credit system, the digital currency does worse $\mathcal{W}(\overline{\pi}) < W^*$ since trade occurs in meetings in which one of the two traders, the buyer or the seller, has currency, but not otherwise. Although cash-less, the economy remains monetary. In sum, digital currency can help allocate liquidity according to trading needs, moving it from those who have it and do not currently need it to those who do not currently have it but need it, through short-term loans without enlarging its stock.

12.5 Labor

For a long time, unemployment has been considered incompatible with the equilibrium of the labor market. The search model we are examining instead shows that unemployment can be rationalized as an equilibrium phenomenon.

12.5.1 Job Search

Consider a model of the labor market in which companies hire one worker at a time, meeting them individually and randomly. Denoting with n_v the number of vacancies of companies and n_u the number of unemployed people at a given point in time, suppose that companies and workers are matched bilaterally according to a function with constant returns to scale that gives the number of matches N as

$$N = n_v^{\sigma} n_u^{1-\sigma}$$

with $\sigma \in (0, 1)$. This function captures in reduced form the imperfections that prevent the possibility of arranging a competitive labor market. For simplicity, suppose that work relationships last for one period and then dissolve.

Denote by $n \equiv n_v/n_u$ the ratio of vacancies to unemployed workers, known as the tightness of the labor market. The fraction of meetings in the number of vacancies represents the probability that a single company will meet a worker, $N/n_v = n^{\sigma-1}$ and the number of meetings in the number of unemployed represents the probability for a person to find a job offer $N/n_u = n^{\sigma}$.

We will assume that a match between a company and a worker produces an output z, which reflects the productivity of a company-worker pair, and the worker is paid a wage w. Opening a vacancy costs κ. Companies compete among themselves for vacancies.

In any period, a company needs to pay the cost κ in order to open a vacancy, obtaining $z - w$ if the vacancy is filled, which happens with probability $n^{\sigma-1}$ provided the job offer is made and accepted, but nothing otherwise. Since there is free entry at the stage of the opening of vacancies, competition will drive the expected profits to zero, $n^{\sigma-1}(z - w) = \kappa$, which gives

$$n = \left(\frac{z - w}{\kappa} \right)^{\frac{1}{1-\sigma}}. \tag{12.2}$$

An unemployed person earns a non-negative unemployment subsidy $s < z$. This can be interpreted, more generally, as the workers' outside option. In any period, an unemployed person expects to earn a salary, w, when hired by a company, that occurs with probability n^{σ} provided the job offer is made and accepted, or to receive the subsidy, s, with the complementary probability.

12.5.1.1 Wage Bargaining

Once a company and worker have met, they are locked in a situation of bilateral monopoly, since each side has something valuable to offer to the opposite side. In a bilateral monopoly, the wage is indeterminate. Consider, for instance, the following wage determination game. Each side of the transaction announces, independently and simultaneously, a wage. If the two announcements coincide, the company will pay such a wage to the worker; otherwise, the two part their ways. This game has a continuum of equilibria for any wage $w \in [s, z]$. As a consequence, there will also be a continuum of equilibrium values of market tightness and unemployment rates. This is a version of the unanimity game proposed by Nash as a non-cooperative foundation of situations of negotiation and bargaining.

To resolve the indeterminacy, Nash proposed using a procedure known as Nash bargaining. We will follow the idea of Nash and assume that the company and the worker bargain over the determination of the wage, according to the Nash bargaining procedure, that identifies the wage that maximizes the product of the surplus of the company, $z - w$, and the surplus of the worker, $w - s$, using the parameter $\nu \in [0, 1]$ as the bargaining power of the company. This is the only procedure that satisfies four natural requirements in this environment, namely that the bilateral gains from trade should be exhausted, the two sides should be willing to engage in the bargaining, the solution should be scale invariant and independent of irrelevant alternatives. Accordingly, the wage is chosen to maximize the so-called Nash product

$$(z - w)^{\nu}(w - s)^{1-\nu},$$

whose solution reflects in part the productivity of the worker within the company, z, and in part his or her outside option, namely the unemployment subsidy, s, giving

$$\hat{w} = (1 - \nu)z + \nu s, \tag{12.3}$$

where the productivity and the unemployment benefit are combined through the bargaining power of the company and the worker. The stronger the power of the worker in the bargaining, the closer the wage will be to his or her productivity, and, vice versa, the stronger the power of the company in the bargaining, the closer the wage will be to the outside option of the worker, namely the unemployment subsidy. Notice that the wage does not reflect the tightness of the labor market, n, since the negotiation occurs bilaterally between a single worker and the company after they have already matched. Thus, the wage will not help internalize the externalities that workers and companies exert on each other due to frictional matching.

12.5.1.2 Incentives

For companies to be willing to offer jobs to workers, it should be the case that $z \geq w$. For workers to be willing to accept job offers, it should be the case that $w \geq s$. These two conditions are verified simultaneously if $w \in [s, z]$. Given the wage determined in equation (12.3) with $\nu \in [0, 1]$, companies have the incentive to offer jobs, since $\hat{w} \leq z$, and workers have the incentive to accept offers, since $\hat{w} \geq s$. Since $\hat{w} \in [s, z]$, the situation is an equilibrium.

12.5.1.3 Unemployment

To compute the equilibrium labor market tightness and unemployment, substitute the wage (12.3) into condition (12.2), obtaining

$$\hat{n} = \left[\frac{\nu(z - s)}{\kappa}\right]^{\frac{1}{1-\sigma}}. \tag{12.4}$$

In a stationary equilibrium, the fraction of people who find a job, $n^\sigma n_u$, and the fraction of employed people, $1 - n_u$, should coincide in every period, giving $n^\sigma n_u = 1 - n_u$. Therefore, the unemployment rate satisfies the condition $n_u = (1 + n^\sigma)^{-1}$, into which we plug (12.4), obtaining the equilibrium unemployment rate

$$\hat{n}_u = \frac{\kappa^{\frac{\sigma}{1-\sigma}}}{\kappa^{\frac{\sigma}{1-\sigma}} + [\nu(z - s)]^{\frac{\sigma}{1-\sigma}}}. \tag{12.5}$$

Therefore, unemployment is positive in equilibrium. The reason why there is equilibrium unemployment is that the matching of workers and companies is frictional with ex-post wage bargaining rather than mediated by a competitive labor market. Notice that wage and market tightness are increasing, while the unemployment rate is decreasing in productivity z. This extends the real business cycle theory to a setting with unemployment.

12.5.1.4 Policy

Consider the effect of two policy interventions on the unemployment rate, namely an increase in the unemployment subsidy and the introduction of a minimum wage. From equation (12.5), it follows that an increase in the subsidy, s, increases the equilibrium unemployment, since it increases the outside option of the workers who become pickier about accepting or rejecting the job offers. The introduction of a minimum wage is irrelevant if the minimum wage is less than or equal to the equilibrium wage (12.3). If the minimum wage is higher than (12.3), then, substituting it into (12.2) and using this condition to determine the unemployment, it is easy to see that the equilibrium unemployment is higher than without the minimum wage. This is because companies are less willing to open vacancies when the wage is higher.

12.5.2 Inefficiency

We adopt a notion of constrained efficiency assuming that the planner cannot eliminate the frictions connected with the matching technology. Therefore, market tightness is still given by the zero-profit condition (12.2) and unemployment is still determined by $n_u = (1 + n^\sigma)^{-1}$.

The efficient allocation can be determined by maximizing the expected profit of companies $n^{\sigma-1}(z - w)$ with weight $\vartheta > 0$, and the expected benefit of workers $n^\sigma(w - s)$ with weight $1 - \vartheta > 0$. The aim is to choose the market tightness, n, and the wage, w, to maximize the welfare function

$$W(w, n) = \vartheta n^{\sigma-1}(z - w) + (1 - \vartheta)n^\sigma(w - s).$$

The first-order condition with respect to the wage w gives $\vartheta = n/(1 + n)$. The first-order condition with respect to the market tightness n is

$$(\sigma - 1)\vartheta n^{\sigma-2}(z - w) + \sigma(1 - \vartheta)n^{\sigma-1}(w - s) = 0.$$

Inserting $\vartheta = n/(1+n)$ into this condition, we obtain the constrained efficient wage

$$w^* = (1-\sigma)z + \sigma s,$$

that reflects both the productivity of the worker and his or her outside option, through the elasticity of the matching probability, given by σ. By condition (12.2) with w^*, the tightness of the constrained efficient market is

$$n^* = \left[\frac{\sigma(z-s)}{\kappa}\right]^{\frac{1}{1-\sigma}}.$$

By condition $n_u = (1+n^\sigma)^{-1}$ with n^*, the constrained efficient unemployment rate is

$$n_u^* = \frac{\kappa^{\frac{\sigma}{1-\sigma}}}{\kappa^{\frac{\sigma}{1-\sigma}} + [\sigma(z-s)]^{\frac{\sigma}{1-\sigma}}}.$$

The equilibrium wage, the equilibrium market tightness, and the equilibrium unemployment $(\hat{w}, \hat{n}, \hat{n}_u)$ are different from the constrained efficient values (w^*, n^*, n_u^*), except when $\nu = \sigma$. This is known as the *Hosios condition*, from the name of the economist who discovered this property. Since ν captures the bargaining power of companies and σ the elasticity of the matching function, there is no reason to expect these parameters to be related in any way. In other words, these parameters are only equal by sheer chance. Therefore, in general, the job search equilibrium is constrained inefficient.

12

12.5.2.1 Externalities

There are two externalities at work. First, there is a congestion externality since every additional unemployed person looking for a job lowers the probability that other unemployed workers will find a job and every additional company lowers the probability that other companies will fill their vacancies; second, there is a thick market externality since every additional person looking for a job increases the probability that companies will fill their vacancies and every additional company increases the probability that unemployed people will find a job. Being the wage determined by bargaining ex-post, after the company-worker match has been formed, these externalities are not internalized by the traders through the wage.

When $\nu > \sigma$, the unemployment rate is too small relative to constrained efficiency, since the unemployed and the companies search too much for job matches, failing to internalize the congestion externality that prevails in this scenario; when $\nu < \sigma$, instead, the unemployment rate is inefficiently large, as the unemployed and the companies search too little, failing to internalize the thick market externality that prevails in this case.

12.5.2.2 Competitive Labor Search

Arranging the labor market so that companies can compete to attract workers posting their wage offers and workers can observe all the job offers and apply for the best offers while still being matched randomly to companies if several workers end up applying for the same job offers leads to a constrained efficient solution with frictional unemployment. The reason is that ex-ante wage posting, unlike ex-post bargaining, allows us to internalize the search externalities on both sides of the labor market, allowing us to achieve (w^{*}, n^{*}, n_u^{*}). The literature that assumes this type of wage setting process is known as the competitive labor search literature. Suppose that, at the outset, firms can announce the wage they are willing to offer to the workers and the unemployed are informed of these announcements and can choose to approach the firms offering the highest wages. The random and exogenous allocation mechanism we saw earlier will come into play, whereby the probability of a single firm hiring a worker depends on how many firms are offering a given wage w relative to the number of unemployed people who are trying to get a job at that wage, and the probability of an unemployed person to get a job at a given wage also depends on the number of unemployed people who are looking for a job at that wage level relative to the number of firms offering it. The ratio of job offers to the number of unemployed, which we denote by n, now indicates the ease of finding a job for each wage offer. The unemployed are aware of the wage offers available for their choice, which operate on that information. In equilibrium, workers will have to be indifferent among the various offers in expected value, balancing a higher wage with a lower probability of getting the job offer. On the other hand, the firm chooses the wage to maximize the expected profit. The combination of these effects leads to the fulfillment of the Hosios condition. The economic reason for this result lies in the fact that firms can compete with each other in an attempt to attract workers, thus activating the competitive mechanism.

12.5.2.3 Natural Rate of Unemployment

The model with a competitive labor market does not have equilibrium unemployment. The competitive labor search model has a frictional level of equilibrium unemployment that reflects what is called, following a terminology coined by Milton Friedman, the *natural rate of unemployment*. The labor search model with bargaining features a more-than-frictional level of unemployment when the bargaining power of the company is smaller than the elasticity of the matching function, violating the Hosios condition. The unemployment rate generated by the labor search model with bargaining fluctuates over time in a countercyclical manner with respect to both productivity and income. However, the fluctuations are an order of magnitude smaller than what is observed in the data. As in the original competitive version, the real business cycle model augmented with search also needs an amplification mechanism for productivity shocks, as in the original market version. The multiplicity of equilibria of the search model suggests an alternative interpretation of business cycles in which there is no single natural rate of unemployment, but multiple long-run equilibrium unemployment rates that emerge as the outcome of the traders' expectations coordination on alternative expansion or recession scenarios. In such a view, the unemployment is not necessarily a short-run phenomenon destined to gravitate back to its unique long-run rate but a potentially persistent phenomenon as observed during the Great Depression of the 1930s in several countries.

12.6 Conclusion

When trade is bilateral and unmediated by markets or contracts as in the search-and-matching model, strategic effects are pervasive, giving rise to multiple equilibria. With the absence of double coincidence of wants, the absence of commitment, and the traders' anonymity, loan repayment cannot be enforced, opening up a role for fiat money as a medium of exchange. In the labor market with search-and-matching frictions, unemployment emerges as an equilibrium phenomenon. Congestion and thick market externalities are responsible for the constrained inefficiency of the equilibrium. Competition among the companies can correct the inefficiency.

12.7 Literature

The coconut model is a simplified version of the barter model with coordination failures presented by Peter Diamond in the famous paper *Aggregate Demand Management in Search Equilibrium*. The literature on sentiments is surveyed in the paper by George-Marios Angeletos entitled *Frictional Coordination*. The monetary search model is a simplified version of the model contained in the paper entitled *A Search-Theoretic Approach to Monetary Economics* by Nobuhiro Kiyotaki and Randall Wright. The extension of the model to divisible goods is due to Alberto Trejos and Randall Wright in their paper *Search, Bargaining, Money, and Prices*. The short- and long-term effects of monetary policy are examined in the paper by Neil Wallace entitled *Short-Run and Long-Run Effects of Changes in Money in a Random-Matching Model*. The characterization of money as an imperfect form of memory is contained in the paper *Money is Memory* by Narayana Kocherlakota. The exposition of the search model of unemployment is a simplified version of the model contained in the book by Christopher Pissarides entitled *Equilibrium Unemployment Theory*. The literature on competitive labor search was initiated by Espen Moen in the paper *Competitive Search Equilibrium*.

Exercises

1. Consider the barter model. Let traders discount the future at the rate $\beta < 1$ and derive the utility u from the consumption of a coconut and the cost c of picking a coconut.

  - Suppose $u = 2$, $c = 1$ and $\beta = 1/3$. Calculate the equilibrium of the model.
  - Suppose $u = 2$, $c = 1$ and $\beta = 2/3$. Compute the equilibria of the model.
2. Consider the money search model with indivisible goods. Let the fraction of money holders be m, the discount factor of traders be $\beta < 1$, the utility of consuming one unit of the good that a trader craves, u, and the cost of producing one unit of the good that the trader can produce, c.
   - Compute the equilibria when $m = 1/2$, $\beta = 1/2$, $u = 8$ and $c = 1$.
   - Derive the efficient allocation.
3. Consider the money search model with divisible goods. Let the fraction of money holders be m and the discount factor be $\beta < 1$. Suppose that the utility and cost functions are, respectively, $u(y) = \frac{y^{1-\epsilon}}{1-\epsilon}$ and $c(y) = y$, where $y \geq 0$ is the quantity of the good traded in the bilateral meetings and the buyers make take-it-or-leave-it offers to the sellers.
   - Calculate the equilibrium amount of production in each meeting and the aggregate amount.
   - Calculate the efficient amount of production.
   - Calculate the effect of a change in M on the equilibrium total output and ex-ante welfare.
4. Consider the job search model.
   - Suppose $z = 3$, $c = 1$, $s = 1$, $\nu = \sigma = 1/2$. Calculate the equilibrium wage, the equilibrium market tightness, and the unemployment. Compare with constrained efficiency.
   - Suppose $z = 3$, $c = 1$, $s = 1$, $\nu = 1/3$, $\sigma = 1/2$. Calculate the equilibrium wage, the equilibrium market tightness, and the unemployment. Compare with constrained efficiency.

References

Angeletos GM (2018), Frictional Coordination, Journal of the European Economic Association, 16: 1–44

Diamond P (1982), Aggregate Demand Management in Search Equilibrium, Journal of Political Economy, 90: 881–894

Kiyotaki N, Wright R (1993), A Search-Theoretic Approach to Monetary Economics, American Economic Review, 83: 63–77

Kocherlakota N (1998), Money is Memory, Journal of Economic Theory, 81: 232–251

Moen E (1997), Competitive Search Equilibrium, Journal of Political Economy, 105: 385–411

Pissarides C (1990), Equilibrium Unemployment Theory, MIT Press

Trejos A, Wright R (1995), Search, Bargaining, Money, and Prices, Journal of Political Economy, 103: 118–141

Wallace N (1997), Short-Run and Long-Run Effects of Changes in Money in a Random-Matching Model, Journal of Political Economy, 105: 1293–1307

Training Day

Advanced macroeconomic theory uses dynamic programming as its standard analytical tool. The idea consists in exploiting the stationarity properties embedded, for instance, in the standard dynastic macroeconomic model to reduce the problem of finding infinite sequences of optimal choices to the simpler problem of finding the optimal short-run response given the current state and extending it recursively into the future. This part of the book provides an introduction to these recursive methods that can be useful to address material treated in more advanced macroeconomic courses. As a foretaste, we show how these methods can be applied to the dynastic model with capital accumulation and the search and matching monetary model with divisible money.

Dynamic Programming

L. Ferraris, *Macroeconomic Theory*, Classroom Companion: Economics,
https://doi.org/10.1007/978-3-031-88740-6_13

More advanced treatments of macroeconomic theory make extensive use of recursive methods, which we have not used in this introductory textbook. In this chapter, we provide a brief overview of dynamic programming, namely the mathematical tool that allows us to simplify the treatment of sequential choice problems over the infinite horizon by reducing them to recursive problems mapping the current state into optimal choices for the near future. The key is the correspondence between vector spaces that are apparently very different but mathematically equivalent, that is, the spaces of certain types of infinite sequences and those of certain types of functions. We apply these techniques to the dynastic model in its version with capital accumulation and with cash payments and to the monetary search-and-matching model with divisible money. We begin with some mathematical preliminaries on vector spaces.

13.1 Vector Space

A real vector space X is a linear space of elements called vectors that can be summed, that is, for any pair of vectors $\mathbf{x}, \mathbf{y} \in X$, their sum belongs to the space $\mathbf{x} + \mathbf{y} \in X$; and multiplied by real numbers, that is, for any vector $\mathbf{x} \in X$ and real number $\alpha \in \mathbb{R}$, their product belongs to the space $\alpha\mathbf{x} \in X$. The null vector is the neutral element of addition and the unit the neutral element of multiplication. Vector addition fulfills the associative and commutative properties, while scalar multiplication fulfills the distributive property with respect to vector addition. The distance between two vectors, $d(\mathbf{x}, \mathbf{y})$ for $\mathbf{x}, \mathbf{y} \in X$, is a symmetric relation that gives a non-negative real number for any pair of vectors of the space and obeys the triangular inequality, namely, given three vectors, the distance between a pair of them is not greater than the sum of the distances between the other pairs. A vector space endowed with the distance between vectors is a metric vector space.

13.1.1 Banach Space

A sequence is a finite or infinite ordered string of elements in the space. A sequence in a metric vector space is a *Cauchy sequence* if beyond a certain element of the sequence, all subsequent elements are arbitrarily close to each other. A sequence in a metric vector space converges to a vector of the space if, beyond a certain element of the sequence, all the subsequent elements are arbitrarily close to that vector. A metric vector space is *complete* if any Cauchy sequence converges to a vector that belongs to that space. A complete metric vector space is a Banach space.

13.1.2 Contraction

An operator is a function that transforms the vectors of a metric vector space into the vectors of the same space. An operator $T : X \to X$ is a *contraction* if the distance between the values that the operator takes for any pair of vectors is uniformly smaller than the distance between the vectors themselves, that is, $d(T(\mathbf{x}), T(\mathbf{y})) \leq \gamma d(\mathbf{x}, \mathbf{y})$ for $\mathbf{x}, \mathbf{y} \in X$, where $\gamma \in (0, 1)$ is independent of the choice of vectors. The Contraction Mapping Theorem guarantees that a contraction that transforms a Banach space into itself has exactly one fixed point, that is, the transformation leaves exactly one vector of the space unchanged. Hence, there is one and only one vector $\mathbf{x}^* \in X$ such that $T(\mathbf{x}^*) = \mathbf{x}^*$ if the operator $T : X \to X$ is a contraction and X is a Banach space.

13.2 Principle of Optimality

According to the *principle of optimality*, a sequence of optimal decisions must remain optimal at any time starting from any consequence of past decisions. This is a principle of sequential rationality analogous to the concept of subgame perfect equilibrium adopted for games in extensive form.

13.2.1 Sequences vs Functions

We will first define a sequential optimization problem and then a functional one. The application of the principle of optimality ensures the equivalence of their solutions.

13.2.1.1 Sequential Problem

First, we formulate the optimization problem in sequential form. Let $\mathbf{x} \equiv \{x_t\}$ be a sequence of real numbers with t running in positive integers. Let $\mathcal{G}(x_t, x_{t+1}) \geq 0$ represent the feasibility constraint of the maximization problem and $\mathcal{U}(x) = \sum_{t=1}^{\infty} \beta^{t-1} \mathcal{F}(x_t, x_{t+1})$ the real-valued function that represents the objective function of the maximization problem, with $\beta \in (0, 1)$. The sequential optimization problem identifies a sequence that maximizes the objective function subject to the feasibility constraint for any initial value $\bar{x}$. Suppose that a solution exists. Let $\mathbf{x}^*$ be the sequence that solves the problem and U^* be the corresponding value of the objective function in the solution.

13.2.1.2 Functional Problem

Next, we formulate the optimization problem in functional form. Let $\mathcal{V}(x)$ be the function that satisfies the following problem

$$\mathcal{V}(x) = \max \mathcal{F}(x, \varkappa) + \beta \mathcal{V}(\varkappa),$$

where the maximization consists in finding the function $\varkappa(x)$ that satisfies the feasibility constraint, that is, $\mathcal{G}(x, \varkappa) \geq 0$ for any x. The functional optimization problem identifies the functions $\mathcal{V}(x)$ and $\varkappa(x)$ for any feasible x. The function $\mathcal{V}(x)$ is the value function and $\varkappa(x)$ the policy function. Suppose that a solution exists. Let $\varkappa^*$ be the sequence of choices implied by the optimal policy function and let V^* be the value function which together constitutes the solution of the problem.

13.2.2 Equivalence

Bellman's Theorem guarantees that the sequential and functional problems have equivalent solutions, that is, $u^*=v^*$ and $\mathbf{x}^* = \varkappa^*$, if the function $\mathcal{F}(\cdot)$ is bounded and the feasibility set is not empty. The theorem formalizes the principle of optimality by identifying the solution of the optimal choice problem of an infinite sequence of decisions with the solution of an essentially static choice problem of functions that constitute the optimal answer in each period starting from the current situation and extended recursively to all future periods.

13.3 Dynastic Model

We now apply this general setting to the economic problem of finding the optimal path of the capital stock or money balances chosen by a rational long-lived representative agent, as described in the dynastic model with capital accumulation or cash-in-advance model examined in the text. The optimal choice problem to be solved regarding the dynastic model is sequential in nature. Its transformation into a problem in equivalent functional form serves to simplify its solution. If the principle of optimality can be applied, the sequential problem and the functional problem will have the same solution. Hence, one can proceed by deriving the solution of the simpler of the two, that is typically the one expressed in functional form, being essentially a static problem.

13.3.1 Capital Accumulation

13 We describe the problem of the choice of the optimal capital accumulation by the dynasty in sequential and functional form. Then, we apply Bellman's theorem, thus proving that the two problems have the same solution. Finally, we show that the solution exists and characterize it.

13.3.1.1 Sequential Problem

In the dynastic model with capital accumulation, the sequences to be optimally determined are: *i.* the consumption sequence, $\mathbf{c} \equiv \{c_t\}$, and *ii.* the capital stock sequence, $\mathbf{k} \equiv \{k_t\}$. The initial capital stock is $e \geq 0$. The production function $f(k_t)$ is differentiable, strictly increasing, and concave in capital, fulfilling the boundary conditions. Moreover, without capital, nothing can be produced, that is, $f(0) = 0$. Capital depreciates completely in production. Feasibility requires $c_t = f(k_t) - k_{t+1} \geq 0$. Define the function $G(k_t, k_{t+1}) \equiv f(k_t) - k_{t+1}$. The dynasty chooses consumption and capital for each period to maximize the objective function $U(\mathbf{c}) = \sum_{t=1}^{\infty} \beta^{t-1} u(c_t)$, with $\beta \in (0, 1)$, subject to feasibility. The utility function $u(c_t)$ is differentiable, strictly increasing, and concave in consumption, fulfilling the boundary conditions. Substituting consumption into the objective function, the optimum problem in sequential form consists in finding a sequence of capital stocks $\mathbf{k}$ that maximizes life-time utility $U(\mathbf{k}) = \sum_{t=1}^{\infty} \beta^{t-1} u(G(k_t, k_{t+1}))$ with $G(k_t, k_{t+1}) \geq 0$ in all periods.

13.3.1.2 Functional Problem

Define $G(k, \kappa) \equiv f(k) - \kappa$. The optimum problem in functional form is

$$V(k) = \max u(G(k, \kappa)) + \beta V(\kappa),$$

where the aim is to find the functions $V(k)$ and $\kappa(k)$, satisfying the constraint $G(k, \kappa) \geq 0$, that represents the feasibility constraint.

13.3.1.3 Bellman's Principle

By the properties of the production function, there exists a positive value of the capital stock, $\bar{k}$, such that $\bar{k} = f(\bar{k})$, since the average productivity is decreasing in the stock of capital and the boundary conditions hold. We will restrict our attention to the values of the capital stock that belong to the closed and bounded interval $[0, \bar{k}]$, implying that the feasibility constraint will be automatically satisfied. Moreover, the functions $u(\cdot)$ and $f(\cdot)$ are bounded over such an interval, since they are continuous. As a consequence, Bellman's theorem applies immediately to this setting. Therefore, if a solution exists, it is the same for the two problems.

13.3.1.4 Existence of the Solution

Next, we show that there is a solution. In the text, we have shown that the sequential problem has a solution. Here, we will show that the problem in functional form has a solution by applying the contraction mapping theorem. To do so, first, we need to show that the value function and the policy function belong to a Banach space. Since the utility function and the production function are continuous and we have restricted the space of the stock of capital to a closed and bounded interval, these functions are also bounded. Therefore, the vector space we consider is the space of continuous and bounded functions defined over a closed and bounded interval. In order to apply the contraction mapping theorem, we assign a distance concept to that space, transforming it into a metric space so that we can define a contraction on it. Since the functions are bounded on the interval $[0, \bar{k}]$, it is natural to use as the distance between pairs of functions the maximum difference between the values that the functions take on the interval itself, called the maximum distance. This metric vector space is complete, so it is a Banach space. Given the continuity and strict concavity of the utility and production function defined in a closed and bounded interval, the Theorem of the Maximum guarantees that the optimal choice can be obtained as a continuous function of k, that is, $\kappa(k)$, and the value function, $V(k)$, is also continuous. Therefore, the policy and value functions are continuous, defined on a closed and bounded interval; hence, they are bounded. As a consequence, they belong to the Banach space. Let's use them to define the following operator

$$T(V(k)) = u(G(k, \kappa(k))) + \beta V(\kappa(k)),$$

that transforms a Banach space in itself, $T : X \to X$. We only have to show that the operator $T(\cdot)$ is a contraction. Given the properties of the fundamentals, Blackwell's Theorem guarantees that $T(\cdot)$ is a contraction. Hence, the contraction mapping theorem applies, guaranteeing that there is a unique value function that satisfies the functional optimization problem. Therefore, there is a unique solution to the functional optimization problem.

13.3.1.5 Stationary Equilibrium

Under the stated assumptions in the fundamentals, the function $V(k)$ turns out to be at least once differentiable, so the solution of the functional problem can be characterized using the apparatus of optimization by first-order conditions that extend its applicability to functional spaces. In particular, the function $\kappa(k)$ can be characterized implicitly by the optimality condition $\beta V'(\kappa) = u'(G(k, \kappa))$. Together with the envelope condition $V'(k) = f'(k)u'(G(k, \kappa))$, the optimality condition allows us to derive the stationary solution, namely the capital stock that remains invariant over time, with $\kappa(k) = k$, as $k^* = f'^{-1}(1/\beta)$. The capital rental rate is equal to its marginal product, that is, $r = f'(k^*) = \beta^{-1}$. There is also the trivial stationary solution in the case where the initial capital stock is nil.

Example 13.1

Suppose that the utility function is $u(c) = \ln c$, the production function is $f(k) = k^\alpha$. In this case, we can solve the problem in functional form directly using the guess-and-verify method. We guess that the value function is an affine transformation of the utility function, namely that $V(k) = a + b \ln k$, where a and b need to be determined. The functional equation becomes

$$a + b \ln k = \max \quad \ln\left(k^\alpha - \kappa\right) + \beta(a + b \ln \kappa).$$

Computing the first-order condition with respect to κ, we obtain $\kappa = \beta b k^\alpha / (1 + \beta b)$ that we can insert back into the previous condition, obtaining

$$a(1 - \beta) + [b - \alpha(1 + \beta b)] \ln k + (1 + \beta b) \ln(1 + \beta b) = \beta b \ln \beta b.$$

We can use b to eliminate the term that multiplies $\ln k$, obtaining $b = \alpha/(1 - \alpha\beta)$, which we can plug back into the equation that determines the capital function, getting

$$\kappa(k) = \alpha\beta k^\alpha.$$

Consumption is given by $c(k) = (1 - \alpha\beta)k^\alpha$, which is positive, since $\alpha\beta < 1$, therefore the feasibility constraint is satisfied. Finally, setting a to satisfy the condition for the value function, we obtain

$$V(k) = \frac{(1 - \alpha\beta)\ln(1 - \alpha\beta) + \alpha\beta \ln \alpha\beta}{(1 - \beta)(1 - \alpha\beta)} + \frac{\alpha}{1 - \alpha\beta} \ln k.$$

13.3.1.6 Productivity Shocks

Let us introduce uncertainty in the model. Suppose that the economy is hit by shocks to the total factor productivity every period. The production function is $y_t = z_t k_t^\alpha$ in each period. The total factor productivity is subject to random shocks, distributed independently and identically. We examine directly the recursive representation of the model. We denote by ζ the next period shock. The sequential problem can be written in recursive form as

$$V(k,z) = \max u(G(k,\kappa)) + \beta \mathbb{E} V(\kappa,\zeta),$$

with $\kappa \in [0,\bar{k}]$. The capital rental rate is equal to the marginal product of capital. Assuming that z is distributed over a compact interval with distribution function $\pi(z)$, the expectation of the future value is calculated as $\mathbb{E}V(\kappa,\zeta) = \int V(\kappa,\zeta)\pi(\zeta)d\zeta$. The solution for capital accumulation is a function that depends on two state variables, namely current capital and current shock to productivity, $\kappa(k,z)$. The solution is found by solving the optimality and envelope conditions analogous to the previous case without shocks.

13.3.2 Cash in Advance

Consider the monetary model in which a dynasty representative of a unit continuum of dynasties works for a company representative of a unit continuum of companies that produce the final output. Payments must be made in cash, whose stock in nominal terms is M at all times.

13.3.2.1 Sequential Problem

The company produces the final output with a technology represented by a linear production function in labor input, $y_t = \ell_t$. The dynasty chooses sequences of consumption $\mathbf{c}$ and labor supply $\mathbf{l}$ to maximize life-time utility $U(\mathbf{c},\mathbf{l}) = \sum_{t=1}^{\infty} \beta^{t-1}[u(c_t) - v(l_t)]$, with $\beta \in (0,1)$. The utility of consumption is differentiable, strictly increasing, and strictly concave; the disutility of labor is differentiable, strictly increasing, and convex. The boundary conditions apply. The real wage is w_t every period. Consumption must be financed with cash in hand. Real balances are denoted with m_t in every period. The budget constraint of the dynasty is $c_t + m_{t+1} = w_t l_t + m_t$ and the cash-in-advance constraint is $c_t \le m_t$. Solve the budget constraint for consumption, obtaining $c_t = w_t l_t + m_t - m_{t+1}$. The dynasty chooses sequences of real balances $\mathbf{m}$ and labor supply $\mathbf{l}$ to maximize life-time utility $U(\mathbf{m},\mathbf{l}) = \sum_{t=1}^{\infty} \beta^{t-1}[u(w_t l_t + m_t - m_{t+1}) - v(l_t)]$ subject to the cash-in-advance constraint $m_{t+1} \ge w_t l_t$ and the non-negativity constraint for consumption $w_t l_t + m_t \ge m_{t+1}$ every period. The company maximizes profits, giving $w_t = 1$. The output, labor, and money market all clear, with $c_t = y_t$, $l_t = \ell_t$, and $m_t = M/p_t$ at all times. The model in sequential form has been solved in the text. Next, we reformulate it in functional form.

13.3.2.2 Functional Problem

Denote by m current real balances. Under the given assumptions about the fundamentals, there exists a unique $l^* > 0$ such that $u'(l) = v'(l)$. Henceforth, we restrict our attention to the interval $[0, l^*]$. Moreover, to satisfy the cash-in-advance constraint and the non-negativity of consumption, we restrict attention to real balances that belong to the interval $[wl, wl + m]$. To solve the functional problem, one needs to find the value function $V(m)$ and the policy functions $\mu(m)$ and $l(m)$ that solve the following problem

$$V(m) = \max u(wl + m - \mu) - v(l) + \beta V(\mu),$$

with $\mu \in [wl, wl + m]$ and $l \in [0, l^*]$. The equivalence of the sequential and functional optimization problems follows immediately from the fact that the intervals identified by the constraints are not empty and the objective function is bounded on such intervals, being continuous.

13.3.2.3 Existence of the Solution

The maximum theorem guarantees that there is a solution to the functional optimization problem in the form of continuous policy functions $\mu(m)$ and $l(m)$ together with a continuous value function $V(m)$. Continuous functions in closed and bounded intervals are bounded. Hence, we can work in the space of continuous and bounded functions endowed with the maximum distance that is a Banach space.

Define the operator

$$T(V(m)) = u(wl(m) + m - \mu(m)) - v(l(m)) + \beta V(\mu(m)),$$

that maps the Banach space into itself. By Blackwell's theorem, the operator is a contraction; hence, the contraction mapping theorem applies, and there exists a unique value function that solves the functional problem together with the policy functions identified above.

13

13.3.2.4 Stationary Monetary Equilibrium

Under the stated assumptions, the value function is also differentiable. Let $\lambda \geq 0$ be the multiplier of the cash-in-advance constraint. Ignore, for the moment, the non-negativity constraint of consumption and the upper bound on labor. The first-order condition with respect to μ gives $\lambda = u'(wl + m - \mu) - \beta V'(\mu)$ and the first-order condition with respect to l is $[u'(wl + m - \mu) - \lambda]w = v'(l)$ that can be written as $\beta V'(\mu)w = v'(l)$ using the previous optimality condition. Using the envelope condition $V'(m) = u'(wl + m - \mu)$, write the complementary slackness condition, $\lambda(\mu - wl) = 0$, as $[V'(m) - \beta V'(\mu)](\mu - wl) = 0$. In a stationary monetary equilibrium, the real balances are invariant in time, $\mu(m) = m$. Since $\beta < 1$, the multiplier is strictly positive, and hence the cash-in-advance constraint binds $\mu = wl$. The equilibrium real wage is $w = 1$. Consequently, $c = y = l = \mu = m$. Using the optimality condition for labor and the envelope condition with $\mu = m$, we obtain

$$v'(l) = \beta u'(l),$$

that determines the equilibrium employment $\tilde{l} > 0$. Hence, consumption is positive. The equilibrium employment satisfies $v'(\tilde{l})/u'(\tilde{l}) = \beta < 1 = v'(l^*)/u'(l^*)$, therefore, given the properties of the fundamentals $\tilde{l} < l^*$. The price level is $p = M/\tilde{l}$.

Example 13.2

Suppose that the utility of consumption is $u(c) = \ln c$ and the disutility of labor is $v(l) = l$. We can solve the problem in functional form directly using the guess-and-verify method. The guess is $V(m) = a + b \ln m$, where a and b need to be determined. The functional equation becomes

$$a + b \ln m = \max \quad \ln(wl + m - \mu) - v(l) + \beta(a + b \ln \mu) + \lambda(\mu - wl),$$

where we have included the cash-in-advance constraint with its multiplier. The first-order condition with respect to l gives $\lambda = \frac{1}{wl+m-\mu} - \frac{1}{w}$, and with respect to μ gives $\frac{1}{wl+m-\mu} - \lambda = \frac{\beta b}{\mu}$. Inserting the former condition into the latter, we obtain $\mu = \beta b w$. Since the cash-in-advance constraint binds, we have $l = \beta b$. Plug these values into the functional equation, together with the complementary slackness condition $\lambda(\mu - wl) = 0$, obtaining

$$a(1 - \beta) + (b - 1) \ln m = -\beta b + \beta b \ln \beta b w.$$

Use b to eliminate the term that multiplies $\ln m$, obtaining $b = 1$. The wage is $w = 1$ by the optimization of the company. Hence, we obtain $\mu = m = l = c = y = \beta$. Finally, setting a to satisfy the previous condition for the value function, we obtain

$$V(m) = \frac{\beta(\ln \beta - 1)}{1 - \beta} + \ln m.$$

The price level is $p = M/\beta$. Efficiency requires $l^* = 1$.

13.4 Monetary Search Model

Next, we apply the recursive methods to a simplified version of the monetary search model with divisible money that provides a foundation for the role of cash as a means of payment.

13.4.1 Foundation of Money

Consider an economy with two types of perishable commodities. Each period is divided into two sub-periods, morning and afternoon. The trade of the first type of commodity happens in the morning, whereas the second type of commodity is traded in the afternoon. There is a continuum of identical dynasties whose preferences for consumption and work in the morning are represented by the function $u(c) - v(l)$ with the usual properties, and preferences for consumption and work in the afternoon are represented by a linear function. Independently every period, with probability $\pi \leq 1/2$ a dynasty becomes a consumer of the good traded in the morning, with probability π becomes a producer of such a commodity and with probability $1 - 2\pi$ remains inactive until the afternoon. The technology to produce the morning good that can only be operated by the sellers is represented by a linear production function, $y = l$. The dynasties cannot acquire this commodity on credit, since they are anonymous during the morning and cannot commit to future actions. Fiat money is available in a time-invariant amount M to help trade the morning commodity. The morning commodity is traded bilaterally with the buyers making take-it-or-leave-it offers to the sellers of cash payment $\hat{m}$ in real terms in exchange for an amount of the commodity $y = c$ to be consumed immediately. Morning trade occurs in the spirit of the matching model of money examined in the text but with divisible money. The afternoon commodity can be produced by all dynasties with a technology represented by a linear production function and is traded in a competitive market at a price p in units of the morning commodity. Efficiency requires $u'(c) = v'(l)$, with $c = l = y$.

13.4.1.1 Bargaining

By bargaining with take-it-or-leave-it offers, buyers will exhaust the available cash, $\hat{m} = m$, offering money to acquire the amount of the morning commodity that makes sellers indifferent between accepting or rejecting offers. Thus, we obtain the indifference condition $v(l) = \hat{m}/p$, which equates the disutility of labor to the linear utility of the money acquired in terms of the consumption of the afternoon, whose price is p. Since the function $v(\cdot)$ is invertible, $\hat{m} = m$ and $c = y = l$, we have $c = v^{-1}(m/p) \equiv c(m/p)$.

13.4.1.2 Monetary Equilibrium

Due to the linearity of the utility in the afternoon, the choice of cash for the future, denoted with μ, is independent of current cash holdings; therefore, all dynasties, no matter what happened during the morning, will choose to accumulate the same amount of cash in the afternoon for the future. Therefore, the distribution of money holdings across the dynasties will be degenerate at equilibrium. We focus on stationary equilibria in which the real variables are time-invariant. The value function of a dynasty before knowing the morning type is

$$V(m) = \pi[u(c(m/p)) - m/p] + m/p - \mu/p + \beta V(\mu).$$

Thus, the optimality condition for the choice of balances μ is $p^{-1} = \beta V'(\mu)$; the envelope condition in m is $V'(m) = p^{-1}[\pi u'(c(m/p))c'(m/p) + 1 - \pi]$. Since the stock of money is constant in a stationary equilibrium, the price level p is time-invariant. Combining these two conditions with $c'(m/p) = 1/v'(l)$, $c = l$, and $\mu = m$, we obtain the equation that determines the morning employment, output, and consumption in stationary equilibrium

$$1 = \beta \left[\pi \frac{u'(l)}{v'(l)} + 1 - \pi \right].$$

Notice that employment income and consumption are inefficiently low in monetary equilibrium, since $u'(l)/v'(l)$ decreases in l and $1 - \beta(1 - \pi) > \beta\pi$, with $\beta < 1$. This is a variant of the equilibrium condition obtained in the cash-in-advance model. The difference is that not all the cash is spent on consumption since a fraction π of the traders become sellers and a fraction $1 - 2\pi$ remain inactive during the morning. Hence, only a fraction π of the dynasties manage to spend their cash while the remaining fraction, $1 - \pi$, keeps its initial cash holdings idle until the afternoon when its payoff in terms of consumption is linear.

13.4.1.3 Monetary Policy

Suppose that the monetary authority can alter the stock of currency at a constant net rate γ over time, using lump-sum taxes or transfers. The equilibrium condition becomes

$$1 = \frac{\beta}{1 + \gamma} \left[\pi \frac{u'(l)}{v'(l)} + 1 - \pi \right].$$

The optimal policy is the Friedman rule, as usual in pure cash economies without distributional issues, since setting $\gamma = \beta - 1$ in the previous equation gives $u'(l) = v'(l)$. However, notice that in this economy with information and enforcement limitations, lump-sum taxes may not be feasible, since traders may hide cash, and therefore the best incentive compatible policy may be no intervention.

13.4.2 Monetary Loans

Consider now what happens when idle cash balances can be rewarded with interest. Suppose that the dynasties have the option of lending each other money at the beginning of every period after finding out whether they will be buyers, sellers, or inactive in the morning but before trading the morning commodity. Assume that there is an institution that guarantees the reimbursement of the loans with nominal interest $i \geq 0$ during the afternoon of the same period or the loan is secured by some collateral. The stationary equilibrium condition is now given by

$$1 = \beta \left[\pi \frac{u'(l)}{v'(l)} + (1 - \pi)(1 + i) \right],$$

since cash does not remain idle anymore in the hands of the sellers and the inactive dynasties but can be lent out to the buyers, thus, earning an interest that is paid out in the afternoon. Suppose that the mechanism that makes loans feasible is competitive, so that the gross nominal interest rate is equal to the marginal rate of substitution between consumption and work, namely $1 + i = u'(l)/v'(l)$, which can be inserted into the previous equilibrium condition to obtain $v'(l) = \beta u'(l)$. This equation coincides with the equilibrium condition of the cash-in-advance model that in turn is the same condition derived for the life-cycle model. Therefore, stationary equilibrium employment, consumption, and output are exactly the same as in the cash-in-advance model and the overlapping generations model. The nominal interest rate is $i = \beta^{-1} - 1 > 0$. Since inflation is nil, this is also the real interest rate.

13.5 Conclusion

In fairly general situations, the principle of optimality allows the transformation of a sequential dynamic optimization problem into a functional static one. The standard dynastic model in its real and monetary versions can be solved using dynamic programming tools. Recursive methods have wide applicability in macroeconomics. We have shown how they can be applied to the dynastic model with capital accumulation, cash-in-advance and a version of the monetary search-and-matching model with divisible money.

13.6 Literature

A standard reference for this material is the book by Robert Lucas and Nancy Stokey *Recursive Methods in Economic Dynamics*. The book by Lars Ljungqvist and Thomas Sargent *Recursive Macroeconomic Theory* covers many recent applications of dynamic programming to macroeconomics. The divisible money monetary search model is a simplified version of the model in the paper *A Unified Framework for Monetary Theory and Policy Analysis* by Ricardo Lagos and Randall Wright. A book-length introduction to the monetary search model with divisible money is Edward Nosal and Guillaume Rocheteau (2017), *Money, Payments, and Liquidity*.

References

Lagos R, Wright R (2005), A Unified Framework for Monetary Theory and Policy Analysis, Journal of Political Economy, 113, 463–484

Ljungqvist L, Sargent T (2018), Recursive Macroeconomic Theory, MIT Press

Lucas R Jr, Stokey N (1989), Recursive Methods in Economic Dynamics, Harvard University Press

Nosal E, Rocheteau G (2017), Money, Payments, and Liquidity, MIT Press

Conclusion

L. Ferraris, *Macroeconomic Theory*, Classroom Companion: Economics,
https://doi.org/10.1007/978-3-031-88740-6_14

The aim of this book was to introduce the reader to modern macroeconomic theory. The common thread has been the general equilibrium model with competitive markets originally developed by Arrow and Debreu and extended in several directions by subsequent generations of economic theorists. The key aspect of this approach to macroeconomic theorizing is the identification of individual preferences and production possibilities as exogenous data and the prices and allocations as endogenous outcomes of the market interaction. We have shown that the attractive, but sometimes counterfactual, properties of the standard market model can be progressively weakened as different imperfections are added to the model, ranging from borrowing limits to incomplete markets, private information, and strategic interaction. In particular, the efficiency of equilibrium allocation disappears as the trade interaction becomes ridden with imperfections, opening up some room for policy intervention that is otherwise unnecessary. The typical role of policy is to compensate for market imperfection, providing a substitute for missing risk-sharing or consumption smoothing options when everything else fails. In strategic situations with private information, the policy intervention should be conceived more ambitiously as institutional design to elicit the private information and incentivize the socially desirable behavior.

A major consequence of taking the preferences and technologies of forward-looking, rational agents as data of the problem is that public authorities should conceive of policy intervention as a strategy, namely a complete plan of actions to be taken in all possible future contingencies, rather than a momentary piecemeal action. When designing policy interventions, the authorities need to find ways to tie their hands in order to be able to credibly commit to an ex ante optimal complete strategy and stick to it at times when the temptation to alter such a strategy will be strong. To avoid the problem of time inconsistency in policy intervention, the adoption of policy rules that cannot be easily changed under the pressure of events is recommended.

Regarding more specifically fiscal policy, in the standard macroeconomic model with unfettered markets, taxation that is not lumpsum distorts the optimal decisions of the traders and lumpsum taxation used to finance public expenditures reduces private consumption and is in the best case irrelevant for the well-being of traders. Whether public programs should be financed with outright taxation or issuing government debt is a matter of indifference whenever the traders anticipate the future burden of taxation to finance the reimbursement of government debt. Capital income should not be taxed except possibly in the very short run. Short-run stabilization policy, if necessary at all, is better left to monetary policy. In sum, fiscal policy is at best irrelevant. In incomplete market models, traders tend to save excessively over-accumulating capital relative to the efficient benchmark to self-insure against adverse income shocks. In this case, fiscal policy can play a role in providing additional risk-sharing options and reducing the excessive accumulation of capital through public saving instruments such as government debt. Capital income may be taxed to reduce its over-accumulation. When traders have private information about their ability to generate income, the optimal taxation scheme trades off the provision of insurance with the provision of incentives to work. The resulting optimal tax scheme turns out to be regressive in income to discourage people from shirking.

As regards monetary policy, in the standard macroeconomic model with unfettered markets, monetary policy has the only role of fixing the price level to control inflation. With short-run nominal rigidity, monetary policy can have real effects, although any systematic attempt to use it as a tool to boost income quickly runs into problems, leading to inflation without income benefits. In monetary economies, optimal monetary policy drives the cost of holding money, that is, the nominal interest rate, to zero, thus minimizing the distortion in the optimal savings decisions of the private sector. This is achieved by making money relatively scarce, through contractionary monetary policy that induces a deflation. In incomplete market monetary models, traders may find themselves short of cash when most needed, hence, expansionary monetary policy that insures those traders providing them with additional means of payment is sometimes part of the optimal monetary policy scheme that trades off the distortion induced on the saving decisions of the private sector with the implicit insurance provided by inflationary policy. Expanding temporarily the liquidity available during a financial crisis may help the private sector relax borrowing restrictions, thus avoiding a deeper recession and recovering sooner from its consequences. Both deposit insurance and macroprudential policy can play a role in preventing liquidity crises. This is the lesson learned from the Great Recession.

Supplementary Information

L. Ferraris, *Macroeconomic Theory*, Classroom Companion: Economics,
https://doi.org/10.1007/978-3-031-88740-6

Appendices

Modern macroeconomics is based on the foundations provided by economic theory. In this appendix, we introduce the reader to such foundations. In particular, after a quick review of real analysis, we present the basic elements of general equilibrium, game theory, and mechanism design. In a nutshell, general equilibrium studies the market interaction of rational people in non-strategic situations; game theory studies the strategic interaction of rational people in the institutional void; mechanism design identifies the institutional structure required to coordinate in a socially satisfactory manner the strategic interaction of rational people.

The *Arrow-Debreu* model of general economic equilibrium contains the standard theory of economic value with complete, perfect, and competitive markets. The economy is conceived as follows. Taking into account their preferences for consumption, production possibilities, and the initial distribution of available commodities, traders optimally determine their demand and supplies of such commodities as a function of the prices whose formation they consider to be outside of their control. Then, the optimal demand and supply schedules are submitted to the market mechanism that determines the prices to balance demand and supply in all markets. Finally, the allocation of resources is implemented to deliver the commodities to the traders. In sum, an economic equilibrium is an allocation of resources together with the market prices that sustain them such that nobody is willing to change choice given prices and prices adjust to clear the markets. Thus, economic value, represented by the market price, reflects and balances the interplay of the private valuations of the traders given the property rights over the existing resources, the preferences for consumption, and the production technologies. The influence of strangers on the personal decisions of each trader occurs exclusively through the market prices, without any direct effect on individual preferences. The resulting allocation cannot be improved socially by external intervention, adopting Pareto efficiency—essentially a unanimity criterion—as a standard to measure social improvements. With complete and perfectly functioning competitive markets, the entire life-time wealth of the traders is always fully liquid, being readily available at no cost to finance any purchase. If traders individually make full and rational use of their wealth, redistributing existing resources among them cannot improve individual decisions without hurting at least someone. Hence, the decisions taken independently by a mass of fully rational people coordinated by the market mechanism give rise to socially optimal outcomes. Moreover, it can be shown that such outcomes are at least locally determinate, making the predictions of the model sharp and empirically testable.

At the other end of the spectrum, non-cooperative *game theory* studies the strategic interaction of people deciding rationally over a complete plan of action in all possible circumstances and taking into account all the available information but without the help of any coordination mechanism. In a strategic interaction—called a game, the influence of strangers, unmediated by any institutional mechanism, directly affects the individual preferences or personal rewards of each participant in the game. An equilibrium is a list of complete plans of action for all the participants such that nobody is willing to unilaterally change the personal plan. There are strategic situations, such as the famous prisoners' dilemma, whose only equilibrium is inefficient in the sense of Pareto. Hence, uncoordinated fully rational people deciding optimally for themselves can give rise to socially wasteful outcomes. Other strategic situations, such as the so-called coordination games, feature multiple equilibria. Hence, uncoordinated fully rational people deciding optimally for themselves can give rise to indeterminate outcomes. In some coordination games, the equilibria are Pareto ordered, with the selection among equilibria left to extraneous coordination devices.

The theory of *mechanism design* aims to find the coordination mechanisms that allow the attainment of the efficient allocation of resources when participants have access to private information that can be used to strategically manipulate the outcomes. With private information, the markets may not be able to allocate the resources efficiently since rational and strategic traders would try to exploit their superior information to game the system in their favor. In this case, institutional arrangements or contracts designed to limit these manipulation attempts by the participants taking into account that they may have some private information helps achieve the efficient allocation of resources if not in the full Pareto sense, at least in an incentive compatible second-best sense. The remarkable result is that the vastly complicated problem of the design of mechanisms with private information can be reduced to a relatively simple linear programming problem thanks to the so-called Revelation Principle, whose application allows us to formulate the problem of the optimal institutional design taking into account the limitations imposed by the presence of private information through some incentive conditions adjoined to an otherwise standard maximization problem without loss of generality. Mechanism design shows that, in very general situations, it is possible to design institutions for the coordination of fully rational and strategic people that achieve socially desirable outcomes making them reveal truthfully their private information.

Appendix A: Mathematics

In this appendix, we will present in an intuitive manner some basic notions of calculus, optimization, dynamical systems, and probability. A standard reference for this material is Rudin W (1976), Principles of Mathematical Analysis, McGraw-Hill.

Calculus

Calculus is a mathematical tool to study continuous change. The aim is to find the marginal change of a variable whose value depends on another variable when the latter changes infinitesimally. To describe infinitesimal changes, the variable should vary in the continuum, that is, be a real number. We assume that the reader is familiar with the standard notation for the operations, order, and equivalence relations over the reals.

Real Numbers

The real numbers whose set is denoted by $\mathbb{R}$ are the completion of the rationals. In real numbers, it is possible to define all the operations for rational numbers, namely, the sum, difference, product, division by a number other than zero, and exponentiation. The absolute value of a real number, denoted with $|x|$, is the maximum between x and $-x$, that is, $|x| \equiv \max\{x, -x\}$. The distance between two real numbers, x and y, is their difference taken in absolute value, $|x - y|$.

A vector, denoted with $\mathbf{x}$, is an ordered string of a finite number of reals, in which x_n corresponds to the n-th component of the vector, with $n = 1, ..., N$ for $N \geq 2$. The space containing such vectors is the N-times product of the reals, denoted by $\mathbb{R}^N$. The notion of distance between numbers can be extended to the vector case, using, for example, the Euclidean distance. This is also known as the Euclidean space.

Compactness

A closed interval in the reals, denoted by $[a, b]$ with $a, b \in \mathbb{R}$ and $a < b$, contains all the reals between the extremes, including the extremes. An open interval, denoted with (a, b), does not include the extremes. The interval is bounded if there exist numbers $c, d \in \mathbb{R}$, such that c is smaller and d is larger than all elements of the interval. A closed and bounded interval is compact.

More generally, a closed and bounded subset of a Euclidean space is compact, with the obvious extensions of the notions of closedness and boundedness from intervals to neighborhoods.

Convexity

A set $X \subseteq \mathbb{R}^N$ is convex if for all pairs of vectors $\mathbf{x}, \mathbf{y} \in X$ and any $\alpha \in [0, 1]$, then $\alpha\mathbf{x} + (1 - \alpha)\mathbf{y} \in X$. A hyperplane in $\mathbb{R}^N$ is a vector $\mathbf{p}$ and a real number a, such that $\mathbf{px} = a$ for $\mathbf{x} \in \mathbb{R}^N$. The *Separating Hyperplane Theorem* guarantees that there exists a hyperplane that separates two disjoint non-empty convex subsets of $\mathbb{R}^N$, so that the two sets lie on opposite sides of the hyperplane.

Functions

To study the effect of the change of a real variable on another real variable, we need to relate the latter to the first unambiguously. Therefore, we introduce the concept of a real-valued function of a real variable and the tools to capture mathematically continuous change.

Continuity

Given two sets $X, Y \subseteq \mathbb{R}$, a function $f : X \to Y$ is a rule that assigns to every element $x \in X$ one and only one element $y \in Y$. A real-valued function $f(x)$ defined over the reals tends to l if for every $\epsilon > 0$ there is $\eta > 0$ such that for any $x \in X$ if $|x - \bar{x}| < \eta$ then $|f(x) - l| < \epsilon$. This can be written as

$$\lim_{x \to \bar{x}} f(x) = l.$$

The function $f(x)$ is continuous at a point $\bar{x} \in X$ if, for any $\epsilon > 0$ there is $\eta > 0$ such that for any $x \in X$ if $|x - \bar{x}| < \eta$ then $|f(x) - f(\bar{x})| < \epsilon$. In other words, the function is continuous in $\bar{x}$ if $l = f(\bar{x})$. The function is continuous in X if it is continuous at every point in X.

The *Intermediate Value Theorem* guarantees that if the real-valued function $f(x)$ is continuous in the interval $[a, b] \subseteq \mathbb{R}$, it will assume all values in the interval $[\min\{f(a), f(b)\}, \max\{f(a), f(b)\}]$. If $f(x)$ is continuous in $x \in [a, b] \subseteq \mathbb{R}$ and the function assumes opposite sign at the extremes of the interval, that is, $f(a)f(b) < 0$, the intermediate value theorem implies the existence of a zero of the function within the interval, namely a $z \in (a, b)$ such that $f(z) = 0$.

Given two sets $X \subseteq \mathbb{R}^N$ and $Y \subseteq \mathbb{R}$, a real-valued function $f : X \to Y$, is a rule that assigns to each vector $\mathbf{x}$ in the domain of definition of the function one and only one real value, $y = f(\mathbf{x})$. Given two sets $X \subseteq \mathbb{R}^N$ and $Y \subseteq \mathbb{R}^M$, a vector-valued function $F : X \to Y$, is a rule that assigns to each vector $\mathbf{x}$ in the domain of definition of the function one and only one vector, $\mathbf{y} = F(\mathbf{x})$. The notion of continuity adopted above extends to real-valued and vector-valued functions.

Brouwer's Fixed Point Theorem guarantees that a continuous function $F : X \to X$ that maps a non-empty compact and convex set $X \subseteq \mathbb{R}^N$ in itself has a fixed point, namely a $\mathbf{x}^* \in X$ such that $\mathbf{x}^* = F(\mathbf{x}^*)$. Kakutani's fixed point theorem extends this result to set-valued functions, also known as correspondences, with the appropriate notion of continuity.

Differentiability

Given two sets $X, Y \subseteq \mathbb{R}$, a function $f : X \rightarrow Y$ is differentiable at a point $\overline{x} \in X$ for $h \in \mathbb{R}$ if

$$\lim_{h \to 0} \frac{f(\overline{x}+h) - f(\overline{x})}{h},$$

exists finite. This is denoted by $f'(\overline{x})$, which is called the derivative of the function at the point $\overline{x}$. The function is differentiable if it is differentiable at all $x \in X$. The function $f'(x)$ is the derivative of $f(\cdot)$ with respect to x. The first derivative of the first derivative, that is, the second derivative of the function, is denoted with $f''(x)$. If $f'(x) > 0$ for all $x \in X$, the function increases monotonically in x; if $f''(x) < 0$ for all $x \in X$, the function is strictly concave in x.

The main rules of differentiation are the following. The derivative of the sum of two functions is the sum of the derivatives of each function; the derivative of the product of two functions is the sum of the product between the derivative of each function and the other function undifferentiated; the derivative of the inverse function is the inverse of the derivative; the derivative of the composite function with another function that constitutes its argument is the derivative of the first function multiplied by the derivative of the second with respect to its argument.

For a real-valued function of a vector, $f(\mathbf{x})$, the notion of differentiability with respect to each component of the vector $\mathbf{x}$ is analogous. To obtain the partial derivative with respect to a component of the vector, the derivative with respect to that component is computed keeping the other components unchanged. The partial derivative of the function $f(\mathbf{x})$ in relation to the component x_n is denoted by $f_{x_n}(\mathbf{x})$.

Given three sets $X, Y, Z \subseteq \mathbb{R}$, consider a function $f : X \times Z \rightarrow Y$ that is differentiable with respect to both arguments. The *Implicit Function Theorem* guarantees that, if the function $f(x, z)$ is differentiable at a point $(\overline{x}, \overline{z}) \in X \times Z$ with $f(\overline{x}, \overline{z}) = 0$ and has a non-zero partial derivative $f_x(\overline{x}, \overline{z})$, then, there exists an open interval $A \subseteq Z$ containing $\overline{z}$ and a function $\phi : A \rightarrow X$, such that $\overline{x} = \phi(\overline{z})$, with $f(\phi(z), z) = 0$ and for $z \in A$ the derivative is

$$\phi'(z) = -\frac{f_z(\phi(z), z)}{f_x(\phi(z), z)}.$$

In other words, under a regularity condition, the implicit function can be made explicit locally and the derivative of the explicit function can be computed using only the partial derivatives of the original implicit function, in particular taking the negative of their ratio. The reason can be seen totally differentiating the implicit function $y = f(x, z)$, obtaining $dy = f_x(x, z)dx + f_z(x, z)dz$ that, at the point $(\overline{x}, \overline{z}) \in X \times Z$ with $f(\overline{x}, \overline{z}) = 0$, gives $\frac{dx}{dz} = -\frac{f_z(\overline{x}, \overline{z})}{f_x(\overline{x}, \overline{z})}$ since the value of the function is kept fixed, $dy = 0$. The notion of differentiability extends to vector-valued functions $F : X \rightarrow Y$ with $X \subseteq \mathbb{R}^N$, $Y \subseteq \mathbb{R}^M$ component by component. The vector that collects partial derivatives with respect to each variable is called the gradient and is denoted by $\nabla F(\mathbf{x})$.

Optimization

To characterize rational behavior, in the text, we have made extensive use of optimization. Optimization is the branch of mathematics that identifies the maximum or minimum of a function, possibly subject to constraints.

Maximum

Let $f : \mathbb{R} \to \mathbb{R}$ be the a function that represents the objective to be maximized. An element $\hat{x} \in \mathbb{R}$ is a maximum point if $f(\hat{x}) \geq f(x)$ for any other $x \in \mathbb{R}$. The value $f(\hat{x})$ is the maximum of the function. An unconstrained maximization problem consists in identifying the points at which the function reaches its maximum value.

Let $g : \mathbb{R} \to \mathbb{R}$ be the a function that represents the constraint. Let the constraint set be $C \equiv \{x \in \mathbb{R} : g(x) \leq 0\}$. An element $\hat{x} \in C$ is a maximum point of $f(x)$ if $f(\hat{x}) \geq f(x)$ for any other $x \in C$. A constrained maximization problem consists of identifying the points at which the function reaches its maximum value within the constraint set.

Weierstrass' Theorem guarantees that a continuous real-valued function defined over a compact interval of the reals attains its maximum.

Let the constraint set, $C(\theta)$, depend on a parameter $\theta \in \Theta \subseteq \mathbb{R}$. Consider the maximization of $f(x)$ over $C(\theta)$. Let $M(\theta)$ denote the set of maximum points for every $\theta \in \Theta$ and $F(\theta)$ the maximum value of $f(x)$ as a function of the parameter.

The *Theorem of the Maximum* guarantees that, if $C(\theta)$ is compact and convex for any $\theta \in \Theta$ and continuous in θ and $f(x)$ is continuous and strictly concave in $x \in C(\theta)$, then $M(\theta)$ is not empty, single-valued and continuous in θ and $F(\theta)$ is continuous in θ.

Maximization

Consider the unconstrained maximization problem, denoted as $\max_{x \in \mathbb{R}} f(x)$. Suppose that the function $f(x)$ is at least twice differentiable in $x \in \mathbb{R}$. Suppose that the function is strictly concave in x. The necessary and sufficient condition to identify the optimum is $f'(x) = 0$.

The constrained maximization problem, denoted $\max_{x \in C} f(x)$, includes the restriction $g(x) \leq 0$. Suppose that the objective and constraint functions are at least twice differentiable, the objective function is strictly concave, and the constraint function is concave. By the *Kuhn-Tucker's Theorem*, there exists a real number $\lambda \geq 0$ such that $f'(\hat{x}) = \lambda g'(\hat{x})$ and $\lambda g(\hat{x}) = 0$ are necessary and sufficient conditions for the optimum. The latter equation is called the complementary slackness condition.

Example B.1 Consider the function $f(x) = 2x - x^2$, with $x \in \mathbb{R}$. The function is strictly concave, since $f''(x) = -2$. The necessary and sufficient condition for the optimum is $f'(x) = 2 - 2x = 0$. Hence, the maximum point is $\hat{x} = 1$ and the maximum value is $f(\hat{x}) = 1$.

Example B.2 Consider the same function $f(x) = 2x - x^2$ defined over the reals, with $x \leq a$, where a is a real number. Thus, the constraint is represented by the linear function $g(x) = x - a \leq 0$. The necessary and sufficient conditions are $2 - 2x = \lambda$ and $\lambda(x - a) = 0$. Inserting λ into the second condition, obtain $(1 - x)(x - a) = 0$. Hence, if $a \geq 1$, the solution is $\hat{x} = 1$ with $\lambda = 0$, while if $a < 1$, the solution is $\hat{x} = a$, with $\lambda = 2(1 - a) > 0$. In sum, $\hat{x} = \min\{a, 1\}$. The maximum value is $f(\hat{x}) = 2a - a^2$ for $a < 1$ and $f(\hat{x}) = 1$ for $a \geq 1$.

Dynamical Systems

Dynamical systems describe mathematically the evolution of a system through differential equations in continuous time or difference equations in discrete time. Since in the text we have considered only discrete-time problems, we will discuss difference equations exclusively.

One-Dimensional Dynamics

A one-dimensional discrete-time dynamic system is a difference equation $x_{t+1} = f(x_t)$ for $t \in \mathbb{N}$, i.e. running over the natural numbers, where $f : A \to \mathbb{R}$, with $A \subseteq \mathbb{R}$ open. Let the initial condition be denoted by $\overline{x}$. The evolution function, $x_t = g(\overline{x})$, gives the current value of the variable at any time as a function of the initial condition. The sequence of values generated by the evolution function is the trajectory of the dynamical system. A fixed point of $f(\cdot)$ is an element $x^* \in A$ such that $x^* = f(x^*)$, i.e. a value that remains invariant over time, also known as a stationary state. A fixed point is locally stable if the trajectories that start near it remain close to it. The local stability is determined by linearly approximating the function around the fixed point, that is, computing its derivative and evaluating it at the fixed point. A fixed point x^* of $f(\cdot)$ is locally stable if $|f'(x^*)| < 1$ and locally unstable if $|f'(x^*)| > 1$. The knife-edge cases are critical points at which the stability properties of the system change. Let $f^2(x) = f(f(x))$ denote the application of the function twice to the point x. If $x^* = f^2(x^*)$ for $x^* \in A$, but $x^* \neq f(x^*)$, then, x^* is a periodic point of period 2 and the corresponding trajectory is a cycle.

Let $\alpha \in (a, b)$ with $a, b \in \mathbb{R}$ and $x_{t+1} = f(x_t, \alpha)$ be a family of difference equations indexed by α, with $f(x^*, \alpha) = x^*$ for all $\alpha \in (a, b)$. A bifurcation is a change in the stability property of a fixed point as α changes. When a so-called *period-doubling bifurcation* occurs as α crosses a critical value, a cycle emerges in an open interval containing the fixed point. Suppose $f(x_t, \alpha)$ is differentiable in both variables. The critical value $\hat{\alpha}$ such that a flip bifurcation occurs is identified by the condition $f_x(x^*, \alpha) = -1$, under the regularity condition $f_{x\alpha}(x^*, \hat{\alpha}) \neq 0$.

Example B.3 Consider the function $f(x_t) = x_t^2$ with the initial condition $\overline{x}$. The trajectory is given by the evolution function $g(\overline{x}) = \overline{x}^{2^t}$. There are two stationary states, $x^* = 0$ and $x^* = 1$. The first is stable since $f'(0) = 0 < 1$ and the second is unstable since $f'(1) = 2 > 1$.

Example B.4 Consider the function $h(x_t, \alpha) = x_t(2 - x_t^\alpha)$, with $\alpha > 0$. There are two stationary states, $x^* = 0$ and $x^* = 1$. The first is unstable since $h_x(0, \alpha) = 2$ for any α. Whether the second is stable or unstable depends on the value of α, since $h_x(1, \alpha) = 1 - \alpha$. When α crosses the value 2, a period-doubling bifurcation occurs and a cycle emerges close to the second stationary state.

Two-Dimensional Dynamics

A two-dimensional discrete-time dynamical system is $\mathbf{x}_{t+1} = F(\mathbf{x}_t)$, with $F : \mathbb{R}^2 \to \mathbb{R}^2$. A fixed point is $\mathbf{x}^*$ such that $\mathbf{x}^* = F(\mathbf{x}^*)$. The local stability of a fixed point can be evaluated approximating linearly the system around the fixed point. This is done by computing the eigenvalues of the Jacobian matrix evaluated at the fixed point. The Jacobian matrix of the system is the two-by-two matrix containing the first derivatives of each equation with respect to each variable. Its determinant D is given by the product of the main diagonal elements minus the product of the elements off the main diagonal and its trace T is the sum of the main diagonal elements. Define the discriminant $\Delta \equiv (T/2)^2 - D$. The two eigenvalues are the solution of the characteristic equation $\lambda^2 - T\lambda + D = 0$, namely $\lambda_{1,2} = T/2 \pm \sqrt{\Delta}$. If $\Delta < 0$, the eigenvalues are complex conjugated and the trajectories of the system spiral toward or away from the fixed point or circle around it indefinitely, with the critical values determined by $D = 1$ and $|T| \leq 2$. If $\Delta \geq 0$, the eigenvalues are real and distinct if and only if $\Delta > 0$. If both eigenvalues are smaller than one in absolute value, the fixed point is stable; if both are larger than one in absolute value, the fixed point is unstable; if one is larger and one is smaller than one in absolute value, the fixed point is a saddle. The critical values are determined by the conditions $|1 - T + D| = 0$ and $|1 + T + D| = 0$, depending on whether the determinant and trace are positive or negative.

Probability

Suppose that an experiment is performed under controlled conditions, whose random outcomes indexed by $s \in \mathcal{S}$ are recorded. For the moment, we will consider the set $\mathcal{S}$ as finite with a total number $S \geq 2$ of outcomes. We define an event e as a subset of the outcomes of the experiment and the probability of such an event, $\pi(e)$, as the ratio of the number of outcomes in which the event occurs to the total number of outcomes of the experiment. Probability is therefore a real number belonging to the unit interval, $\pi(e) \in [0, 1]$. An event with zero probability is impossible, while an event with unit probability is certain.

The calculus of probabilities gives the probability that more complex events occur from the known probability of simpler events. The probability of the occurrence of at least one of two mutually incompatible events, that is, such that their intersection is zero, is given by the sum of the probabilities of the two events. The probability of one event given the realization of another event is called the conditional probability of the first event given the second. If this probability is equal to the unconditional probability of the first event, then the two events are said to be independent. The probability of two events occurring simultaneously is given by the product of the probability of one event occurring and the conditional probability of the other event upon the occurrence of the first event. If two events are independent, the probability of both occurring is given by the product of the probabilities of the occurrence of each event. Two events are equiprobable if they have the same probability of occurrence. Two events are complementary if one and only one of the two events will necessarily occur. Therefore, two complementary events are mutually incompatible. The sum of the probabilities of complementary events is unitary. A set of events is complete if one and only one of the events in the set will necessarily occur. The events of a complete set are, therefore, mutually incompatible with each other. The sum of the probabilities of a complete set of events is unitary. The probability of an event belonging to a complete set consisting of a finite number of equiprobable events is equal to one divided by the total number of events. These computational rules allow the following three properties to be derived. First, the probability of at least one of a set of events occurring is never greater than the sum of the probabilities of the individual events. Second, given a complete set of events obtained as subsets of the outcomes of an experiment, the total probability of the realization of any outcome of the experiment is given by the sum of the conditional probabilities of the outcome upon the occurrence of each event in the set, each weighted with the probability that the corresponding event will occur. Third, given a complete set of events obtained as subsets of the results of an experiment, the conditional probability of each event at the occurrence of a given outcome of the experiment is the product of the conditional probability of the outcome at the occurrence of the particular event and the probability of the occurrence of the event itself divided by the total probability of the outcome of the experiment. This is the *Bayes' rule*.

Random Variables

A random variable is an assignment of a real number for each possible outcome of an experiment, x_s for every $s \in \mathcal{S}$. The value taken by the random variable at an outcome is its realization. A probability distribution of a random variable gives the probability of each of its possible realizations, $\pi_s \in [0, 1]$, with $\sum_s \pi_s = 1$. Two distributions are mutually independent if the realization of one of the two random variables does not affect the realization of the other.

A summary measure describing the characteristics of a probability distribution is the mean of the distribution, or its expected value, defined as the sum of the possible realizations of the random variable, each weighted with its own probability of realization, $m \equiv \sum_s \pi_s x_s$. The mean of the realizations with equal weights is called the arithmetic mean. The average of the sum of two probability distributions is equal to the sum of the averages of the two distributions. If two distributions are mutually independent, the mean of the products of the two distributions is equal to the product of their means.

Another summary measure often used is the variance, which provides a measure of the dispersion of a probability distribution around its mean, given by the sum of the square deviations of the realizations of the random variable from the mean, weighing each deviation by its probability of realization $v \equiv \sum_s (x_s - m)^2 \pi_s$. The standard deviation is the square root of the variance $d \equiv \sqrt{v}$. The covariance between two random variables is, by definition, the difference between the expected value of their product and the product of their expected values. The correlation index is used to measure the statistical relationship between two random variables. The correlation index between two random variables is given by the ratio of their covariance to the product of their mean square deviations.

The *law of large numbers* says that if a set of N random variables has mutually independent probability distributions, the same mean m, and standard deviation d, the arithmetic mean of the random variables is arbitrarily close to the mean m for N sufficiently large.

A random process is a collection of random variables indexed by time. A random process has the Markov property if the behavior of the process in the future is stochastically independent of its behavior in the past given its current state. A martingale is a stochastic process for which, at a particular time, the conditional expectation of the next value is equal to the present value, regardless of prior values.

Measure

Let us now generalize the previous considerations to more general sets. Let $\mathcal{S}$ be a set and Σ a family of subsets of $\mathcal{S}$ such that: i. the empty set and the entire set belong to the family; ii. if a set belongs to the family, its complement also belongs to the family; iii. if a countable number of sets belong to the family, its union also belongs to the family. A family that satisfies these conditions is called a σ-algebra. The pair $(\mathcal{S}, \Sigma)$ is a measurable space. A measure is a real-valued function $\pi(\sigma)$ with $\sigma \in \Sigma$ such that: i. the empty set has measure zero; ii. the measure is non-negative; iii. the measure of a countable union of pairwise disjoint sets is the sum of their measures. The triple $(\mathcal{S}, \Sigma, \pi)$ is a measure space. If the measure of the entire set is unitary, the measure $\pi(\sigma)$ is the probability of the event $\sigma \in \Sigma$ and the measure space is called a probability space. A real-valued function $f(s)$ with $s \in \mathcal{S}$ is measurable with respect to the σ-algebra if the sets $\{s \in \mathcal{S} : f(s) \leq x, \forall x \in \mathbb{R}\}$ belong to the σ-algebra. If the measure space is a probability space, the measurable function is a random variable. The measurable function $f(s)$ is integrable if the sum of the absolute values of the areas of the regions between the graph of f and the x-axis is finite. The integral is $\int f d\pi = \int f^+ d\pi - \int f^- d\pi$, where $f^+(s) \equiv \max\{f(s), 0\}$ and $f^-(s) \equiv \max\{-f(s), 0\}$. If π is a probability, the integral is the expectation of the random variable.

Appendix B: Economic Theory

In this appendix, we offer a brief introduction to the Arrow-Debreu general equilibrium model of competitive trade, to game theory, and to mechanism design, namely the theory that designs optimally the trading institutions so as to try to overcome the presence of private information. A standard reference for this material is Mas Colell A, Whinston M, Green J (1995), Microeconomic Theory, Oxford University Press.

General Equilibrium

The representation of the market interaction in the Arrow-Debreu model works as follows. Before the markets open for trade, all traders decide separately and simultaneously their demands and supplies for each available commodity at all possible prices, taking the prices as parameters. This gives rise to demand and supply schedules that are independently and simultaneously submitted by each trader to the facility that operates the markets. The traders commit to deliver or agree to receive, when the markets open, the amount of the commodities implied by their demand and supply schedules at any given price. The job of the market facility is to find the prices that equate demand and supply for all commodities, that is, clear markets. The markets open, and then the traders deliver and receive the commodities. Finally, consumption occurs.

At the heart of the Arrow-Debreu representation, there is a single budget constraint that allows each trader to finance all conceivable expenditures within the limits imposed by the overall life-time income. Together with the insatiability of traders, this characteristic makes it impossible for market equilibrium allocations to be improved by external intervention relative to the Pareto criterion. At a competitive equilibrium, the traders exploit all the substitution possibilities offered by the markets, spending all the resources available over their life-time. This is enough to guarantee efficiency, without the need for any redistribution of resources enacted by some external agency.

We begin the exposition with this static version of the Arrow-Debreu model of a competitive market economy. Later, we include a finite time horizon, and uncertainty.

Static Model

We first consider a model of pure exchange. Subsequently, we will extend the model to include production. A pure exchange competitive market economy is populated by individuals with an endowment of some commodities who would like to trade such an endowment to obtain other commodities for consumption purposes. The exchange of commodities occurs through competitive markets. The model determines economic value, namely the market prices, from the private characteristics of the traders, namely endowments and preferences, which are called the fundamentals.

Fundamentals

The model is characterized by a given number of commodities and consumers. There is no obsolescence or innovation in commodities and no change in the population of consumers. Consumers have an initial endowment of the existing commodities and preferences over the commodities representing their private valuation for them. Consumers have property rights over their initial endowments, so the exchange is voluntary.

There are many traders, indexed by $i \in \mathcal{I}$. The set $\mathcal{I}$ may be finite, countably infinite, or uncountable, depending on the circumstances. Strictly speaking, perfect competition requires an atomless continuum of agents. Here, we consider a finite number of consumers. Each consumer i is interested in consuming at least some of the available commodities. There is a finite set $\mathcal{J}$ of commodities whose total number is J, indexed by $j \in \mathcal{J}$. The commodity space is $X \subseteq \mathbb{R}^J_+$. Each consumer i has an initial endowment of commodities, represented by the column vector $\mathbf{e}^i \in X$. The bundle comprising the amounts of the commodities obtained by the consumer i is denoted by the column vector $\mathbf{x}^i \in X$. The j-component of this vector is denoted by $x^i_j \in \mathbb{R}_+$ for $j \in \mathcal{J}$.

For consumers to be able to choose among bundles of commodities, they need to have a criterion to order the bundles in the consumption set. The criterion adopted here is the following.

Assume that each consumer is characterized by a binary relation, denoted with $\succsim$ defined on the consumption space X, which orders the elements of the commodity space. This binary relation reflects the preferences of consumers for commodities in the sense that, for any two elements $\mathbf{x}, \mathbf{y} \in X$, $\mathbf{x} \succsim \mathbf{y}$, means that $\mathbf{x}$ is preferred or indifferent to $\mathbf{y}$. We assume that the binary relation satisfies the following four requirements.

- *Reflexivity*. For any $\mathbf{x} \in X$, $\mathbf{x} \succsim \mathbf{x}$.
- *Completeness*. For any $\mathbf{x}, \mathbf{y} \in X$, either $\mathbf{x} \succsim \mathbf{y}$ or $\mathbf{y} \succsim \mathbf{x}$.
- *Transitivity*. For any $\mathbf{x}, \mathbf{y}, \mathbf{z} \in X$, if $\mathbf{x} \succsim \mathbf{y}$ and $\mathbf{y} \succsim \mathbf{z}$, then $\mathbf{x} \succsim \mathbf{z}$.
- *Continuity*. For any $\mathbf{x}, \mathbf{y} \in X$, such that $\mathbf{x} \succsim \mathbf{y}$, there exists a $\mathbf{z} \in X$, such that $\mathbf{x} \succsim \mathbf{z} \succsim \mathbf{y}$.

Reflexivity is a minimal assumption that requires the ability to identify objects. Completeness is a more demanding requirement, as it assumes that all possible bundles are pairwise comparable. It excludes the indecisiveness that arises from the inability to compare different situations. Transitivity is also demanding, as it requires the choices of the consumer to be fully consistent, without going through recurring cycles in the process of choice. It excludes the capriciousness that arises from changing one's mind about an unchanged situation. These requirements embed the notion of rationality of preferences typically assumed in economic theory. A binary relation that satisfies reflexivity, completeness, and transitivity is called a *preference relation*. The continuity requirement, in Euclidean space, implies continuity in the usual sense. It avoids sudden jumps in preferences, preventing wildly different evaluations of similar situations and allowing the comparison of situations at the margin. A preference relation that satisfies continuity is called continuous. A real-valued function $U : X \to \mathbb{R}$, represents the preference relation $\succsim$ over X, if, for any $\mathbf{x}, \mathbf{y} \in X$, $\mathbf{x} \succsim \mathbf{y} \Leftrightarrow U(\mathbf{x}) \geq U(\mathbf{y})$. The real-valued function that represents the preference relation is called a *utility function*. It can be shown that continuous preference relations can be represented by continuous utility functions. This property is convenient since it allows us to reduce the problem of comparing vectors of choices to a simpler comparison of real numbers using the binary relation "greater or equal," $\geq$, which orders completely the real line.

The representation of preferences through a utility function is unique only up to monotonically increasing transformations. In other words, any two utility functions that are related by a monotonically increasing transformation represent the same preferences and, hence, are equivalent from the point of view of the problem of choice. This means that the units of measurement and the scale of utility can be changed without changing the underlying preferences and choice problem. Thus, utility is an ordinal concept, not a cardinal one.

Henceforth, we assume that every consumer is endowed with a continuous preferences relation, so that we can consider directly their utility representation. Thus, the preferences of each trader i are represented by the continuous utility function $U^i(\mathbf{x}^i)$. This function represents the way in which the trader privately evaluates the consumption of a bundle of commodities.

The traders are assumed to be rational in the sense that they try to identify their best available consumption option among the feasible ones. In other words, the consumption choices of traders are such that they maximize their utility subject to any constraint they may face.

Rational Choice

So far, we have described how consumers privately value different consumption bundles. It is time to describe the economic constraints on the traders' choice. The traders are constrained by their budget when choosing how much to consume. There is an institution that enforces budget constraints, preventing traders from exceeding their budget. For trade to happen, private valuations must be made compatible. This is the task of the market institution. There is a perfectly competitive market for the trade of claims of commodities. The commodities are traded at prices $\mathbf{p}$, a row vector of prices one for every commodity expressed in abstract units of account. Consumers have no influence on prices and consider them as parameters beyond their control. This reflects the assumption that the market is perfectly competitive. The consumption choice $\mathbf{x}^i$ of every trader i must satisfy the following restriction $\mathbf{p}\mathbf{x}^i \leq \mathbf{p}\mathbf{e}^i$, that is, the *budget constraint*. The LHS of the constraint represents the total expenditures of the trader, and the RHS the total value of his or her endowment. Thus, a trader's expenditures cannot exceed his or her income. This is expressed in vector notation with the usual inner product between the row vector of prices and the column vector of consumption choices, representing the value of a bundle of commodities. It is assumed that the total value of the endowment of any consumer is finite; otherwise the constraint would never bind the trader's choice. Notice that the budget constraint has two notable features that will be crucial for the analysis to follow. First, there is a price for every commodity that the traders value as potential objects of consumption, meaning that every desirable commodity is marketed. There are no commodities that are potentially desirable for consumption purposes but cannot be traded in the market, although, in principle, some commodity may be free, i.e. traded at zero price. Second, the prices enter linearly in the budget constraint. This reflects the competitive nature of trade that excludes a non-linear dependence of prices from the quantities traded, as would have happened if some of the traders had market power. It is convenient to define

$$B^i(\mathbf{p}) = \{\mathbf{x}^i \in X : \mathbf{p}\mathbf{x}^i \leq \mathbf{p}\mathbf{e}^i\},$$

as the budget set, namely the trader's choices that are budget feasible. Thus, we now have an economic constraint on the choice of the traders to consume. We can turn to their optimal choice.

Each trader i chooses $\mathbf{x}^i \in B^i(\mathbf{p})$ to maximize $U^i(\mathbf{x}^i)$, taking the given prices. The optimal choice of the consumer i is not necessarily a function but may be a correspondence, depending on the assumed properties of the utility function. Observe that multiplying all prices by the same value does not change the budget set, that is, homogeneous of degree one in prices. Hence, the optimal choice of the consumer is homogeneous of degree zero in prices. Next, we describe the interaction of consumers through the competitive markets.

Competitive Equilibrium

Market participants trade in an idealized sense in this model. Before the market opens, the consumers decide their demands and supplies of each commodity at any feasible price, and then submit to the market facility their demand and supply correspondences, committing to deliver the amount of the commodities implied by their demand and supply schedules at any price that may arise in the market. Once the market facility receives the demands and supplies of the consumers, it computes the prices that equate the aggregate demand and supply for all commodities, i.e. the marker facility determines the price that clears the markets. Then, the equilibrium price is announced and the commodities are delivered to each consumer and, finally, consumed. The delivery of commodities is enforced by the market institution at no cost and without failure.

The traders submit their optimal choices to the market facility, whose job is to determine the price that guarantees that aggregate demand does not exceed aggregate supply, namely

$$\sum_{i \in \mathcal{I}} x_j^i \leq \sum_{i \in \mathcal{I}} e_j^i,$$

for every commodity $j \in \mathcal{J}$. These are the market clearing conditions. We allow for the possibility that the supply may exceed the demand for some commodity, with freely available commodities traded at zero price. Let $\mathbf{x} = (\mathbf{x}^i)_{i \in \mathcal{I}}$ be an allocation of commodities among traders. A competitive equilibrium is a situation in which the traders do not want to change their decisions and the aggregates are compatible.

Definition B.1 A *competitive equilibrium* is a pair $(\mathbf{x}, \mathbf{p})$ such that the traders choose optimally their demand for the commodities given the prices and the prices clear the markets.

If the utility functions of all consumers are strictly increasing, the equilibrium price is bound to have only strictly positive components, and excess supply cannot arise as an equilibrium; hence, markets exactly clear. In addition, with strictly increasing utility functions, consumers exhaust their budget constraints at optimum. Henceforth, we work under the assumption that the utility functions are strictly increasing for all the consumers. If the binding budget constraints of the agents are taken into account, among the market clearing conditions, one is redundant. This is called *Walras Law*. Due to the homogeneity of degree zero of demand and the validity of Walras law, the model exhibits one degree of nominal indeterminacy and, as a consequence, can determine only the relative and not absolute prices. This means that one of the commodities can be chosen as the unit of account.

Under relatively mild assumptions on the fundamentals, a competitive equilibrium can be shown to exist as an application of *Kakutani's Fixed Point Theorem*. We will prove the existence of competitive equilibrium with a different approach later. The proof of the existence of equilibrium is an important achievement, as it confirms that a logically coherent theory of market value based entirely on the consumers' private valuations of the commodities and their aggregation through market signals can be constructed in a logically consistent way.

Example B.1 Suppose that there are two traders with identical preferences for the consumption of two commodities represented by the utility function $U(\mathbf{x}^i) = \alpha u(x_1^i) + \beta u(x_2^i)$ with $\alpha, \beta > 0$ but having opposite endowments: the first trader has a positive endowment of the first commodity, $e_1^1 = z > 0$, and nil of the second, $e_2^1 = 0$, while the second trader vice versa. The utility function $u(\cdot)$ is differentiable, strictly increasing, and concave. Define the relative price of the two commodities as $p \equiv p_2/p_1$ and let $x_2^1 \equiv x$. The optimality conditions for the first trader give $p\alpha u'(z - px) = \beta u'(x)$. The optimality of the second trader, together with the clearing of the market for the second commodity, gives $p\alpha u'(px) = \beta u'(z - x)$. These two conditions immediately give the competitive equilibrium relative price $\hat{p} = \beta/\alpha$ and the consumption of the second commodity for the first trader $x_2^2 = \hat{x} = \frac{\alpha z}{\alpha+\beta}$. By the budget constraint of the first trader, his or her equilibrium consumption of the first commodity is $x_1^1 = z - \hat{p}\hat{x} = \frac{\alpha z}{\alpha+\beta}$ and the consumption of the other trader is $x_j^2 = z - \hat{x} = \frac{\beta z}{\alpha+\beta}$ for both j. In other words, the two traders smooth their consumption across the two options, splitting it in proportion α to β. This is the only competitive equilibrium.

Uniqueness

After having established that a competitive equilibrium exists, the next pressing question is to figure out whether the model can make determinate predictions about market outcomes, namely, whether the equilibrium is unique for any set of fundamentals. It turns out that in a very general sense, the equilibrium is not globally unique. It is possible to find restrictions on the behavior of demand that imply the global uniqueness of equilibrium. One such restriction is called *gross substitutability*. Two commodities are gross substitutes if an increase in the price of one commodity decreases the (gross) demand for that commodity and increases the (gross) demand for the other. Gross substitutability implies global uniqueness of the equilibrium. Global uniqueness may be a desirable property, especially if one is interested in making sharp predictions, for instance, for policy purposes, but gross substitutability is a very restrictive assumption. Fortunately, under relatively mild assumptions on the fundamentals, the competitive equilibrium enjoys a weaker but still desirable property, which is local uniqueness. An equilibrium price is locally unique if there is no other equilibrium price arbitrarily close to it. A theory that has locally unique equilibria is locally determinate. Assuming that utility functions are differentiable, it can be shown that, typically, the competitive equilibria are locally unique; hence, the Arrow-Debreu theory is locally determinate. This makes local comparative statics exercises meaningful.

Core Allocations

The popular notion of competition involves the idea of having alternative options for trade, while the traders of the Arrow-Debreu model have no alternative options other than trading in the existing market at given prices. One may wonder whether this is the appropriate notion of competition.

A powerful way to capture alternative trade possibilities is the *core*. Define a coalition as a group of consumers who can commit to stick together for the purpose of achieving a mutually advantageous outcome. A coalition can block a feasible allocation if there exists an alternative allocation that is feasible using only the resources of the coalition such that every consumer in the coalition is better off with the alternative than the original allocation. A feasible allocation that cannot be blocked by any coalition of consumers is in the core.

Under the maintained assumptions, the competitive equilibrium allocations are in the core. To see that this is the case, proceed by contradiction. Suppose that there exists a coalition that can block a competitive equilibrium allocation. Then, every member of the coalition must be better off with the new allocation. This implies that the new allocation is not budget feasible for the consumers in the coalition at the competitive equilibrium prices, or they would have chosen it. This, in turn, implies that the new allocation cannot be attainable by the coalition alone, by feasibility.

The converse is not, in general, true. There are allocations in the core that are not competitive equilibrium allocations. This can be easily seen by considering an example with two commodities and two consumers. The core allocations for such an economy are represented by the contract curve, namely the set of allocations at which the two consumers are at least as well off as at their initial endowment. The contract curve, in general, contains more allocations than the competitive equilibrium allocation, which is the allocation on the contract curve supported by the competitive equilibrium prices. However, when the number of consumers is large, the converse also holds. As the size of the economy increases, the size of the core shrinks until, in the limit, only the competitive equilibrium allocations survive. Thus, for sufficiently large economies, the Arrow-Debreu notion of perfect competition coincides with the notion that there are no feasible individually and socially advantageous alternative trading possibilities left to be exploited.

No-Surplus Allocations

Perfect competition can also be seen as a situation in which every trader appropriates his or her marginal contribution to the well-being of society. The marginal contribution of a trader can be estimated by computing the value that would be missing if such a trader were to be removed from the system. Define a *no-surplus allocation* as a feasible allocation in which all traders obtain their marginal contribution to the well-being of society. In an economy with a continuum of traders, competitive equilibrium and no-surplus allocations coincide. In this view, market competition is conceived as the only way to exactly reward each individual for the personal contribution to society. The restriction to economies in which traders are negligible cannot be dispensed with, since otherwise the contribution of a trader would become non-marginal. Indeed, at the competitive equilibrium of an exchange economy with a finite number of traders, each of them is rewarded for the last unit of the endowment they contribute not for all the infra-marginal units.

Efficiency

One of the aims of the theory is to compare the allocations of commodities among traders according to a criterion of social optimality. We would like to have a criterion to compare competitive equilibrium allocations, to understand whether they can be improved in some yet to be defined sense by some redistributive scheme possibly devised by the public authority. However, judging the social desirability of allocations would seem to require making interpersonal comparisons among consumers. These comparisons are prevented by the ordinal nature of utility. The appropriate criterion for comparing different allocations without making interpersonal comparisons is the notion of *Pareto efficiency*. An allocation $\mathbf{x}$ is feasible if $\sum_i x^i_j \leq \sum_i e^i_j$ for every commodity $j \in \mathcal{J}$. A trader is weakly better off consuming the bundle $\mathbf{x}^i$ than the alternative bundle $\mathbf{y}^i$ if $U^i(\mathbf{x}^i) \geq U^i(\mathbf{y}^i)$ and is strictly better off if the inequality is strict.

Definition B.2 A feasible allocation $\mathbf{x}$ is *Pareto efficient* if there is no feasible alternative allocation $\mathbf{y}$ that makes everyone weakly better off and someone strictly better off.

The concept is coherent with ordinal utility, which does not allow for interpersonal comparisons. Being essentially a unanimity criterion, the notion of Pareto efficiency does not order allocations completely, as there are, in general, several allocations that are not Pareto comparable. However, it is sufficiently tight so as to exclude some allocations as Pareto-dominated. The *First Welfare Theorem* states that any competitive equilibrium is Pareto efficient, under the assumption that the utilities are strictly increasing.

Proposition B.1 If the traders' utilities are strictly increasing, any competitive equilibrium is Pareto efficient.

Proof

The argument is by contradiction. Take any competitive equilibrium allocation $\mathbf{x}$. Suppose that there is an alternative feasible allocation $\mathbf{y}$ that makes everyone at least as well off and someone strictly better off. A competitive equilibrium allocation is optimal for all traders subject to budget constraints. When the utility is strictly increasing, traders exhaust their budget. Hence, any alternative allocation that makes everyone at least as well off and someone strictly better off should violate the budget of the traders who are made better off; otherwise, it would have been chosen by them. Since all traders are on their budget and one trader is over budget, the allocation cannot be feasible at positive market prices. In fact, aggregating the budgets of traders, we get $\mathbf{p} \sum_i \mathbf{y}^i > \mathbf{p} \sum_i \mathbf{e}^i$ which implies a violation of feasibility for at least one commodity, since prices are all positive due to the strict monotonicity of the utilities. □

The First Welfare Theorem requires that the traders are insatiable, which is implied by their utilities being increasing, to ensure that they exhaust their budget. Should some traders optimally choose not to spend all their resources, obviously, there may exist a Pareto-improved redistribution that takes the resources of these traders who do not exhaust their budget and gives them to those who have exhausted their budget. If all traders already exhausted their budget, such a redistribution does not exist. When utility is increasing in consumption, traders have the incentive to exhaust their budget. Hence, given the budget available to traders, its allocation across commodities achieved by trade in perfectly competitive markets cannot be improved upon by any redistribution enacted even by a benevolent authority, as the substitution possibilities offered by market trade have already been fully exploited by the consumers. The hallmark of efficiency is the presence of a single budget constraint with linear prices. This result is the conceptual cornerstone on which market economies are built.

The next question is whether all the Pareto efficient allocations can be decentralized as competitive equilibria. The *Second Welfare Theorem* states that any Pareto-efficient allocation can be decentralized through market trade, possibly redistributing initial endowments when the utility functions of all traders are concave. The proof is a direct application of the separating hyperplane theorem for convex sets.

Negishi's Problem

The problem of identifying Pareto-efficient allocations can be made operational through the so-called *Negishi's problem*. Assume that the traders' utilities are twice differentiable, strictly increasing, and strictly concave. Using individual weights $\vartheta^i > 0$ with $\sum_i \vartheta^i = 1$, whose vector is denoted by ϑ, define the social welfare function

$$W(\mathbf{x}) = \sum_{i \in \mathcal{I}} \vartheta^i U^i(\mathbf{x}^i).$$

Define the feasibility set as $F = \{\mathbf{x} \in X^I : \sum_i \mathbf{x}^i \leq \sum_i \mathbf{e}^i\}$. An allocation solves Negishi's problem if it maximizes the social welfare function among feasible allocations, that is, $\max_{\mathbf{x} \in F} W(\mathbf{x})$. The next proposition shows that we can find all the efficient allocations by solving Negishi's problem.

Proposition B.2 An allocation is Pareto efficient if and only if it solves Negishi's problem.

Proof

Suppose that an allocation solves Negishi's problem but is not Pareto efficient. Since $\vartheta^i > 0$ for all i, a Pareto improvement would increase $W(\mathbf{x})$ that contradicts the premise. To see that the converse also holds, note that by the second welfare theorem, under the stated assumptions on utilities, the efficient allocation $\mathbf{x}^*$ satisfies the marginal conditions in vector notation $\nabla U^i(\mathbf{x}^{i*}) = \lambda^i \mathbf{p}$ for all traders, which equate the marginal utilities of traders with the market prices of commodities through the Lagrange multipliers of the budget constraints of traders $\lambda^i > 0$. Under the stated assumptions on utilities, the feasibility constraints of Negishi's problem are binding. The necessary and sufficient conditions for the optimum of Negishi's problem are $\vartheta^i \nabla U^i(\mathbf{x}^{i*}) = \mathbf{p}$ for all traders, where $\mathbf{p}$ is the vector of the shadow prices of the feasibility constraints. Setting ϑ^i so that $\vartheta^i = 1/\lambda^i > 0$ for every trader, we find that $\mathbf{x}^*$ is the solution to Negishi's problem. □

The solution of Negishi's problem identifies efficient allocations that can be used to prove that a competitive equilibrium exists, showing that the solution verifies not only feasibility and optimality but also the traders' budget constraints.

Proposition B.3 There exists a competitive equilibrium.

Proof

First, identify efficient allocations through the maximization of the Negishi problem. For every vector of normalized positive weights ϑ there is a Pareto-efficient allocation $\mathbf{x}(\vartheta)$ and, according to the second welfare Theorem, there is a price vector $\mathbf{p}(\vartheta)$ that supports the allocation. We only need to make sure that the allocation is budget feasible for all traders. Under the monotonicity assumption of utility, the budget constraints of the traders are satisfied at equality, which gives I equations $\mathbf{p}(\vartheta)\left[\mathbf{e}^i - \mathbf{x}^i(\vartheta)\right] = 0$ for each $i \in \mathcal{I}$. By Walras' law the number of equations is reduced by one, so that we have a system of $I - 1$ equations to determine the $I - 1$ dimensional normalized vector ϑ. With strictly increasing and strictly concave utility functions, the optimal choices $\mathbf{x}^i(\vartheta)$ are continuous functions according to the maximum theorem. Define for every i and any vector of normalized positive weights the continuous function

$$T^i(\vartheta) \equiv \frac{\max\left\{0, \vartheta^i + \mathbf{p}(\vartheta)\left[\mathbf{e}^i - \mathbf{x}^i(\vartheta)\right]\right\}}{\sum_i \max\left\{0, \vartheta^i + \mathbf{p}(\vartheta)\left[\mathbf{e}^i - \mathbf{x}^i(\vartheta)\right]\right\}}. \tag{B.1}$$

Let $\mathbf{T}(\vartheta)$ be the continuous vector-valued map that collects such functions. Since $\mathbf{x}^i(\vartheta)$ and $\mathbf{p}(\vartheta)$ are continuous and the set of normalized weights is compact, the map can be extended continuously to the boundary of the set of normalized weights. Thus, $\mathbf{T}(\vartheta)$ continuously maps the set of normalized weights, a compact and convex set, to itself. By *Brouwer's Fixed Point Theorem*, the map has a fixed point, that is, a ϑ^* such that $\mathbf{T}(\vartheta^*) = \vartheta^*$. At the fixed point, (B.1) gives $\vartheta^{i*} = \vartheta^{i*} + \mathbf{p}(\vartheta^*)\left[\mathbf{e}^i - \mathbf{x}^i(\vartheta^*)\right]$, for every i, therefore, the corresponding allocation satisfies the budget constraint for all traders. □

Example B.2 Continuing with the above example, denote by $\vartheta^1 \in (0, 1)$ the weight of the first trader and $1 - \vartheta^1$ the weight of the second trader. Using the binding feasibility constraint $x_j^1 + x_j^2 = z$ for each j, the first-order condition for the optimum is $\vartheta^1 u'(x_j^1) = (1 - \vartheta^1)u'(z - x_j^1)$ for each commodity for the first trader and, by feasibility, also for the other trader. This gives equal consumption across the two commodities for each trader. The competitive equilibrium allocation derived above meets these conditions for $\vartheta^1 = \frac{u'(z-\hat{x})}{u'(\hat{x})+u'(z-\hat{x})}$. The other efficient allocations for different values of the weight can be decentralized redistributing the initial endowments.

Externality

The general cause of the failure of markets to ensure efficient allocation of resources is externalities, in which people do not fully capture the benefits or bear the costs of their choices. Externalities are distinguished in direct and indirect. An externality is direct if it directly affects the fundamentals. Direct externalities include pollution generated by emissions, increasing returns to scale in production, strategic effects, and asymmetric information. An externality is indirect if it works through the change in the incentive or relative price system, which in turn affects people's choices and their well-being, as in the case of the pecuniary externality, which occurs when markets are incomplete or borrowing is limited.

Production

We now introduce production in the general equilibrium model. Suppose that there are $h \in \mathcal{H}$ productive units or companies, where the set may be finite, countably infinite, or uncountable, depending on the specifications. Here, we take the set of companies to be finite. A productive unit or company is represented by a production set $Y^h \subseteq \mathbb{R}^J$. A productive plan $\mathbf{y}^h \in Y^h$ has negative entries representing inputs, positive entries representing output, and zero entries for commodities that are not used as inputs or produced as output in the specific productive plan. The set Y^h allows for inaction, that is, $\mathbf{0} \in Y^h$, is closed and convex for every h. The objective of companies is to maximize profits. A company h chooses $\mathbf{y}^h$ to maximize $\mathbf{p}\mathbf{y}^h$. The description of the traders remains the same. With production, market clearing should be written as

$$\sum_{i\in\mathcal{I}} x_j^i \leq \sum_{i\in\mathcal{I}} e_j^i + \sum_{h\in\mathcal{H}} y_j^h$$

for all $j \in \mathcal{J}$. Provided that the production process in aggregate requires the use of some input and is irreversible, the existence, local determinacy, and efficiency of equilibrium continue to hold even in the setting with production.

In the macroeconomic literature, since there is typically a single commodity available for final consumption, production is often introduced by assuming the existence of a production function that represents the underlying technology that converts a vector of inputs $\mathbf{x}$ into a single output y, $f(\mathbf{x}) = y$. The typical production function has at most two inputs, often identified as labor and capital, and meets the following requirements. With a single input, the production function is assumed to be continuously differentiable twice, strictly increasing, and weakly concave. With two inputs, the production function is assumed to be twice differentiable, strictly increasing and concave in each input separately, and exhibit constant returns to scale when changing both inputs by the same factor, namely for any positive κ, $f(\kappa x_1, \kappa x_2) = \kappa f(x_1, x_2)$.

Example B.3 A production function with constant return-to-scale is $y = f(x_1, x_2) = x_1^{\alpha} x_2^{1-\alpha}$ with $\alpha \in (0, 1)$, since for any $\kappa > 0$, $(\kappa x_1)^{\alpha} (\kappa x_2)^{1-\alpha} = \kappa x_1^{\alpha} x_2^{1-\alpha} = \kappa y$.

Time and Uncertainty

The extension of the general equilibrium model to time and uncertainty was first discussed by Debreu in his *Theory of Value* in axiomatic form, redefining commodities so as to include the time dimension and the state of uncertainty in their description. Consumers are assumed to be able to trade claims contingent on the state of uncertainty and the date of delivery of the commodities before the opening of the markets. Then, the market mechanism computes and announces the equilibrium prices, allowing the delivery of the commodities to happen at the appropriate time and contingency. In this way, the model has an immediate extension to a finite time horizon with uncertainty.

Other ways of capturing trade over time and with uncertainty were developed subsequently by Roy Radner, leading to a representation in which trade occurs sequentially using assets that deliver income in future contingencies rather than commodities as in the Arrow-Debreu representation with contingent commodity claims. Once income is delivered, commodity trade occurs in spot markets that open and clear at each date. Since the traders exchange commodities over time rather than trading claims ex-ante, they need to form expectations about the prices that will clear the spot commodity markets in the future.

If the traders have rational expectations over such prices and there are enough assets to transfer income to all dates and across all states of uncertainty, the sequential and Arrow-Debreu representations are equivalent. We first consider the time dimension and then the economy with uncertainty.

Time Horizon

We examine first an economy with a finite time horizon. When the economy unfolds over time, the economy may be represented with trade occurring in the ex-ante idealized market of Arrow-Debreu or in spot markets that open at each point in time. An economy with a finite time horizon can be subsumed under the previous static framework including the time dimension in the notation for the goods and allowing consumers to trade claims of dated commodities. With a time horizon of T periods, the consumption space becomes $X = \mathbb{R}_+^{JT}$ with $\mathbf{x}^i \in X$ denoting the entire bundle of dated commodities for the trader i. The endowment of consumer i for all dated commodities is $\mathbf{e}^i \in X$. The utility function of the consumer is still $U^i(\mathbf{x}^i)$. Provided that consumers can trade claims contingent on the date, the maximization problem of consumers remains formally identical to the static version, with the single life-time budget constraint represented by $\mathbf{px}^i \leq \mathbf{pe}^i$. Market clearing applies to every dated commodity. The model is formally identical to the static one. A competitive equilibrium is guaranteed to exist by the same argument used for the static model, the local determinacy result still applies, and the welfare theorems hold for this case as well.

The model admits an alternative, equivalent representation in terms of sequential trade. Consider an economy with a competitive lending market in which traders can lend to and borrow from each other at a market interest rate. Market clearing applies to all dated commodities and loans at every date. The agents have perfect foresight of the spot prices and interest rates that will emerge at future dates. The model can be reduced to the previous version with contingent claims for the delivery of commodities recovering the single life-time budget constraint of the model with contingent claims.

Example B.4 Consider the previous example by reinterpreting the index $j = 1, 2$ as time $t = 1, 2$, that is, with two dated commodities. Let $\alpha = 1$ and $\beta < 1$. The competitive equilibrium allocation has constant consumption over time for both traders with $x^1 = \frac{z}{1+\beta}$ and $x^2 = \frac{\beta z}{1+\beta}$. The relative price is $p = \beta$, and therefore the implicit net interest rate is $p^{-1} - 1 = \beta^{-1} - 1 > 0$. According to the loan interpretation, the first trader lends resources to the second at interest $r = \beta^{-1} - 1$.

The extension of the model to an infinite time horizon with dynasties living for ever, typical of macroeconomics, requires defining the preferences of the dynasties over infinite sequences of consumption. Let X be a linear vector space containing infinite sequences $\mathbf{x} = (x_1, x_2, ...) \in X$ of non-negative amounts of the only commodity available in each time period $t \in \mathbb{N}$, endowed with the inner product between vectors. Let $\mathbf{x}_a \in X$ denote the sequence beginning with quantity a of the commodity in the first period and $\mathbf{x}_{ab} \in X$ the sequence with consumption equal to a in the first period and b in the second period. We define the following two requirements for preferences over consumption sequences.

- *Stationarity.* For any pair $\mathbf{x}, \mathbf{y} \in X$ and any a, $\mathbf{x} \succeq \mathbf{y} \Leftrightarrow \mathbf{x}_a \succeq \mathbf{y}_a$.
- *Independence from initial trade-off.* For any pair $\mathbf{x}, \mathbf{y} \in X$ and any a, b, c, d, $\mathbf{x}_{ab} \succeq \mathbf{x}_{cd} \Leftrightarrow \mathbf{y}_{ab} \succeq \mathbf{y}_{cd}$.

Continuous preference relations that are stationary and independent from initial trade-offs can be represented by a continuous life-time utility function expressed in the time-separable and discounted form with time discount $\beta < 1$, as follows

$$U^i(\mathbf{x}^i) = \sum_{t=1}^{\infty} \beta^{t-1} u^i(x_t^i).$$

The endowment of dynasty i is a sequence $\mathbf{e}^i \in X$. Trade occurs in a competitive Arrow-Debreu market for date contingent commodities at non-negative prices $\mathbf{p} = (p_1, p_2, ...)$. Thus, the budget set of the dynasty i is $B^i(\mathbf{p}) = \{\mathbf{x} \in X : \mathbf{p}\mathbf{x}^i \leq \mathbf{p}\mathbf{e}^i\}$. Each dynasty chooses $\mathbf{x}^i \in B^i(\mathbf{p})$ to maximize $U^i(\mathbf{x}^i)$. Market clearing requires $\sum_i x_t^i \leq \sum_i e_t^i$ for all periods t. The infinite dimensionality of the consumption space brings about some technical difficulties relative to its finite-horizon counterpart. However, the key descriptive and normative properties survive.

Example B.5 Suppose there are two dynasties with alternating and opposite endowments but identical preferences for consumption represented by the life-time time-separable, discounted utility above with the same spot utility function, $u(\cdot)$, which is differentiable, strictly increasing, and concave. The first dynasty has a positive endowment $e_t^1 = z$ when $t = 2n - 1$ and $e_t^i = 0$ when $t = 2n$ with $n \in \mathbb{N}$, and the second dynasty vice versa. Letting $\vartheta \in (0, 1)$ be the welfare weight for the first dynasty and $1 - \vartheta$ for the second, we can solve the efficient allocations maximizing $\vartheta U(\mathbf{x}^1) + (1 - \vartheta)U(\mathbf{x}^2)$ subject to the binding feasibility constraint $x_t^1 + x_t^2 = z$. Efficiency requires $\vartheta u'(x_t^1) = (1 - \vartheta)u'(z - x_t^1)$ for all periods, which implies constant consumption for the two dynasties over time, $x_t^i = x^i$ for all t and both i. By the welfare theorems, efficient allocation is also competitive equilibrium allocation. We need to find competitive equilibrium prices. Solving the maximization of the first dynasty, denoting by $\lambda \geq 0$ the multiplier of the life-time budget constraint, we obtain the first-order condition $\beta^t u'(x_t^1) = \lambda p_t$. Since the utility function strictly increases in consumption, the budget constraint is binding and, hence $\lambda > 0$. Since the allocation is constant over time, define a constant $c \equiv u'(x^1)/\lambda$. From the first-order condition, we obtain the price $p_t = c\beta^t$ in all periods t. Take the budget constraint of the dynasty $\sum_t p_t x_t^1 = \sum_t p_t e_t^1$, insert the alternating endowment and the constant profile of consumption with the price $p_t = c\beta^t$, obtaining $\frac{x^1}{1-\beta} = \frac{z}{1-\beta^2}$, that is, $x^1 = \frac{z}{1+\beta}$. By market clearing, the consumption of the other dynasty is $x^2 = \frac{\beta z}{1+\beta}$. Hence, market trade provides perfect consumption smoothing opportunities, but allocates consumption unequally between the two dynasties with a declining profile of prices over time that implies a positive implicit net interest rate $\frac{p_t}{p_{t+1}} - 1 = \beta^{-1} - 1 > 0$ at all times. The sequential trade version has the dynasty with the endowment loan and the other borrow resources at interest $r = \beta^{-1} - 1$.

Uncertainty

Uncertainty is introduced in the model assuming that there are states of nature that may be realized with some probability. The uncertainty model behaves differently depending on whether there are enough market instruments that consumers can use to protect against uncertainty. We will distinguish situations in which markets are complete, i.e. full insurance is possible, or incomplete, that is, full insurance cannot be achieved. With uncertainty, we will need a notion of expected utility. Before discussing market issues, we introduce some notation and definitions for this purpose.

First, we describe uncertainty, the space of commodities, and traders' preferences. Uncertainty can be subsumed in the standard framework as follows. Suppose that there is a finite set $\mathcal{S}$ of uncertainty states, whose total number is S, indexed by $s \in \mathcal{S}$ and the consumption space is defined as $X = \mathbb{R}_{+}^{JS}$. There is an initial period, which is the planning period, before the uncertainty is realized. The trader i has a state contingent endowment bundle $\mathbf{e}_s^i$ for each state s, with $\mathbf{e}^i \in X$. Let $\mathbf{x}_s^i$ be the bundle of consumption of consumer goods i in state s, with $\mathbf{x}^i \in X$, and let π_s be the non-negative probability that state s arises, with $\sum_{s \in \mathcal{S}} \pi_s = 1$. Let $\Delta(X)$ be the space of probability distributions over X. We define the following requirement for preferences over probability distributions over the consumption set.

- *Independence from irrelevant alternatives.* For any $\mathbf{x}, \mathbf{y}, \mathbf{z} \in \Delta(X)$ and $\alpha \in [0, 1]$, $\mathbf{x} \succsim \mathbf{y}$ implies $\alpha\mathbf{x} + (1 - \alpha)\mathbf{z} \succsim \alpha\mathbf{y} + (1 - \alpha)\mathbf{z}$.

Under this independence axiom, continuous preferences relations can be represented by the continuous *Von Neumann-Morgenstern (VNM) expected utility* function

$$\mathbb{E}U^i(\mathbf{x}^i) = \sum_{s \in \mathcal{S}} \pi_s u_s^i(\mathbf{x}_s^i),$$

which is the weighted average of utility for consumption in the different states, using the probability of the realization of each state as weight. Notice that the utility function itself may depend directly on the state. The VNM expected utility representation is unique up to affine transformations and, hence, is cardinal. This representation is not required for the fundamental theorems concerning the existence of equilibrium and welfare properties but is convenient for applications. We consider two formulations of the model, one with state contingent commodity claims and one with financial assets.

If claims for the delivery of commodities contingent on the state of uncertainty can be traded before their realization, the budget constraint can be written as before. Market clearing is required to hold for all state contingent commodities. The model is formally equivalent to the Arrow-Debreu formulation without uncertainty. Simply, the definition of a commodity has been extended to include the state of uncertainty in its description. Its existence is established with the same argument as used before. The welfare theorems hold for this model. An equivalent formulation involves the exchange of contingent claims for only one commodity that serves to transfer resources across states of uncertainty. This formulation is due to Radner and shows that full insurance does not require the use of contingent claims on all the commodities.

Example B.6 Consider the previous static example with two commodities, interpreting the index $j = 1, 2$ as states of uncertainty $s = 1, 2$, i.e. with state contingent commodities. Let the parameters $\alpha = \pi$ and $\beta = 1 - \pi$. The competitive equilibrium allocation has constant consumption between states for both consumers with $x^1 = \pi z$ and $x^2 = (1 - \pi)z$. The relative price is $p = \frac{1-\pi}{\pi}$. The same allocation can be achieved with insurance provided by competitive insurance companies at an actuarially fair price.

Another formulation of the model has financial assets, traded before the realization of uncertainty, and used to transfer income between states of uncertainty. Suppose that there is a set $\mathcal{A}$ of assets, whose total number is A, indexed by $a \in \mathcal{A}$. A portfolio of assets for the consumer i is a column vector $\theta^i \in \mathbb{R}^A$, with θ_a^i denoting the demand, if positive, or the supply, if negative, of the asset a. The price of assets is a row vector $\phi \in \mathbb{R}^A$, with ϕ_a being the price of the asset a, and their returns are represented by the matrix R, of dimension $S \times A$, listing the state-by-state payoff of each asset, with the payoff of asset a in state s denoted with r_{sa}. The payoffs may be expressed in units of one of the commodities, of a bundle of commodities, or in abstract units of account, i.e. in monetary terms. When $A = S$, a stylized but convenient return matrix is the identity matrix, representing the so-called Arrow securities. The budget constraint for the acquisition of the assets before the realization of uncertainty, in the initial period, is

$$\phi\theta^i = \sum_{a \in \mathcal{A}} \phi_a \theta^i_a \leq 0$$

The budget constraint in every state s is

$$\mathsf{p}_s \mathbf{x}^i_s \leq \mathsf{p}_s \mathbf{e}^i_s + \sum_{a \in \mathcal{A}} r_{sa} \theta^i_a$$

where p_s is the vector of spot commodity prices at contingency s. The budget set of trader i can be written as

$$B^i(\phi, \mathsf{p}) = \{(\mathbf{x}^i, \theta^i) \in X \times \mathbb{R}^A : \quad \phi\theta^i \leq 0, \quad \mathsf{p}\Box(\mathbf{x}^i - \mathbf{e}^i) \leq R\theta^i\}$$

where the box product $\Box$ between vectors $\mathbf{y}, \mathbf{z} \in X$ is $\mathbf{y}\Box\mathbf{z} = (\mathbf{y}_1\mathbf{z}_1, ..., \mathbf{y}_S\mathbf{z}_S)$. Each trader i chooses $(\mathbf{x}^i, \theta^i) \in B^i(\phi, \mathsf{p})$ to maximize his or her expected utility, $\mathbb{E}U(\mathbf{x}^i)$. An important concept for economies with financial assets is arbitrage. An arbitrage portfolio allows its holder to get a positive payoff at no cost. When utility is strictly increasing, consumers' optimization implies that there should not be unexploited profitable asset trading opportunities, in other words, arbitrage opportunities are incompatible with the traders' optimization. In turn, this implies the requirement that asset prices should reflect their returns through some vector that reflects the consumers' private valuations. Moreover, when there are enough assets to insure against the uncertainty, which requires having access to a number of assets that is at least as large as the number of states of uncertainty, namely when the markets are complete, all private valuations coincide. In this case, the asset prices reflect their discounted returns, $\phi = \lambda R$, using the common marginal rates of substitution of the traders, represented by the vector λ, as discount factors.

Finally, we describe market clearing. Market clearing requires the balance of aggregate demand and supply for all commodities in all contingencies and the balance of aggregate demand and supply of financial assets, that is, $\sum_{i \in \mathcal{I}} \theta^i_a = 0$ for every $a \in \mathcal{A}$. Consumers form expectations about the spot prices in each state. A further equilibrium requirement for this model is that these expectations should be rational in the sense that the spot prices expected to prevail in each state do clear the markets when the state realizes. The competitive equilibrium of this model with financial assets is a rational expectation equilibrium.

When markets are complete, the model can be reduced to the contingent claims version described above, since for every trader we have, with increasing utility functions, by no-arbitrage, that $\phi\theta^i = \lambda R\theta^i = 0$, which can be used in the budget constraints to obtain $\mathbf{p}(\mathbf{x}^i - \mathbf{e}^i) \leq \lambda R\theta^i = 0$, where $\mathbf{p} = \lambda \mathrm{p}$ is the Arrow-Debreu ex-ante vector of prices. Hence, we obtain the single budget constraint of the Arrow-Debreu model with trade in contingent commodities. Therefore, all the properties derived therein continue to hold, including the two welfare theorems.

Example B.7 Consider the previous example with two consumers and two states of uncertainty. Suppose that there are two Arrow securities such that R is the identity matrix. The budget constraint for the initial acquisition of the securities by the trader i is $\phi_1\theta_1^i + \phi_2\theta_2^i = 0$. The budget constraint of trader i in the first state is $\mathrm{p}_1 x_1^i = \mathrm{p}_1 e_1^i + \theta_1^i$ and in the second state $\mathrm{p}_2 x_2^i = \mathrm{p}_2 e_2^i + \theta_2^i$. Define $\phi \equiv \phi_2/\phi_1$ and $\theta \equiv \theta_2^i$. The initial budget constraint gives $\theta_1^i = -\phi\theta^i$, which we can plug into the first state budget constraint obtaining $\mathrm{p}_1 x_1^i = \mathrm{p}_1 e_1^i - \phi\theta^i$. From the second state budget constraint, we get $\theta^i = \mathrm{p}_2(x_2^i - e_2)$, which we can plug back into the previous constraint by obtaining $\sum_s p_s x_s^i = \sum_s p_s e_s^i$ where $p_s \equiv \phi_a \mathrm{p}_s$ with $a = s$. This is the single budget constraint of the original model. Since the market clearing conditions for the commodities are the same as before, the competitive equilibrium allocation is the same.

Incomplete Markets

If the overall number of available assets is smaller than the total number of states of uncertainty, the model has an incomplete set of financial assets, hence, only partial insurance against uncertainty can be achieved. In this case, the model cannot be reduced to its contingent claim representation, as the marginal rates of substitutions are not equalized across traders. As a consequence, generally the welfare properties of the equilibrium are lost. Moreover, even the local determinacy property may become problematic.

There are three main cases for the financial asset structure. First, a real asset structure that pays in units of the numeraire commodity; second, a real asset structure that pays in a bundle of commodities; and third, a nominal asset structure, paying off in monetary units. When markets are incomplete, the existence of equilibrium is unproblematic for the first and third cases, since the rank of the return matrix is unaffected by the spot prices of the commodities. In the second case, instead, the rank of the return matrix varies endogenously with spot commodity prices, and this may create discontinuities in the demand function, potentially compromising the existence of equilibrium. However, it can be shown that discontinuities occur only rarely and that existence is guaranteed generically in the space of fundamentals.

The question of whether equilibrium is locally determinate or not is subtle with incomplete markets and depends on the nature of the assets. With numeraire assets and real assets, since the payoffs of the assets are proportional to spot prices, the homogeneity properties of the budget constraints that apply to the complete markets version of the model still apply, and the equilibrium has one degree of nominal indeterminacy but no real indeterminacy. The number of equilibria is finite, and generically they are all locally isolated. When the securities are nominal, a change in the price level matters since the asset payoffs are independent of spot prices. For example, if all the prices double, the purchasing power of assets is halved. With complete markets, these changes in the purchasing power of assets are undone by a change in the portfolio choice before the realization of uncertainty. With incomplete markets, changes in purchasing power cannot be fully absorbed. Hence, with nominal assets, there is an equilibrium indeterminacy in real terms. One way to resolve the indeterminacy is to have the market facility distribute money for trade after the realization of the uncertainty by fixing the stock of money, M_s, in the state s. This gives rise to a new quantity theory equation for each state of uncertainty that pins down the price level in each state. Since in an economy with nominal assets, the indeterminacy is real, namely, it affects the allocations by varying the stock of money, the market facility can alter allocations and generate real effects, i.e. changes in the allocation of commodities.

To see that the first Welfare Theorem does not apply with incomplete markets, consider the previous example with two states and one commodity per state without assets. In this case, the budget constraint of any trader i is $p_s x_s^i \leq p_s e_s^i$ in all states s. Thus, the income available in some state s cannot be used to finance consumption in a different state s'. The only equilibrium has consumption of the endowment in the good state and no consumption otherwise. This is clearly inefficient if utility is strictly concave. The hallmark of market incompleteness is the presence of a multiplicity of budget constraints that cannot be reduced to the single budget constraint of the standard Arrow-Debreu representation.

The notion of Pareto efficiency may be considered too strong for this environment with a given exogenous asset structure, as it compares the allocation achieved with the existing assets to a benchmark in which all possible reallocations of income are feasible. Arguably, the appropriate notion is one of constrained Pareto efficiency, in which feasible reallocations of income are restricted to be those that can be obtained using the available assets. With this limited notion of efficiency, for instance, without any asset, there would be no possibility of redistributing income, and the autarky equilibrium could not be improved upon, thus being constrained efficient. Except in peculiar circumstances, namely, when there are no assets or there is only one good per state, or utility is quasi-linear or all the consumers have identical homothetic utility, the rational expectations equilibrium of the model with financial assets is not constrained Pareto efficient. The reason why even constrained Pareto efficiency typically fails in incomplete markets economies is that there are *pecuniary externalities* that are not internalized by consumers, as seen in the text.

As a last observation, suppose that the uncertainty is extrinsic in the sense that neither the utility functions nor any of the endowments depend on the state. With extrinsic uncertainty, a rational expectations equilibrium in which the allocation is state dependent is called a *sunspot equilibrium*. If utilities are strictly concave, with complete markets, sunspot equilibria cannot exist, since any Pareto-efficient allocation is state-independent, and the traders risk averse. With complete markets and strictly concave utilities, the Second Welfare Theorem holds. Hence, at any competitive equilibrium, the allocation is state-independent. However, if markets are incomplete, sunspot equilibria sometimes exist. In other words, there exist situations in which extrinsic uncertainty that is unrelated to the fundamentals ends up affecting market outcomes at a rational expectations equilibrium.

This occurs because of the beliefs of consumers about market outcomes that become self-fulfilling.

Enforcement

In the Arrow-Debreu model, the traders are implicitly assumed to be able to commit to deliver the commodities in the appropriate states at the appropriate time, according to the claims of contingent commodities they exchanged at the beginning of the economy. This is presumably guaranteed by an authority that enforces the claims with punishments for non-compliance.

Abandoning the assumption that the market institution can freely enforce the delivery of the commodities on each date after the claims have been traded, a model is obtained in which consumers can default on their promises to deliver the commodities. One possibility is to consider a situation in which the default on a promise is punished with the permanent exclusion from the market ever thenceforth.

Consider an economy with an infinite time horizon. At each point in time, on top of the budget constraint, every trader faces an extra individual rationality constraint in every period, since if a trader decides to default, will be permanently excluded from market trade and, hence, the only available option will consist of consuming the endowment from that time onward. Thus, traders choose consumption to maximize life-time utility, subject to the life-time budget constraint and the individual rationality constraint. The markets for all commodities clear at all times. Taking the perspective that there exists an institution that enforces the punishment of default with the permanent exclusion from the market facility, one is led to define the consumption space as the set of bundles that satisfy the individual rationality constraints for every trader. With this redefinition of the consumption set, the first Welfare Theorem holds for this economy, by the same argument used in the case without default. Hence, the equilibrium allocation will be constrained efficient. An example of such an economy is solved in the text, showing that consumption smoothing may be less than perfect when traders are impatient.

Game Theory

Game theory is the mathematical theory that studies the strategic interaction of rational decision makers. There are two main approaches to game theory. The non-cooperative approach conceives the strategic situation as one in which the decision makers cannot explicitly communicate with each other and cannot enforce any agreement among themselves. Each decision maker decides on his or her own about a complete plan of action to be taken during the interaction with the other decision makers. The objective of non-cooperative game theory is to find a profile of such complete plans of action for every decision maker that would not be changed unilaterally by any of them. Cooperative game theory conceives the strategic situation as one in which there are communication possibilities among the decision makers and agreements among groups of them can be enforced. The objective of cooperative game theory is to find a way to allocate the benefits and costs of the interaction among the decision makers that would not be rejected by any single decision maker or group of them.

Complete Information

Consider non-cooperative finite strategic form games with complete information, namely simultaneous move games with a finite set of players $\mathcal{I}$ and a finite action space X^i for each player $i \in \mathcal{I}$ in which all the relevant aspects of the game are common knowledge among the players. An action profile is a vector $\mathbf{x} = (x^1, ..., x^I)$ that lists an action $x^i \in X^i$ for every player $i \in \mathcal{I}$. Each player i has preferences on the action profiles represented by a utility function $u^i(\mathbf{x})$, also known as the payoff of the player. The strategic element comes from the fact that, unlike the previous market model, the utility of each player depends *directly* on the actions of the other players. The players can randomize over their action spaces independently from each other, obtaining strategies that are probability distributions on their action spaces, denoted by $\sigma^i \in \Delta(X^i)$ for every i. A strategy profile $\sigma = (\sigma^1, ..., \sigma^I)$ is a vector of strategies, one for each player. Let the expected VNM utility of player i be denoted by $U^i(\sigma) = \mathbb{E}u^i(\mathbf{x})$. The game is played as follows. First, all players independently and simultaneously select a strategy. Then, payoffs are realized. Let σ^{-i} be the vector of strategies of all players other than i.

Definition B.3 A strategy profile σ is a *Nash equilibrium* if $U^i(\sigma) \geq U^i(\sigma^{-i}, \hat{\sigma}^i)$ for all alternative strategies $\hat{\sigma}^i \in \Delta(X^i)$, for all players $i \in \mathcal{I}$.

Thus, a strategy profile is a Nash equilibrium if no one gains by unilaterally changing the chosen strategy. John Nash proved the existence of equilibrium for any finite game in strategic form, namely a static simultaneous move game played by a finite number of players with a finite number of options. For this reason, this equilibrium notion is called Nash equilibrium. The existence proof is a direct application of Kakutani's fixed point theorem.

Example B.8 Consider a game in which two players, say 1 and 2, choose whether to cooperate (C) or defect (D). The payoffs are represented in the following two-by-two matrix, where the first number in each entry represents the payoff of the first player and the second number the payoff of the second player, with $\gamma \in \mathbb{R}$.

1/2	C	D
C	1,1	$-1,\gamma$
D	$\gamma,-1$	0,0

Setting $\gamma = 2$, we obtain an instance of the famous *Prisoners' Dilemma*. The Prisoners' Dilemma has one Nash equilibrium in which both players defect. The reason is that defecting is a dominant strategy for each player, which gives a higher payoff than cooperation for every choice of the opponent. Notice that the equilibrium is inefficient, since it is strictly dominated for both players by another strategy combination in which both cooperate, which unfortunately is not an equilibrium. Therefore, the Prisoners' Dilemma is the ultimate example of the socially damaging effect of strategic interaction among rational people. Being afraid that cooperation will not be reciprocated, the players do not cooperate to begin with.

Equilibrium Concept

The Nash equilibrium concept is compelling as a solution concept, since situations in which someone could gain by changing strategy unilaterally cannot be stable unless the players are irrational. However, Nash equilibrium does not rule out situations in which the players take weakly dominated options, as in the game in which two players obtain a unit payoff if they both cooperate (C) and zero whenever somebody defects (D). This game has two Nash equilibria (C,C) and (D,D), as it is easy to check since deviating unilaterally from (C,C) lowers the payoff, and deviating unilaterally from (D,D) does not increase it. However, playing D is weakly dominated by C for each player since the payoff obtained from playing the latter action is always at least the same and sometimes higher than the payoff obtained from the former action. This equilibrium is eliminated by a refinement of the Nash equilibrium concept called *trembling hand perfect equilibrium* in which players are assumed to tremble when they make their choices, so that even when they are meant to choose D, they may still pick C, although with a small probability. For a situation to be a trembling hand perfect equilibrium, it has to be robust to unilateral deviations for arbitrarily small but positive trembles of the players. Since playing D always gives 0, while playing C gives a, possibly small, but still positive amount for any positive tremble, the combination (D,D) does not survive as a trembling hand perfect equilibrium. Hence, the requirement that equilibrium should be stable against these trembles refines the Nash equilibrium notion, eliminating equilibria in weakly dominated strategies. The reason is that with the trembles, playing D is dominated for each player, who knows that the opponent will play C with a perhaps tiny but still positive probability.

In extensive-form games, namely games in which the players' actions unfold over time, refinements using a sequential rationality requirement eliminate some equilibria that are supported by imputing suboptimal behavior of the equilibrium path. A simple example is the following extensive-form game with two players and two actions each, playing sequentially. The first player chooses first and may decide to stay out, playing O, or enter the game, playing E. In the former case, the two players obtain payoffs (1,3) respectively, while in the latter case the second player gets to choose between a punishing action, P, which gives payoff 0 to both players or a rewarding action, R, that gives payoffs 2 to both players. The strategy profile in which the first player plays O for sure and the second player plays P with a probability that is equal or larger than the probability with which plays R is a Nash equilibrium in which the first player stays out of the game expecting the second player to play harshly with sufficiently high probability if given the chance to play. However, this equilibrium seems unreasonable, since the implicit threat of the second player to play harshly if given the chance is not credible, given that playing P is dominated by R for the second player if he or she gets the chance to play. The only reason why this situation is a Nash equilibrium is that the punishment never happens on the equilibrium path, since the first player stays out of the game. There is also another equilibrium in which the first player enters and the second gets the reward. Adding to the Nash equilibrium notion, the sequential rationality requirement that choices should be optimal for the players starting at any decision point eliminates any equilibrium in which the second player chooses P, since the punishing action is dominated by the rewarding one, when the second player is given the chance to play. The resulting *subgame perfect equilibrium* notion, which includes the sequential rationality requirement, eliminates the unreasonable equilibria leaving only (E,R) as an equilibrium, as it can be checked using backward induction, i.e. starting with the optimal choice of the second player at the end of the game, which is unambiguously R, and moving backward to the best response of the first player to such a choice, which is also unambiguously E. However, equilibrium concepts based on the notion of perfection do not completely characterize rational behavior in strategic situations. Consider a game between two players, in which the first player has a choice between staying out of the game or entering. The first option gives a small but positive payoff to both players, while following the second option the two players will play a simultaneous move game in which they can either cooperate or defect. If both players cooperate, they get a large positive payoff; if only one of the two players cooperates and the other defects, the former gets an equally large negative payoff, while the latter gets nothing; if neither cooperates, both players get nothing. This game has two Nash equilibria that are also trembling hand perfect and subgame perfect, one in which the first player enters the game and both players cooperate, one in which the first player stays out of the game and both players plan to choose defection with higher probability than cooperation should the game turn out to be played. The second equilibrium is not entirely compelling, since planning to defect upon entering the game does not seem rational for the first player, who always has the option to get a positive payoff staying out of the game. The second player should be able to figure this out, which would make defection unreasonable on his part. In other words, should the game be played contrary to what the equilibrium stipulates with the first player entering the game, the second player could well interpret this unexpected event as evidence that the first player has chosen to enter the game signaling her intention to cooperate. This type of reasoning is based on forward rather than backward induction. The sequential rationality requirement based on backward induction interprets unexpected behavior as a sudden episode of irrationality from which the players will soon recover, going back to their fully rational selves. The reasoning based on forward induction interprets unexpected behavior whenever possible as a signal of the intention to play rationally in the future rather than as a fit of irrationality. The full characterization of rationality includes both backward and forward induction elements.

Inefficiency

Nash equilibrium may be inefficient, as in the case of the prisoners' dilemma. The problem of inefficiency can be addressed by repeating the game indefinitely. Suppose that the Prisoners' Dilemma is played repeatedly for ever. The two players observe each other's choices at the end of each round of play and discount future rewards at the rate $\beta < 1$. Mutual defection is still an equilibrium of the repeated game. However, there are now other equilibria, including indefinite mutual cooperation. Suppose that the players adopt the following strategy. Each player cooperates until the opponent defects, in which case indefinite retaliation begins defecting for ever. The players have the incentive to continue cooperating in every round if the long-term benefit of cooperation is not less than the short-term gain of defection, namely $(1 - \beta)^{-1} \geq 2$. In other words, if the players are sufficiently patient, with $\beta \geq 1/2$, indefinite cooperation is an equilibrium of the game. The players want to maintain the reputation of being cooperators, to enjoy the long-run benefit of cooperation.

The inefficiency of equilibrium can be addressed, also allowing for cooperative transformations of the original game in which the players may be able to communicate or sign binding contracts or correlate their choices, using public signals or a mediator. This latter option leads to the notion of a correlated equilibrium. A correlated strategy is a probability distribution on the set of action profiles. A correlated strategy is a *correlated equilibrium* if nobody wants to unilaterally deviate from it.

Equilibrium Multiplicity

In some games there may be multiple Pareto-ordered equilibria, as in the coordination game between two players with two actions each, known as the *Stag Hunt*, that is obtained from the two-by-two game above with $\gamma = 0$. This game has two pure strategy equilibria, namely (C,C) and (D,D), and a mixed strategy equilibrium in which both players play each action with equal probability.

The problem of the multiplicity of equilibria in coordination games can be addressed assuming that there is a *focal point* identified by an arbitrator or through a negotiation process, for example, according to the Nash bargaining procedure. Alternatively, there may be public signals such as *sunspots* that facilitate coordination on one of the equilibria or there may be an arbitrarily small amount of incomplete information that helps select among equilibria, as we will see next.

Incomplete Information

A Bayesian game is a representation of a game with incomplete or private information. A finite Bayesian game is an extension of a finite strategic form game, in which each player has a finite set of possible information states or types and a probability distribution over the possible types of all other players given their type representing their belief about their opponents' private information. The utility of each player depends on the action profiles and the type profiles of all the players, so that the opponents' private information is potentially payoff relevant for the player. The type spaces and the probability distributions are common knowledge among the players, but the realization of the type is private information of each player. The game is played as follows. First, the types are selected. Then, the players, knowing their own type but not their opponents' types, choose independently and simultaneously their strategies. Finally, the private information is publicly revealed and the payoffs are realized. Given the private information of a player, a strategy is a probability distribution on the player's action space. A *Bayesian equilibrium* is a Nash equilibrium of the Bayesian representation of the game with private information.

Global Game

Incomplete information can be used as a selection device when there are multiple equilibria. To see the point, consider the stag hunt game, that is, the game in the two-by-two matrix above with $\gamma = 0$. Suppose that the players are uncertain about their payoffs, so that, where a 0 appears in the bi-matrix, there is $x \in [-2, 2]$ instead. The value of x is determined, before the game is played, by performing a random variable that is uniformly distributed in the given interval. Each player i receives a private signal about this value, x^i, which is the realization of a random variable that is distributed independently and uniformly in the interval $[x - \varepsilon, x + \varepsilon]$. Therefore, there is private information about the realization of the random variable that determines the payoffs. This is a game with incomplete information about the payoffs. The underlying game with common knowledge of the payoffs has only one equilibrium, namely (C,C), if $x < -1$, two pure strategy equilibria, namely both (C,C) and (D,D) if $x \in [-1, 1]$ together with one mixed strategy equilibrium, in which C is played with probability $(x + 1)/2$ by both players if $x \in (-1, 1)$, and only one equilibrium, namely (D,D), if $x > 1$. When there are multiple equilibria, (C,C) is Pareto dominant, but (D,D) is risk dominant if $x > 0$. A pure strategy equilibrium is risk dominant with respect to the alternative equilibrium if the product of the payoff deviations arising from it is larger than the product of the payoff deviations arising from the alternative equilibrium.

Suppose that the random draw has given a value $x \in (0, 1)$, so that the underlying game has multiple equilibria and the Pareto-dominated one is risk dominant. With incomplete information but almost common knowledge of payoffs, so that ε is sufficiently close to 0, the only equilibrium surviving is the risk dominant one. The reason is that each player is agnostic about the behavior of the opponent, under the statistical assumptions made above. If one of the two players receives a signal that is smaller than 0 will assign equal probability to the opponent playing any strategy, hence, will have the incentive to play C, while if the signal is larger than 0 will have the incentive to play D. By symmetry, (D,D) is the only surviving equilibrium. Using a similar argument, we can show that the only equilibrium that survives is (C,C) if $x \in (-1, 0)$ and $\varepsilon \approx 0$. Hence, except in the non-generic case in which $x = 0$, the game with an arbitrarily small amount of incomplete information has only one equilibrium, which is the risk dominant in the corresponding complete information game. Therefore, a small departure from common knowledge of payoffs leads to a unique equilibrium, except in very special cases.

Mechanism Design

The Arrow-Debreu formulation assumes that all the information relevant for market trade is held in common among the traders, i.e. is public or common knowledge. The removal of this assumption has far-reaching consequences. Keeping the idea that traders compute their optimal decisions before the market opens and submit them to the market mechanism that searches for an equilibrium, the problem is that the market mechanism ignores any private information the traders might have. This opens up the possibility that traders may exploit their private information to game the system. Thus, a proposed equilibrium allocation may not survive the presence of private information.

Private Information

Imagine that traders are asked to report secretly to the market mechanism not only their requests for the commodities but also any private information they may have. Now, an equilibrium is a situation in which no trader has the incentive to change his consumption decisions and has no incentive to misrepresent his private information, together with the requirement that the traders' choices are mutually compatible. Thus, market prices will not only have the role of giving the incentive to traders to stick to the optimal choice while clearing markets, but also reveal their private information truthfully. This imposes an extra burden on the market mechanism, to insure that truth-telling is incentive-compatible. This line of reasoning applies not only to the market mechanism, but to any institution that is conceived as a way to allow people to communicate their information and coordinate their actions. The key point is that people need to have the incentive to share their private information, so that revealing the private information should be compatible with personal incentives. As a consequence, on top of budget and feasibility constraints, with private information, some other constraints need to be taken into account, namely the constraints that reflect the incentive to reveal the private information. Once these *incentive constraints* are taken into account, the reward schemes and the equilibrium allocations of commodities exhibit features that are quite different from those emerging in economies with public information.

Privacy

There are cases in which private information does not disrupt the functioning of the market mechanism. This occurs with privacy issues, whereby consumers or producers have private information about their personal characteristics that do not directly affect others. For example, consider a seller of a homogeneous commodity whose customers have unobservable private tastes for the commodity. The seller sets up an auction for a unit of the commodity that has no value for him with several potential buyers with different private valuations for the commodity. The best auction to make sure that the commodity is sold to the buyer with the highest valuation is the second-price auction, in which the commodity is sold to the highest bidder, who then pays the second highest bid. This scheme induces the truthful revelation of private information. Indeed, buyers have no incentive to misrepresent their private valuations in a second-price auction since the buyer with the highest valuation appropriates the gain from trade generated by her presence in the auction, while all others would get the commodity only at the cost of paying more than their valuation for it. The problem with this scheme is that the seller may not want to use it. Indeed, the seller may find it optimal to fix a minimum price that needs to be offered for the object that, however, may turn out to be too high, discouraging altogether buyers from bidding. In auction-theoretic terminology, the second-price auction is not budget balanced. The exception occurs when there are at least two buyers with the highest valuation. In this case, one of the two buyers with the highest valuation gets the commodity and the seller gets the highest price. Stiff competition for the object ensures the revelation of private information, efficient allocation, and budget balance. In fact, a much stronger result holds. In privacy settings, the *only* efficient, incentive compatible mechanism that is budget balanced is competitive trade. Instead, when private information directly affects others, competition is not enough to curb incentives leading to inefficiencies. There are mainly two classes of settings in which someone's private information affects directly the payoffs of others, with adverse selection and moral hazard, respectively.

Adverse Selection

A typical situation in which the information held privately by some traders has a direct effect on the other traders' payoffs occurs when there is the so-called *adverse selection* problem, in which some of the traders have private information about a relevant underlying characteristic of the item being traded. The classic example is the market for lemons, that is, used cars in poor condition. The example is as follows. There are several used car sellers. The cars are either in good or bad condition, but this is private information of the sellers, who have private valuations for their cars. Buyers have a higher valuation than sellers for good cars. Lemons are not worth anything. The sellers have the incentive to claim their cars are in good condition, unless the price for good cars and lemons is the same, equal to the average valuation of the buyers for good cars and lemons. If the value of the sellers is higher than the average valuation of the buyers, sellers with good cars will not sell their cars at the market price, although it would be efficient to do so since buyers have a higher value than sellers for good cars. Hence, there will be only lemons in the market for used cars. Anticipating this, no buyer will show up and the market for used cars will shut down. This phenomenon is known as *adverse selection*, since the market selects the quality of cars adversely.

Moral Hazard

The other classic example of a situation in which the private information held by some trader has a direct effect on the other traders' payoffs occurs when the very actions of the traders are private information. This is known as the *moral-hazard* problem. Consider the owner of a company who wants to hire a manager to run a project whose riskiness can be reduced if the manager works diligently on the project but not if the manager shirks. However, whether the manager exerts effort or shirks is his private information, while the outcome of the project is observable also by the owner. Suppose that the owner is risk neutral and the manager is risk averse. The efficient scheme without private information would have the risk neutral party bear all the risk. Hence, the owner would have to pay the manager a positive wage if he exerts the effort independently of the outcome, and nothing if he shirks. However, this scheme is not incentive compatible with private information, as the manager has the incentive to claim that he has exerted the effort and blame the poor outcome of the project on bad luck. The best incentive compatible scheme has imperfect insurance of the risk-averse party, that is, the manager, to induce him to exert the effort rather than shirk.

Information Revelation

Both adverse selection and moral-hazard situations are cases in which the traders exert reciprocal externalities on each other and are inherently strategic. Competition is not powerful enough to curb the traders' countervailing incentives with private information of the adverse selection or moral-hazard type, hence, the recourse to alternative trading arrangements that may help elicit the information held by the traders in private while trying to achieve efficiency. The theory that studies such arrangements is the mechanism design theory.

Mechanisms

Game theory identifies the stable situations, from which nobody would want to unilaterally deviate, in a given strategic interaction. Mechanism design theory identifies the institutional arrangements, called *mechanisms*, that allow the achievement of socially efficient stable situations as outcomes of the strategic interaction induced by the institutional arrangement. A mechanism is a plan that determines how the interaction of the traders will depend on the communication of their private information. Different mechanisms correspond to different institutions that induce different interactions among traders. The task of identifying such arrangements seems daunting, as the mechanisms used to communicate information can be arbitrarily complex.

Revelation Principle

The remarkable result is that any equilibrium outcome of any mechanism, no matter how complex, can be replicated by a simple mechanism, called the direct mechanism, in which each decision maker communicates his private information confidentially to a trustworthy and benevolent mediator who, then, recommends, also confidentially, to each trader what course of action to take in the interaction with the other traders, provided the mediator's suggested plan gives every trader the incentive to reveal his or her private information truthfully and obey the mediators' recommendations. This result, known as the *Revelation Principle*, applies very generally and allows the representation of economies with private information simply including a set of incentive compatibility constraints on top of resource constraints, ignoring the details of how the private information is communicated. Incentive compatibility constraints are of two types. There are adverse or self-selection constraints that ensure that the private information is revealed truthfully by the participants in the mechanism to the mediator and strategic or moral risk constraints that ensure that the mediator's recommendations are obeyed by the participants. If prospective participants have feasible alternative options to the mechanism, there will also be participation or individual rationality constraints to be considered.

The intuitive reason for why the revelation principle applies so broadly is that the mediator, through the direct communication structure, potentially has access to the entire available information, thus, being able to replicate any allocation of any communication system and, thanks to the confidentiality of the communication, potentially is able to make sure that every participant has the incentive to reveal truthfully any information held privately and obey his recommendations, minimizing the possibility that the participants may use their private information to game the system. A direct mechanism is a correlated strategy of the Bayesian representation of the game with incomplete information.

Definition B.4 An *incentive compatible direct revelation mechanism* is a correlated equilibrium of the game with incomplete information.

Mechanisms are sometimes also called *contracts*. Contract theory is an application of mechanism design to a situation in which the designer of the mechanism is one of the parties involved in the interaction that offers a contract to try to maximize his or her own payoffs rather than a welfare criterion for society as a whole.

Efficiency

As regards efficiency, its notion is more subtle with private information than with public information. In particular, with private information, efficiency becomes a property of mechanisms rather than allocations. Extending the notion of Pareto efficiency to mechanism, we have that a mechanism is efficient if there is no other mechanism that, being both physically and incentive feasible, makes some participants in the mechanism better off and nobody worse off. However, the criterion is ambiguous, as we have not specified what information needs to be considered in determining whether participants are made better off or worse off by the mechanism. One possibility is to consider the expected utility payoff of participants as computed before the types are realized. This is the ex-ante welfare criterion. A second possibility is to consider the conditionally expected utility of the participants, given their own but not the other players' types. This is the interim welfare criterion. A third possibility is to consider the conditionally expected utility given the types of all participants. This is called the ex-post welfare criterion. The efficiency concepts normally used with private information are the ex-ante and interim ones.

Two Leading Examples

We illustrate how mechanism design works through two key examples. In the first example of the adverse selection type, there are two parties who are attempting to trade an object for which they have valuations that are private information. In the second example of the type of moral hazard, there are two parties who are engaged in a productive activity with a hidden action by one of the two.

Example B.9 Suppose there is a seller of an indivisible object with possible valuations V and v and a buyer with possible valuations U and u. These possibilities are commonly known to be equally likely and $U > V > u > v = 0$. Moreover, assume that the buyer's high valuation is sufficiently larger than the low valuation $U > 2u$. Efficiency requires trade to happen for sure whenever the buyer has a higher valuation for the object than the seller and never otherwise. The efficient allocation can be decentralized with trade at prices for the object that are in between the valuations of the buyer and the seller. For instance, with symmetric bargaining power between the parties the price would split equally the gains from trade.

Suppose that the valuations of the traders are their private information but there is a benevolent mediator who can talk confidentially to traders and recommend actions to them. Consider the recommendation to trade the object whenever there are gains from trade at a price that splits equally the gains from trade between the two traders. This recommendation is not incentive compatible, since the seller with a low valuation for the object when trading with a high valuation buyer would have the incentive to claim to value the object highly, to get a better price.

Let us determine the best symmetric incentive compatible mechanism for this trading situation with incomplete information. Consider the following confidential recommendation by the mediator to the traders after having collected their reports on their private information. If the seller values the object more than the buyer, trade will not happen, and if the sellers cares little about the object while the buyer values it highly, trade will happen for sure at a price that splits the benefit of trade equally between the two traders. In the other two cases, trade will occur with probability π at a price P paid by the buyer when it has a high value for the seller who also values the object highly, and the price p paid by the buyer when it has a low value for the object to a seller with a low evaluation of the object. To ensure the participation of the buyer, it has to be the case that the price does not exceed his or her valuation, that is, $p \leq u$ for the low value buyer and $P \leq U$ for the high value buyer.

To make sure that the seller when he or she has a low valuation for the object reveals this information truthfully, it has to be the case that the payoff from doing so is not smaller than the payoff that is obtained misrepresenting the information, namely

$$\pi p + U/2 \geq \pi P.$$

To make sure that the buyer when he or she has a high valuation for the object reveals this information truthfully, it has to be the case that the payoff from doing so is not smaller than the payoff that is obtained misrepresenting the information, namely

$$\pi(U - P) + U/2 \geq \pi(U - p),$$

that is equivalent to the previous incentive condition. By symmetry, we set the seller's compensation when both traders have a low value for the object equal to the buyer's compensation when both have a high value for the object, that is, $p = U - P$. Plugging this symmetry condition into the incentive condition, we obtain

$$\pi \leq \frac{U}{2(U-2p)}. \tag{B.2}$$

We consider ex-ante efficiency. The ex-ante welfare with equal weights for the two traders is

$$W(\pi) = \frac{U + \pi(U + u + V)}{4},$$

since trade never occurs when the seller values the object more than the buyer, trade occurs for sure if the sellers cares little about the object while the buyer values it highly, while in the other cases trade happens with probability π. The best symmetric incentive compatible mechanism is a pair (π, p) that maximizes ex-ante welfare $W(\pi)$ subject to the participation constraint, $p \leq u$, and the incentive constraint, (B.2), with $\pi \in [0, 1]$. Since p does not appear in the objective function, let us use it to satisfy the participation constraint at equality, setting $p = u$. Plugging it into the incentive constraint, we get an upper bound on the probability

$$\pi \leq \frac{U}{2(U-2u)} \equiv \overline{\pi},$$

where the upper bound is strictly smaller than 1 if and only if $U > 4u$. Since ex-ante welfare increases with probability π, the optimum has $\pi = \overline{\pi}$. The other price is given by $P = U - u < U$.

Notice that, when the high valuation of the buyer is large, in the optimal mechanism trade does not happen for sure, as efficiency would require, since this would not be incentive compatible, making the allocation impossible to implement. When the buyer has a large high valuation, inducing the truthful revelation of information is especially demanding. The requirement of information revelation places tight restrictions on the allocation, distorting it with respect to efficiency, in particular making trade uncertain.

Example B.10 An entrepreneur can activate a risky project that requires an initial unit investment of resources and can be successful with a product z in the future or a failure without any product. The probability of the project being successful can be influenced by the entrepreneur, who can increase the probability of success from $\rho < 1/2$ to $1 - \rho > 1/2$ spending effort at a cost $c < z$. Assume that the project is valuable if and only if the entrepreneur exerts the effort, that is

$$(1 - \rho)z - c > 1 > \rho z, \tag{B.3}$$

The entrepreneur does not have the resources to begin the project, but there are investors with enough resources to finance it. Suppose everyone is risk neutral and there is no time discount. Efficiency requires to activate the project whenever there is a positive net expected value of the investment. Efficiency can be decentralized with a reward scheme that ensures participation of both the entrepreneur and the investor. Under assumption (B.3), it is always possible to find such a reward.

Suppose now that the effort of the entrepreneur is not observable by the investors, but there is a benevolent mediator who can recommend actions to the parties involved. The mediator recommends that a reward r should be paid by the entrepreneur to investors who provide the initial resources to start the project and suggests to the entrepreneur to exert the effort. The mediator needs to check whether the parties are willing to participate in the mechanism. For investors to be willing to participate, the expected reward should not be less than the investment, that can be written as

$$r \geq \frac{1}{1-\rho}. \tag{B.4}$$

For the entrepreneur to participate, it must be that the expected profit is non-negative $(1-\rho)(z-r) \geq c$, that can be written as

$$z - \frac{c}{1-\rho} \geq r. \tag{B.5}$$

The mediator should also check the incentive of the entrepreneur to follow the recommendation to exert the effort. For this to be the case, the expected profit of the entrepreneur needs to be larger with effort than without, namely $(1-\rho)(z-r) - c \geq \rho(z-r)$, that can be written as

$$z - \frac{c}{1-2\rho} \geq r. \tag{B.6}$$

This inequality is tighter than the participation condition of the entrepreneur (B.5). For the mechanism to be implementable, the incentive condition (B.6) should be compatible with the participation condition of investors (B.4). This requires to satisfy the inequality $F(\rho) \equiv z - c - 1 - (3z - c - 2)\rho + 2z\rho^2 \geq 0$, with ρ smaller than 1/2. Since $F(\rho)$ is quadratic with $F(0) > 0$ and $F(1/2) < 0$, there is a unique $\overline{\rho} < 1/2$ such that $F(\rho) < 0$ for $\rho > \overline{\rho}$. Hence, for ρ sufficiently close to 1/2, the mechanism is not implementable. In fact, if $\rho > (1/2)(1 - c/z)$, the incentive condition (B.6) cannot be satisfied for any positive r. Therefore, if the effort of the entrepreneur is only moderately productive, in the best incentive compatible mechanism a valuable project is not activated, as the reward needed to provide the entrepreneur with the incentive to exert the effort to make it valuable would be incompatible with the reward that guarantees the willingness of the investors to contribute the resources to start the project. Should the entrepreneur be able to count on personal resources to finance the project, condition (B.6) could be relaxed. Thus, with moral hazard, the allocation of property rights over initial resources matters.

Renegotiation

When the ability to enforce the execution of contracts is limited, the expectation of reopening the negotiation during the contractual relationship may inhibit its inception. If some contractual provisions are not enforceable, there may be a *renegotiation* of the contractual terms during its execution, when part of the activity covered by the contract has already taken place. The party that has already provided its contribution may then be held up by the other parties. Such an expectation of extortion could discourage the establishment of contractual relationships that are socially beneficial. As an example, consider an entrepreneur who needs a unit of outside resources to finance a project that generates a short-term payoff that is larger than the initial investment with an even larger long-term payoff, and an investor with a unit endowment of resources. Both parties are risk neutral, and there is no time discount. In the short term, the project can be liquidated at a cost, obtaining less than the initial investment. The entrepreneur's skills are essential to complete the project, but not for the liquidation of the project. The entrepreneur can fully appropriate the project's returns without suffering consequences. The contract between entrepreneur and investor offers a payment to reward the initial investment while, if the payment does not occur, the project is transferred to the investor for liquidation. Suppose that, in case of renegotiation between the parties, the entrepreneur can always force his or her most favorable outcome. This implies that the payment cannot exceed the liquidation value of the project, which is, however, insufficient to remunerate the initial investment. The investor anticipating this outcome, for fear of being held up by the entrepreneur in renegotiation, does not finance the project, despite its positive net present value. Therefore, limited contractual enforcement is a source of inefficiency, leading to individually rational but socially wasteful renegotiation. The literature that deals with these situations is the incomplete contracts literature.

The manufacturer's authorised representative in the EU is Springer Nature Customer Service Centre GmbH, Europaplatz 3, 69115 Heidelberg, Germany. If you have any concerns regarding our products, please contact ProductSafety@springernature.com

Printed and bound by CPI Group (UK) Ltd, Croydon, CR0 4YY
22/06/2025
01905094-0001